Our Culture, What's Left of It

Our Culture, What's Left of It

The Mandarins and the Masses

THEODORE DALRYMPLE

Ivan R. Dee

CHICAGO 2005

www.ivanrdee.com

Most of the contents of this book first appeared in *City Journal*, published
by The Manhattan Institute.

Library of Congress Cataloging-in-Publication Data:
Dalrymple, Theodore
   Our culture, what's left of it : the mandarins and the masses / Theodore
Dalrymple.
      p. cm.
   Most of the contents of this book originally appeared in City journal.
   Includes index.
   ISBN 1-56663-643-4 (alk. paper)
   1. Dalrymple, Theodore. 2. Physicians—Great Britain—Biography.
3. Prison physicians—Great Britain—Biography. 4. Great Britain—
Civilization—1945– I. City Journal (New York, N.Y.) II. Title.
   R489.D357A3 2005
   610'.92—dc22

                              2004027150

For Agnès
With all my love

Contents

Preface

◈ THE FRAGILITY of civilization is one of the great lessons of the twentieth century. At the beginning of that century, optimism that technical and moral progress went hand in hand was, if not quite universal, at least widespread. As the late-nineteenth-century Russian writer V. G. Korolenko put it, man was born for happiness as a bird for flight. Thanks to increasing scientific and technological mastery, humanity would become ever wealthier, ever healthier, and therefore ever happier. Wisdom would follow as a matter of course.

Mankind has indeed become ever wealthier and ever healthier. The fact of progress is obvious. The life expectancy of an Indian peasant, for example, now exceeds by far that of a member of the British royal family at the apogee of British power. In much of the world, poverty is no longer absolute, a lack of food, shelter, or clothing; it is relative. Its miseries are no longer those of raw physical deprivation but those induced by comparison with the vast numbers of prosperous people by whom the relatively poor are surrounded and whose comparative wealth the poor feel as a wound, a reproach, and an injustice.

But if the hope of progress has not proved altogether illusory, neither has the fear of retrogression proved unjustified. The Great War destroyed facile optimism that progress toward heaven on earth was inevitable or even possible. The most civilized of peoples proved capable of the most horrific of organized violence. Then came communism and Nazism, which between them destroyed scores of millions of lives, in a fashion that only a few short decades before would have appeared inconceivable. Many of the disasters of the twentieth century could be characterized as revolts against civilization itself: the Cultural Revolution in China, for example, or the Khmer Rouge in Cambodia. Only ten years ago, in Rwanda, scores of thousands of ordinary people were transformed into pitiless murderers by demagogic appeals over the radio. They achieved a rate of slaughter with their machetes never equaled even by the Nazis with their gas chambers. Who now would bet heavily against such a thing ever happening again anywhere in the world?

One might have supposed, in the circumstances, that a principal preoccupation of intellectuals, who after all are supposed to see farther and think more deeply than ordinary men and women, would be the maintenance of the boundaries that separate civilization from barbarism, since those boundaries have so often proved so flimsy in the past hundred years. One would be wrong to suppose any such thing, however. Some have knowingly embraced barbarism; others have remained unaware that boundaries do not maintain themselves and are in need of maintenance and sometimes vigorous defense. To break a taboo or to transgress are terms of the highest praise in the vocabulary of modern critics, irrespective of what has been transgressed or what taboo broken. A review of a recent biography of the logical positivist philosopher A. J. Ayer, in the *Times Literary Supplement*, enumerated the philosopher's personal virtues. Among them was the fact that he was unconventional—but the writer did not feel called upon to state in what respect Ayer was unconventional. For the reviewer, Ayer's alleged disregard of convention was a virtue in itself.

Of course, it might well have been a virtue, or it might equally well have been a vice, depending on the ethical content and social effect of the convention in question. But there is little doubt that an oppositional attitude toward traditional social rules is what wins the modern intellectual his spurs, in the eyes of other intellectuals. And the prestige that intellectuals confer upon antinomianism soon communicates itself to nonintellectuals. What is good for the bohemian sooner or later becomes good for the unskilled worker, the unemployed, the welfare recipient—the very people most in need of boundaries to make their lives tolerable or allow them hope of improvement. The result is moral, spiritual, and emotional squalor, engendering fleeting pleasures and prolonged suffering.

This is not to say, of course, that all criticism of social conventions and traditions is destructive or unjustified; surely no society in the world can have existed in which there was not much justly to criticize. But critics of social institutions and traditions, including writers of imaginative literature, should always be aware that civilization needs conservation at least as much as it needs change, and that immoderate criticism, or criticism from the standpoint of utopian first principles, is capable of doing much—indeed devastating—harm. No man is so brilliant that he can work out everything for himself, so that the wisdom of ages has nothing useful to tell him. To imagine otherwise is to indulge in the most egotistical of hubris.

Having spent a considerable proportion of my professional career in Third World countries in which the implementation of abstract ideas and ideals has made bad situations incomparably worse, and the rest of my career among the very extensive British underclass, whose disastrous notions about how to live derive ultimately from the unrealistic, self-indulgent, and often fatuous ideas of social critics, I have come to regard intellectual and artistic life as being of incalculable practical importance and effect. John Maynard Keynes wrote, in a famous passage in *The Economic Consequences of the Peace*, that practical men might not have much time for theoretical considerations, but in fact the world is governed by little else than the outdated or defunct ideas of economists and social philosophers. I agree: except that I would now add novelists, playwrights, film directors, journalists, artists, and even pop singers. They are the unacknowledged legislators of the world, and we ought to pay close attention to what they say and how they say it.

Our Culture, What's Left of It

ARTS AND LETTERS

The Frivolity of Evil

WHEN PRISONERS are released from prison, they often say that they have paid their debt to society. This is absurd, of course: crime is not a matter of double-entry bookkeeping. You cannot pay a debt by having caused even greater expense, nor can you pay in advance for a bank robbery by offering to serve a prison sentence before you commit it. Perhaps, metaphorically speaking, the slate is wiped clean once a prisoner is released from prison, but the debt is not paid off.

It would be just as absurd for me to say, on my imminent retirement after fourteen years of my hospital and prison work, that I have paid my debt to society. I had the choice to do something more pleasing if I had wished, and I was paid, if not munificently, at least adequately. I chose the disagreeable neighborhood in which I practiced because, medically speaking, the poor are more interesting, at least to me, than the rich: their pathology is more florid, their need for attention greater. Their dilemmas, if cruder, seem to me more compelling, nearer to the fundamentals of human existence. No doubt I also felt my services would be more valuable there: in other words, that I had some kind of duty to perform. Perhaps for that reason, like the prisoner on his release, I feel I have paid my debt to society. Certainly the work has taken a toll on me, and it is time to do something else. Someone else can do battle with the metastasizing social pathology of Great Britain while I lead a life aesthetically more pleasing to me.

My work has caused me to become perhaps unhealthily preoccupied with the problem of evil. Why do people commit evil?

What conditions allow it to flourish? How is it best prevented and, when necessary, suppressed? Each time I listen to a patient recounting the cruelty to which he or she has been subjected, or has committed (and I have listened to several such patients every day for fourteen years), these questions revolve endlessly in my mind.

No doubt my previous experiences fostered my preoccupation with this problem. My mother was a refugee from Nazi Germany, and though she spoke very little of her life before she came to Britain, the mere fact that there was much of which she did not speak gave evil a ghostly presence in our household.

Later I spent several years touring the world, often in places where atrocity had recently been, or still was being, committed. In Central America I witnessed civil war fought between guerrilla groups intent on imposing totalitarian tyranny on their societies, opposed by armies that didn't scruple to resort to massacre. In Equatorial Guinea the current dictator was the nephew and henchman of the last dictator, who had killed or driven into exile a third of the population, executing every last person who wore glasses or possessed a page of printed matter for being a disaffected or potentially disaffected intellectual. In Liberia I visited a church in which more than six hundred people had taken refuge and been slaughtered, possibly by the president himself (soon to be videotaped being tortured to death). The outlines of the bodies were still visible in the dried blood on the floor, and the long mound of the mass grave began only a few yards from the entrance. In North Korea I saw the acme of tyranny, millions of people in terrorized, abject obeisance to a personality cult whose object, the Great Leader Kim Il Sung, made the Sun King look like the personification of modesty.

Still, all these were political evils, which my own country had entirely escaped. I optimistically supposed that, in the absence of the worst political deformations, widespread evil was impossible. I soon discovered my error. Of course, nothing that I was to see in a British slum approached the scale or depth of what I had witnessed elsewhere. Beating a woman from motives of jealousy, locking her in a closet, breaking her arms deliberately, terrible though it may be, is not the same, by a long way, as mass murder.

More than enough of the constitutional, traditional, institutional, and social restraints on large-scale political evil still existed in Britain to prevent anything like what I had witnessed elsewhere.

Yet the scale of a man's evil is not entirely to be measured by its practical consequences. Men commit evil within the scope available to them. Some evil geniuses, of course, devote their lives to increasing that scope as widely as possible, but no such character has yet arisen in Britain, and most evildoers merely make the most of their opportunities. They do what they can get away with.

In any case, the extent of the evil that I found, though far more modest than the disasters of modern history, is nonetheless impressive. From the vantage point of one six-bedded hospital ward, I have met at least five thousand perpetrators of the kind of violence I have just described and five thousand victims of it: nearly 1 percent of the population of my city—or a higher percentage if one considers the age-specificity of the behavior. And when you take the life histories of these people, as I have, you soon realize that their existence is as saturated with arbitrary violence as that of the inhabitants of many a dictatorship. Instead of one dictator, though, there are thousands, each the absolute ruler of his own little sphere, his power circumscribed by the proximity of another such as he.

Violent conflict, not confined to the home and hearth, spills out onto the streets. Moreover, I discovered that British cities such as my own even had torture chambers: run not by the government, as in dictatorships, but by those representatives of slum enterprise, the drug dealers. Young men and women in debt to drug dealers are kidnapped, taken to the torture chambers, tied to beds, and beaten or whipped. Of compunction there is none—only a residual fear of the consequences of going too far.

Perhaps the most alarming feature of this low-level but endemic evil, the one that brings it close to the conception of original sin, is that it is unforced and spontaneous. No one requires people to commit it. In the worst dictatorships, some of the evil that ordinary men and women do, they do out of fear of not committing it. There, goodness requires heroism. In the Soviet Union in the 1930s, for example, a man who failed to report a political joke to the authorities was himself guilty of an offense that could lead to deportation or death. But in modern Britain, no such conditions exist: the government does not require citizens to behave as I have described and punish them if they do not. The evil is freely chosen.

Not that the government is blameless in the matter—far from it. Intellectuals propounded the idea that man should be freed from the shackles of social convention and self-control, and the government, without any demand from below, enacted laws that promoted unrestrained behavior and created a welfare system that protected people from some of its economic consequences. When the barriers to evil are brought down, it flourishes; and never again will I be tempted to believe in the fundamental goodness of man, or that evil is something exceptional or alien to human nature.

Of course, my personal experience is just that—personal experience. Admittedly I have looked out at the social world of my city and my country from a peculiar and possibly unrepresentative vantage point, from a prison and from a hospital ward where practically all the patients have tried to kill themselves, or at least made suicidal gestures. But it is not small or slight personal experience, and each of my thousands, even scores of thousands, of cases has given me a window into the world in which that person lives.

And when my mother asks me whether I am not in danger of letting my personal experience embitter me or cause me to look at the world through bile-colored spectacles, I ask her why she thinks that she, in common with all old people in Britain today, feels the need to be indoors by sundown or face the consequences, and why this should be the case in a country that within living memory was law-abiding and safe? Did she not herself tell me that, as a young woman during the blackouts in the Blitz, she felt perfectly safe, at least from the depredations of her fellow citizens, walking home in the pitch dark, and that it never occurred to her that she might be the victim of a crime, whereas nowadays she has only to put her nose out of her door at dusk for her to think of nothing else? Is it not true that her purse has been stolen twice in the last two years, in broad daylight, and is it not true that statistics—however manipulated by governments to put the best possible gloss upon them—bear out the accuracy of the conclusions that I have drawn from my personal experience? In 1921, the year of my mother's birth, there was 1 crime recorded for every 370 inhabitants of England and Wales; 80 years later it was 1 for every 10 inhabitants. There has been a twelvefold increase since 1941 and an even greater increase in crimes of violence. So while personal experience is hardly a complete guide to social reality, the historical data certainly back up my impressions.

A single case can be illuminating, especially when it is statistically banal—in other words, not at all exceptional. Yesterday, for example, a twenty-one-year-old woman consulted me, claiming to be depressed. She had swallowed an overdose of her antidepressants and then called an ambulance.

There is something to be said here about the word "depression," which has almost entirely eliminated the word and even the concept of unhappiness from modern life. Of the thousands of patients I have seen, only two or three have ever claimed to be unhappy: all the rest have said they were depressed. This semantic shift is deeply significant, for it implies that dissatisfaction with life is itself pathological, a medical condition, which it is the responsibility of the doctor to alleviate by medical means. Everyone has a right to health; depression is unhealthy; therefore everyone has a right to be happy (the opposite of being depressed). This idea in turn implies that one's state of mind, or one's mood, is or should be independent of the way that one lives one's life, a belief that must deprive human existence of all meaning, radically disconnecting reward from conduct.

A ridiculous *pas de deux* between doctor and patient ensues: the patient pretends to be ill, and the doctor pretends to cure him. In the process, the patient is willfully blinded to the conduct that inevitably caused his misery in the first place. I have therefore come to see that one of the most important tasks of the doctor today is the disavowal of his own power and responsibility. The patient's notion that he is ill stands in the way of his understanding of the situation, without which moral change cannot take place. The doctor who pretends to treat is an obstacle to this change, blinding rather than enlightening.

My patient already had had three children by three different men, by no means unusual among my patients, or indeed in the country as a whole. The father of her first child had been violent, and she had left him; the second died in an accident while driving a stolen car; the third, with whom she had been living, had demanded that she leave his apartment because, a week after their child was born, he decided that he no longer wished to live with her. (The discovery of incompatibility a week after the birth of a child is now so common as to be statistically normal.) She had nowhere to go, no one to fall back on, and the hospital was a temporary sanctuary from her woes. She hoped that we would fix her up with some accommodation.

She could not return to her mother because of conflict with her "stepfather," or her mother's latest boyfriend, who, in fact, was only nine years older than she and seven years younger than her mother. This compression of the generations is also now a common pattern and is seldom a recipe for happiness. (It goes without saying that her own father had disappeared at her birth, and she had never seen him since.) The latest boyfriend in this kind of ménage either wants the daughter around to abuse her sexually or else wants her out of the house as being a nuisance and an unnecessary expense. This boyfriend wanted her out of the house, and set about creating an atmosphere certain to make her leave as soon as possible.

The father of her first child had, of course, recognized her vulnerability. A girl of sixteen living on her own is easy prey. He beat her from the first, being drunken, possessive, and jealous, as well as flagrantly unfaithful. She thought that a child would make him more responsible—sober him up and calm him down. It had the reverse effect. She left him.

The father of her second child was a career criminal, already imprisoned several times. A drug addict who took whatever drugs he could get, he died under the influence. She had known all about his past before she had his child.

The father of her third child was much older than she. It was he who suggested that they have a child—in fact he demanded it as a condition of staying with her. He had five children already by three different women, none of whom he supported in any way whatever.

The conditions for the perpetuation of evil were now complete. She was a young woman who would not want to remain alone, without a man, for very long; but with three children already, she would attract precisely the kind of man, like the father of her first child—of whom there are now many—looking for vulnerable, exploitable women. More than likely, at least one of them (for there would undoubtedly be a succession of them) would abuse her children sexually, physically, or both.

She was, of course, a victim of her mother's behavior at a time when she had little control over her destiny. Her mother had thought that her own sexual liaison was more important than the welfare of her child, a common way of thinking in today's welfare Britain. That same day, for example, I was consulted by a young woman whose mother's consort had raped her many times between the ages of eight and fifteen, with her mother's full knowledge. Her mother had allowed this solely so that her own relationship with her consort might continue. It could happen that my patient will one day do the same thing.

My patient was not just a victim of her mother, however: she had knowingly borne children of men of whom no good could be expected. She knew perfectly well the consequences and the meaning of what she was doing, as her reaction to something that I said to her—and say to hundreds of women patients in a similar situation—proved: next time you are thinking of going out with a man, bring him to me for my inspection, and I'll tell you if you can go out with him.

This never fails to make the most wretched, the most "depressed" of women smile broadly or laugh heartily. They know exactly what I mean, and I need not spell it out further. They know that I mean that most of the men they have chosen have their evil written all over them, sometimes quite literally in the form of tattoos, saying "FUCK OFF" or "MAD DOG." And they understand that if I can spot the evil instantly, because they know what I would look for, so can they—and therefore they are in large part responsible for their own downfall at the hands of evil men.

Moreover, they are aware that I believe that it is both foolish and wicked to have children by men without having considered even for a second or a fraction of a second whether the men have any qualities that might make them good fathers. Mistakes are possible, of course: a man may turn out not to be as expected. But not even to consider the question is to act as irresponsibly as it is possible for a human being to act. It is knowingly to increase the sum of evil in the world, and sooner or later the summation of small evils leads to the triumph of evil itself.

My patient did not start out with the intention of abetting, much less of committing, evil. And yet her refusal to take seriously and act upon the signs that she saw and the knowledge that she had was not the consequence of blindness and ignorance. It was utterly willful. She knew from her own experience, and that of many people around her, that her choices, based on the pleasure or the desire of the moment, would lead to the misery and suffering not only of herself, but—especially—of her own children.

This truly is not so much the banality as the frivolity of evil: the elevation of passing pleasure for oneself over the long-term misery of others to whom one owes a duty. What better phrase than the frivolity of evil describes the conduct of a mother who turns her own fourteen-year-old child out of doors because her latest boyfriend does not want him or her in the house? And what better phrase describes the attitude of those intellectuals who see in this conduct nothing but an extension of human freedom and choice, another thread in life's rich tapestry?

The men in these situations also know perfectly well the meaning and consequences of what they are doing. The same day I saw the patient I have just described, a man aged twenty-five came into our ward, in need of an operation to remove foil-wrapped packets of cocaine that he had swallowed in order to evade being caught by the police in possession of them. (Had a packet burst, he would have died immediately.) As it happened, he had just left his latest girlfriend—one week after she had given birth to their child. They weren't getting along, he said; he needed his space. Of the child, he thought not for an instant.

I asked him whether he had any other children.

"Four," he replied.

"How many mothers?"

"Three."

"Do you see any of your children?"

He shook his head. It is supposedly the duty of the doctor not to pass judgment on how his patients have elected to live, but I think I may have raised my eyebrows slightly. At any rate, the patient caught a whiff of my disapproval.

"I know," he said. "I know. Don't tell me."

These words were a complete confession of guilt. I have had hundreds of conversations with men who have abandoned their children in this fashion, and they all know perfectly well what the consequences are for the mother and, more important, for the children. They all know that they are condemning their children to lives of brutality, poverty, abuse, and hopelessness. They tell me so themselves. And yet they do it over and over again, to such an extent that I should guess that nearly a quarter of British children are now brought up this way.

The result is a rising tide of neglect, cruelty, sadism, and joyous malignity that staggers and appalls me. I am more horrified after fourteen years than the day I started.

Where does this evil come from? There is obviously something flawed in the heart of man that he should wish to behave in this depraved fashion—the legacy of original sin, to speak metaphorically. But if, not so long ago, such conduct was much less widespread than it is now (in a time of much lesser prosperity, be it remembered by those who think that poverty explains everything), something more is needed to explain it.

A necessary, though not sufficient, condition is the welfare state, which makes it possible, and sometimes advantageous, to behave like this. Just as the IMF is the bank of last resort, encouraging commercial banks to make unwise loans to countries that they know the IMF will bail out, so the state is the parent of last resort—or, more often than not, of first resort. The state, guided by the apparently generous and humane philosophy that no child, whatever its origins, should suffer deprivation, gives assistance to any child, or rather the mother of any child, once it has come into being. In matters of public housing, it is actually advantageous for a mother to put herself at a disadvantage, to be a single mother, without support from the fathers of the children and dependent on the state for income. She is then a priority; she won't pay local taxes, rent, or utility bills.

As for the men, the state absolves them of all responsibility for their children. The state is now father to the child. The biological father is therefore free to use whatever income he has as pocket money, for entertainment and little treats. He is thereby reduced to the status of a child, though a spoiled child with the physical capabilities of a man: petulant, demanding, querulous, self-centered, and violent if he doesn't get his own way. The violence escalates and becomes a habit. A spoiled brat becomes an evil tyrant.

But if the welfare state is a necessary condition for the spread of evil, it is not sufficient. After all, the British welfare state is neither the most extensive nor the most generous in the world, and yet our rates of social pathology—public drunkenness, drug-taking, teenage pregnancy, venereal disease, hooliganism, criminality—are the highest in the world. Something more was necessary to produce this result.

Here we enter the realm of culture and ideas. For it is necessary not only to believe that it is economically feasible to behave in the irresponsible and egotistical fashion I have described, but also to believe that it is morally permissible to do so. And this idea has been peddled by the intellectual elite in Britain for many years, more assiduously than anywhere else, to the extent that it is now taken for granted. There has been a long march not only through the institutions but through the minds of the young. When young people want to praise themselves, they describe themselves as "nonjudgmental." For them, the highest form of morality is amorality.

There has been an unholy alliance between those on the left, who believe that man is endowed with rights but no duties, and libertarians on the right, who believe that consumer choice is the answer to all social questions, an idea eagerly adopted by the left in precisely those areas where it does not apply. Thus people have a right to bring forth children any way they like, and the children, of course, have the right not to be deprived of anything, at least anything material. How men and women associate and have children is merely a matter of consumer choice, of no more moral consequence than the choice between dark and milk chocolate, and the state must not discriminate among different forms of association and child rearing, even if such nondiscrimination has the same effect as British and French neutrality during the Spanish Civil War.

The consequences to the children and to society do not enter into the matter: for in any case it is the function of the state to ameliorate by redistributive taxation the material effects of individual irresponsibility, and to ameliorate the emotional, educational, and spiritual effects by an army of social workers, psychologists, educators, counselors, and the like, who have themselves come to form a powerful vested interest of dependence on the government.

So while my patients know in their hearts that what they are doing is wrong, and worse than wrong, they are encouraged nevertheless to do it by the strong belief that they have the right to do it, because everything is merely a matter of choice. Almost no one in Britain ever publicly challenges this belief. Nor has any politician the courage to demand a withdrawal of the public subsidy that allows the intensifying evil I have seen over the past fourteen years—violence, rape, intimidation, cruelty, drug addiction, neglect—to flourish so exuberantly. With 40 percent of children in Britain born out of wedlock, and the proportion still rising, and with divorce the norm rather than the exception, there soon will be no electoral constituency for reversal. It is already deemed to be electoral suicide to advocate it by those who, in their hearts, know that such a reversal is necessary.

I am not sure they are right. They lack courage. My only cause for optimism during the past fourteen years has been the fact that my patients, with a few exceptions, can be brought to see the truth of what I say: that they are not depressed; they are unhappy—and they are unhappy because they have chosen to live in a way that they ought not to live, and in which it is impossible to be happy. Without exception, they say they would not want their children to live as they have lived. But the social, economic, and ideological pressures—and, above all, the parental example—make it likely that their children's choices will be as bad as theirs.

Ultimately the moral cowardice of the intellectual and political elites is responsible for the continuing social disaster that has overtaken Britain, a disaster whose full social and economic consequences have yet to be seen. A sharp economic downturn would expose how far the policies of successive governments, all in the direction of libertinism, have atomized British society, so that all social solidarity within families and communities, so protective in times of hardship, has been destroyed. The elites cannot even acknowledge what has happened, however obvious it is, for to do so would be to admit their past responsibility for it, and that would make them feel bad. Better that millions should live in wretchedness and squalor than that they should feel bad about themselves—another aspect of the frivolity of evil. Moreover, if members of the elite acknowledged the social disaster brought about by their ideological libertinism, they might feel called upon to place restraints upon their own behavior, for you cannot long demand of others what you balk at doing yourself.

There are pleasures, no doubt, to be had in crying in the wilderness, in being a man who thinks he has seen farther and more keenly than others, but they grow fewer with time. The wilderness has lost its charms for me.

I'm leaving—I hope for good.

2004

A Taste for Danger

◈ ON A RECENT VISIT to New York, I stepped from the remarkably rich and elegant world of Madison Avenue into a photographic exhibition entitled "Requiem" at the Newseum. The
stores, galleries, and boutiques of the Upper East Side had given me
great pleasure; but the contemplation of silk ties, no matter how
beautifully designed and exquisitely made, bores me after a while,
and I begin to suffer acutely from *nostalgie de la boue*. I have ex-
plored the dark underside of life for too long to remain contented
with its sunny uplands for more than a few hours at a time.

"Requiem" was an exhibition of photographs of the Vietnam
War taken by photographers who were themselves killed in it. This
gave the exhibition a special poignancy: some of the pictures were
printed from the photographers' last roll of film or were even of
the last thing they saw before their death. It would have taken a
strange kind of intellectual obtuseness or emotional unresponsive-
ness not to have reacted deeply to these photographs of bravery,
cowardice, cruelty, torture, pain, treachery, comradeship, terror,
death, destruction, and inconsolable grief—all in a landscape of
unequaled beauty that had long been home to a delicate and refined civilization. We see, *inter alia*, an aircrew chief weeping after
a failed mission in which his comrades were killed; a woman being
interrogated by having her head held under the water of a river, her
interrogator gripping her by the hair; a failed attempt at mouth-to-
mouth resuscitation of a wounded infantryman; the silhouette of a
dead soldier being hoisted aboard a helicopter. And we read the
last message received from a Cambodian photographer working

for the AP, as the Khmer Rouge entered Phnom Penh: "I alone in post office. . . . I have so numerous stories to cover. . . . I feel rather trembling. . . . Maybe last cable today and forever."

The first pictures in the exhibition, however, were of the Indochinese landscape before the war and extended to every part of it. I doubt that there is a more serene landscape anywhere in the world, and I count myself fortunate to have traveled through it several years after the ending of the war, when the serenity—superficially, at least—had returned. Vietnam was then emerging from its isolation, but visitors were still few. I had the imperial tombs at Hue entirely to myself—not another person in sight or, more important still, within earshot—and I can hardly expect ever again to experience such complete tranquility. The architecture, the gardens, and the landscape were in the most perfect harmony, to be appreciated fully only in silence and solitude.

Of course, hundreds of thousands of people had been killed that I might enjoy my little aesthetic epiphany. I had, unwittingly, taken advantage of a window of opportunity to experience it, for soon afterward, no doubt, the tour buses would start to arrive, with all the ugliness and despoliation that mass tourism entails. There is no contest between Confucius and Coca-Cola. Meanwhile, to the north, the people of puritanical Hanoi had begun to partake of the joys of frivolity for the first time in nearly half a century. Private market stalls had just been permitted, dance halls had opened, and ice cream was available again. To see the innocent pleasure people took in these small things, after so grim a period of history, was moving indeed; but I knew that, in the not distant future, the growth of the tender green shoots of a consumer society would render impossible the kind of quasi-mystical experience that Hue had offered me.

I recalled a passage in Mary McCarthy's book *Hanoi*, written at the height of the conflict in 1968, when she visited that city. Miss McCarthy had a conversation with the prime minister of North Vietnam, Pham Van Dong, about the *quality* (her emphasis) of Vietnamese life. "Material scarcity," she wrote, "is regarded as a piece of good luck. . . . He [Pham Van Dong] spoke of our automobile-TV culture as of something distastefully gross and heavy; Vietnamese ethics are permeated with ideas of lightness and swift pliability: bamboo, bicycles, sandals, straw. . . . With a full-lipped contempt . . . he rejected the notion of a socialist consumer society." It did not occur to Miss McCarthy, who perceived and reported such wonders in Hanoi as the triumph of socialism over acne, to ask at whose behest, or on what moral authority, Pham Van Dong rejected consumer society.

Much as I feel a tension between my own aesthetic and cultural tastes and the preferences of vast numbers of people, I do not conclude, as Miss McCarthy did, that the solution lies in the political dictatorship of a small, like-minded minority. The answer to mass vulgarity is not the rule of snobbery or a forcible return to the world of straw and sandal; but it nevertheless remains a matter of sorrow to me that, with the opportunity for individual participation in the glories of our culture greater than ever before in all our history, the meretricious, the vulgar, and the downright hideous should triumph so easily, should find so eager a reception in the minds of men.

It is strange, perhaps, to speak of aesthetics in the context of an exhibition of photographs of the Vietnam War, but even when the photographs move on from the serene landscape of Indochina to the terrible events of war, it is obvious that the photographers were aesthetes of a kind. With death and terror all around them, they yet had a mind to the composition of their pictures. For their photographs were not just taken unself-consciously but were composed, often brilliantly so. A camera pointed at random, even in the fiercest of action, would not have produced these shattering images.

How could anyone witness these scenes—of scattered corpses, of interrogation under torture by suspension of a suspect upside down, of mortally wounded men dying in the mud, even of a woman correspondent, Dickey Chapelle, being given the last rites after she had stepped on a land mine and her neck had been ripped open by a piece of shrapnel, her head lying in a shining pool of her own blood—how could anyone witness them and still worry about composition? Is this not evidence of a defective sensibility, of an almost psychopathic indifference to human suffering?

No. In a small way, on a scale nothing like that in "Requiem," I too have witnessed scenes of horror in far-flung places: a church in Monrovia, for example, in which six hundred people taking refuge from the civil war were heartlessly slaughtered by the troops of the dictator, and where the silhouettes of the victims' bodies were still visible in the dried blood on the floor; or of the corpses of poor Peruvians in Ayacucho, murdered by the Shining Path guerrillas to discourage other Peruvians from voting as they had just done. The flesh of their faces had been flayed from their skulls, leaving their eerily translucent eyeballs naked and exposed—and I too took photographs while worrying about the angle, the light, the composition.

I was consumed by the need to communicate to others what I had seen for myself, and a bad, uncomposed photograph would never be published. My aesthetic concerns, therefore, were not a sign of any lack of feeling on my part but, on the contrary, of my strength of feeling and character—that, at any rate, is what I told myself. Certainly the desire to inform the world about suffering distances the informer emotionally from that suffering, even his own, but not in the way that a psychopathic perpetrator distances himself from his victims, and not for the same purposes. The photographer of catastrophe is more akin to the doctor, who does not suffer a moral collapse every time he encounters a tragedy:

> The wounded surgeon plies the steel
> That questions the distempered part;
> Beneath the bleeding hands we feel
> The sharp compassion of the healer's art
> Resolving the enigma of the fever chart.

It is only the sentimentalist who imagines that the profundity of a person's response to tragedy is proportional to the length, volume, or shrillness of his lamentation.

But human motives are rarely pure and never simple. One hundred and thirty-five photographers are known to have been killed in the Vietnam War, forty-one of them from countries in which they could easily have lived in peace, prosperity, and perfect honor, without having exposed themselves to the trauma or dangers of war. They knew the risks they ran (as how could they not have known?), and many of them returned for further tours of duty knowing that death was no distant possibility. But away from the war they grew restless, bored, and dissatisfied. I do not think that a desire to inform their fellow citizens of what was happening, laudable though it was, can be the whole explanation of their extraordinary, almost suicidal, conduct.

These photographers hated the war, but they loved it too: for it gave meaning to their lives or at the very least provided a temporary relief from those nagging questions about the meaning of life that even the most complacent of us sometimes ask. Dr. Johnson kicked a stone to establish the reality, which Bishop Berkeley had questioned, of the external world; these photographers established that there was more to life than dull domestic routine by going to war. Vietnam was big enough for the largest ego to lose itself in; it was big enough to give purpose to the most aimless of lives.

I understand this frame of mind only too well: I know the incomparable attractions of danger. Of course, I have never had myself strapped to the wings of an aircraft in a combat zone, as one of the photographers represented in this exhibition did, the better to furnish idle readers back home with a startling photograph of an air raid. But for an ordinary and respectable son of the English middle classes, with a proper profession, I have put myself in the way of a few unusual situations: I have been sought by the South African secret police for having disregarded the laws of apartheid; I have seen the inside of a Balkan police station from the point of view of someone under arrest; I have been deported from Honduras to Nicaragua as a Communist; I have made myself the target of Salvadoran guerrillas for having given a ride to government soldiers; I have been clandestine in East Timor; I have traveled through several civil wars. There are few exhilarations greater than being completely beyond the reach of anyone who might help you—provided of course that the dangerous situation has been freely chosen and not imposed, and that there is somewhere safe to return to when the excitement has either worn off or become overwhelming. Even with these provisos, however, I am only describing what I myself have experienced: I do not prescribe what others ought to experience. And I am happy to acknowledge that, by the standards of many, my tastes are peculiar, even perverse.

Not surprisingly, I have found my frequent returns to the workaday world of mortgages, regular hours, and supermarket shopping less than wholly pleasurable. And when, having returned from a country in which half the population has been displaced and the infrastructure entirely destroyed, I hear complaints about the difficulty of finding taxis in the rain or delays in delivery of the mail, I am apt to grow disdainful. The problem with having lived too long or too frequently in dangerous situations is that one ceases to care very much about the actual content of the existence one is so anxious to preserve. Danger absolves one of the need to deal with a hundred quotidian problems or to make a thousand little choices, each one unimportant. Danger simplifies existence and therefore—again when chosen, not imposed—comes as a relief from many anxieties.

My tastes are neither as uncommon nor as extreme as might at first appear. I have met many people far more avid for the thrill of danger than I. For them, danger is like a drug to which tolerance has developed, so that they require ever-larger doses to experience the same effect. I remember an American photographer in San Salvador—at a time when bombs exploded daily in the city, when Uzi-wielding men of dubious appearance guarded every store, every playground, and every middle-class home, and when the final assault by the guerrillas on the mountainside was expected at any moment—who told me that he was bored by the tameness of the city, that he longed for the real action of napalm and firefights such as happened in the countryside. He was only at inner peace in the midst of bullets, he said. He loved the country, but his commitment to it was only war-deep: if peace, alas, were to break out, he would have to find another conflict to photograph.

An extreme and terminal case, no doubt, but I encounter milder forms of the malady every day. Untold numbers of my patients, with every opportunity to lead quiet, useful, and tolerably prosperous lives, choose instead the path of complication and, if not of violence and physical danger exactly, at least of drama and excitement, leading to sleepless nights and financial loss. They break up marriages, form disastrous liaisons, chase chimeras, and behave in ways that predictably will end in disaster. Like moths to the flame, they court catastrophe. As many have told me, they prefer disaster to boredom.

Those who are not satisfied with their work, or who have no intellectual or cultural interests, and whose coarse emotions have undergone refinement neither by education nor by adherence to civilized custom, are particularly liable to seek out the compensatory complications of domestic disorder and disarray. The perpetually unemployed, for example, lead a crude and frequently violent version of the life portrayed in *Les Liaisons Dangereuses*. Like French aristocrats under the *ancien régime*, they are—thanks to Social Security—under no compulsion to earn a living; and with time hanging heavy on their hands, their personal relationships are their only diversion. These relationships are therefore both intense and shallow, for there is never any mutual interest in them deeper than the avoidance of the ever-encroaching ennui.

The pattern of human self-destruction is confined to no social class or group, however. A distinguished and in many ways admirable Russian writer of the late nineteenth century, V. G. Korolenko, once wrote that man is born for happiness as a bird for flight: to which one is inclined to add, yes, if mice are born for heroism. It would be difficult, in fact, to summarize human nature more inaccurately. Yet social theorists often suppose that human beings have a clear idea what it is they want from life, and behave moreover as if they were rational calculating machines designed to procure it. How many people does each of us know (present company excepted) who claim to seek happiness but freely choose paths inevitably leading to misery?

The photographers represented in "Requiem" were surely both terrified and enthralled, appalled and exhilarated, exhausted and energized, by what they saw and did. Just as the man who fights iniquity is seldom wholly satisfied by its defeat (for what is there for him to do thereafter?), so the anti-war propagandist—as each of these photographers must be accounted—comes to love his ostensible enemy as himself. Like Richard III, he would lament this weak piping time of peace and hate the idle pleasures of these days. For him, peace and peace of mind not merely fail to be synonymous but are almost antonyms.

I learned early in my life that if people are offered the opportunity of tranquility, they often reject it and choose torment instead. My own parents chose to live in the most abject conflictual misery and created for themselves a kind of hell on a small domestic scale, as if acting in an unscripted play by Strindberg. There was no reason external to themselves why they should not have been happy; reasonably prosperous, they lived under as benign a government as they could have wished for. Though they lived together, they addressed not a single word to one another in my presence during the eighteen years I spent in their house, though we ate at least one meal a day together; once, as a child, I was awakened in the night by the raised voice of my mother exclaiming to my father, "You're a wicked, wicked man." Those are the only words I ever heard pass between them. It was like a bolt of lightning on a dark night: dazzling but unilluminating. For the rest, their silences were highly nuanced, expressing resentment, aggression, injured innocence, exasperation, moral superiority, and all the other dishonest little emotions of which the human mind is capable. They continued their absurd, self-dramatizing civil war to the end of my father's life: on his deathbed, my father, by then long separated from my mother, said to me, "Tell her she can come if she wants to," to which my mother's reply was, "Tell him I'll come if he asks me." They stuck to their principles and never did meet: for what is mere death by comparison to a lifelong quarrel?

For a long time I pitied myself: had any child ever been as miserable as I? I felt the deepest, most sincere compassion for myself. Then gradually it began to dawn on me that the education I had received had liberated me from any need or excuse to repeat the sordid triviality of my parents' personal lives. One's past is not one's destiny, and it is self-serving to pretend that it is. If henceforth I were miserable, it would be my own fault: and I vowed never to waste my substance on petty domestic conflict.

It was the time of the Vietnam War. Pictures such as those displayed in "Requiem" seemed to uncritical and arrogant youth to unmask the falseness, the hypocrisy, the hidden but always underlying violence of Western civilization. It was the time of the Glaswegian psychiatrist R. D. Laing, according to whom only the insane were sane in an insane world, while the sane were truly insane. The family was the means by which society passed on and perpetuated its collective madness; and the Cambridge social anthropologist Edmund Leach famously said in a series of lectures on the BBC that the nuclear family was responsible not for some but for all of the misery of human existence. (Pol Pot was but a few years away.)

For obvious reasons, I was not entirely well disposed to family life or to the supposed joys of bourgeois existence, and therefore swallowed some of the nonsense whole. Like the photographers, I was only too desirous of escaping what I supposed to be the source of my personal dissatisfactions. But not for very long: for I soon came to realize that the peculiarities of my personal upbringing were not a reliable prism through which to judge the world. The only thing worse than having a family, I discovered, is not having a family. My rejection of bourgeois virtues as mean-spirited and antithetical to real human development could not long survive contact with situations in which those virtues were entirely absent; and a rejection of everything associated with one's childhood is not so much an escape from that childhood as an imprisonment by it.

It was in Africa that I first discovered that the bourgeois virtues are not only desirable but often heroic. I was working in a hospital in what was then still Rhodesia and is now Zimbabwe. I was still of the callow—and fundamentally lazy—youthful opinion that nothing in the world could change until everything changed, in which case a social system would arise in which it would be no longer necessary for anyone to be good. The head nurse on the ward in which I worked, a black woman, invited me to her home in the township for a meal. At that time and in that place, social contact between blacks and whites was unusual, though not actually illegal.

She was a splendid, kindly, hardworking woman. She lived in a township in which there were thousands of tiny, identical, prefabricated bungalows, the size of huts. The level of violence in the township was very great: on Saturday night the floors of the emergency department of my hospital were slippery with still-flowing blood.

In this unpromising environment, I discovered, the nurse had created an extremely comfortable and even pretty home for herself and her aging mother. Her tiny patch of land was like a bower; the inside of her house was immaculately clean, tidy, and well—though cheaply—furnished. I would never laugh again at the taste of people of limited means to make a comfortable home for themselves.

Looking around me in the township, I began to see that the spotlessly clean white uniform in which she appeared every day in the hospital represented not an absurd fetish, not the brutal imposition of alien cultural standards upon African life, but a noble triumph of the human spirit—as, indeed, did her tenderly cared-for home. By comparison with her struggle to maintain herself in decency, my former rejection of bourgeois proprieties and respectability seemed to me ever afterward to be shallow, trivial, and adolescent. Until then I had assumed, along with most of my generation unacquainted with real hardship, that a scruffy appearance was a sign of spiritual election, representing a rejection of the superficiality and materialism of bourgeois life. Ever since then, however, I have not been able to witness the voluntary adoption of torn, worn-out, and tattered clothes—at least in public—by those in a position to dress otherwise without a feeling of deep disgust. Far from being a sign of solidarity with the poor, it is a perverse mockery of them; it is spitting on the graves of our ancestors, who struggled so hard, so long, and so bitterly that we might be warm, clean, well fed, and leisured enough to enjoy the better things in life.

To base one's rejection of what exists—and hence one's prescription for a better world—upon the petty frustrations of one's youth, as surely many middle-class radicals have done, is profoundly egotistical. Unless consciously rejected, this impulse leads to a tendency throughout life to judge the rightness or wrongness of policies by one's personal emotional response to them, as if emotion were an infallible guide. Only connect, was E. M.

Forster's enigmatic injunction to his readers at the end of *Howards End*: to which I should prefer the injunction, Only compare. One's supposed sufferings are then not so great after all and give no special insight into the world as it is or as it should be.

But the overestimation of the importance of one's emotional responses is very widespread. It could be seen in the comment book available to visitors to the "Requiem" exhibition. Most of the visitors who wrote more than a word or two imagined that their personal responses to the pictures were sufficient for them to pass judgment on the war itself, indeed on all war. It seemed to occur to none of them that the justness or otherwise of the war could not be judged by the pictures alone, and that they needed a lot more information to make this judgment—for if such photographs had been published of Allied soldiers and civilians during the Second World War, they might, in the absence of any other information, be taken as evidence of the wrongness of resistance to Nazism.

It is not surprising that emotion untutored by thought results in nearly contentless blather, in which—ironically enough—genuine emotion itself cannot be adequately expressed. "What hurts so much," wrote one person who had visited the exhibition, "is that we humans keep doing this war / killing thing. We must hammer our guns into Plows and STUDY Peace." There were pages and pages of this kind of sentiment, which aimed to combine thought with emotion and missed both. The comment of an Italian stood out like a beacon of truth in this murk of dishonesty: "*É molto emocionante. Se non fosse la guerra, che cosa farebbero i reporter?*"

Very moving. If it weren't for war, what would journalists do?

1998

Why Shakespeare Is for All Time

A DECADE AGO the psychiatrist Peter Kramer published a book called *Listening to Prozac*, which claimed that our understanding of neurochemistry was so advanced that we would soon be able to design—and no doubt to vary—our personalities according to our tastes. Henceforth there would be no more angst. He based his prediction upon the case histories of people given the supposed wonder drug who not merely recovered from depression but emerged with new, improved personalities.

Yet the prescription of the drug (and others like it) to millions of people has not noticeably reduced the sum total of human misery or the perplexity of life. A golden age of felicity has not arrived: and the promise of a pill for every ill remains, as it always will, unfulfilled.

Anyone who had read his Shakespeare would not have been surprised by this disappointment. When Macbeth asks a physician:

Canst thou not minister to a mind diseased,
Pluck from the memory a rooted sorrow,
Raze out the written troubles of the brain,
And with some sweet oblivious antidote
Cleanse the stuffed bosom of that perilous stuff
Which weighs upon the heart?

The physician replies laconically: "Therein the patient / Must minister to himself."

Every day several patients ask me Macbeth's question with regard to themselves—in less elevated language, to be sure—and they expect a positive answer: but four centuries before neurochemistry was even thought of, and before any of the touted advances in neurosciences that allegedly gave us a new and better understanding of ourselves, Shakespeare knew something that we are increasingly loath to acknowledge: there is no technical fix for the problems of humanity.

Those problems, he knew, are ineradicably rooted in our nature; and he atomized that nature with a characteristic genius never since equaled: which is why every time we moderns consult his works, we come away with a deeper insight into the heart of our own mystery.

Take as a test case *Macbeth*, the shortest of his tragedies. The play is a study of ambition, the evil to which ambition leads when unrestrained by ethical inhibition, and the logic of evil once an evil course has been embarked upon. The ambition and the evil are part of man's nature. All that is necessary to understand the play, therefore, is to be human: and if we attend to it closely, we shall have a deeper appreciation of its subject matter than if we read all the philosophy, sociology, criminology, and biology of the past two centuries. Statistics will not lead us to enlightenment about ourselves, any more than the elucidation of the human genome will render Shakespeare redundant. Those who think that an understanding of the double helix is the same as an understanding of ourselves are not only prey to an illusion but are stunting themselves as human beings, condemning themselves not to an advance in self-understanding but to a positive retrogression.

Modern experience has been said to render Shakespeare irrelevant. In *The Gulag Archipelago*, for example, Alexander Solzhenitsyn remarks that Shakespeare's evildoers, Macbeth notably among them, stop short at a mere dozen corpses because they have no ideology. By the sanguinary standards of the twentieth century's totalitarian despots, in other words, Shakespeare's characters are but petty criminals, for (says Solzhenitsyn) it is ideology that "gives evildoing its long-sought justification and gives the evildoer the necessary steadfastness and determination." Since all subject matter shrinks to triviality when compared to the cataclysms of the Holocaust and the Gulag, it follows that a tragedy such as *Macbeth* is of limited relevance to our recent history.

Solzhenitsyn was not alone in this view: indeed, one Russian poet wrote a cycle of sonnets from the Gulag, in which he referred disparagingly to Shakespeare's tragedies as "mere trumpery"— a phrase he repeated many times as a refrain to underline the unprecedented nature of Soviet evil. Just as the German philosopher and social theorist Theodor Adorno said that after Auschwitz there could be no more poetry, so the Russians said that after the Gulag there could be no more *Macbeth*.

They were mistaken. Massacre and genocide have not always been accompanied by an ideology: were the Mongol hordes ideological, and was the ethnic conflict in Rwanda and Burundi ideological? And I have little doubt from my medical practice that radical evil can exist on a large scale without the sanction of an official ideology. Many a man is the Macbeth of his own little world, and the measurement of evil is not the same as a body count.

The Russians' remarks suggest a reading of *Macbeth* that takes the raw plot and the number of deaths as the play's most significant aspects—the kind of interpretation one might expect of a literal-minded person who had seen the play acted upon the stage but had not studied the text very closely. Even on the number of deaths, Solzhenitsyn—one of the last century's great experts on evil, after all—was not quite accurate, for there are more people killed than those whose deaths occur, or are recounted, upon the stage. When Macduff goes to sound out Malcolm, the legitimate heir to the throne who has fled to England, about leading an attempt to overthrow Macbeth, he underscores that reality:

> Each new morn,
> New widows howl, new orphans cry, new sorrows
> Strike heaven in the face.

Shakespeare makes plain that something like totalitarian terror reigns as a direct result of Macbeth's thirst for power: an atmosphere one might have expected Solzhenitsyn to recognize instantly.

Comparatively early in Macbeth's reign, before his evil is clear to everyone, Lennox says:

> And the right-valiant Banquo walked too late,
> Whom you may say, if't please you, Fleance killed,
> For Fleance fled. Men must not walk too late.

Dictatorships traditionally ascribe political murders to people who have fled the scene to escape being murdered too. If they weren't guilty, goes the charge, why did they run away? Lennox's words exactly capture the bitter irony of those impotently caught up in such a dictatorship.

Macbeth boasts that he has spies in the households of potential enemies—an ever-expanding class, of course, with each passing murder: "There's not a one of them but in his house I keep a servant fee'd." Neither spying nor fear were the inventions of Solzhenitsyn's accursed twentieth century, and tyranny is no new invention. It proceeds from the human soul itself.

Shakespeare no less than Solzhenitsyn understood the role of agents provocateurs and entrapment in tyrannies. When Macduff first seeks Malcolm's assistance, Malcolm denies that he is a suitable figurehead for opposition to Macbeth because he has so many vices himself. Where evil reigns, it is best to pretend to be evil oneself. When finally he is convinced that Macduff is sincere, however, he retracts his self-denigration and explains why he has lied in this peculiar fashion:

> Devilish Macbeth
> By many of these trains hath sought to win me
> Into his power, and modest wisdom plucks me
> From over-credulous haste.

When Macduff asks the Thane of Ross, "Stands Scotland where it did?" he replies:

> Alas, poor country,
> Almost afraid to know itself.
>   It cannot
> Be called our mother, but our grave, where nothing,

But who knows nothing, is seen once to smile;
Where sighs, and groans, and shrieks that rend the air
Are made, not marked. . . .

Did this really ring no bells during the Soviet era?

Again, when Malcolm addresses the commanders who are about to do decisive battle with Macbeth's forces, he says:

Cousins, I hope the days are near at hand
That chambers will be safe.

He doesn't say "our chambers," the chambers of a small clique of aristocratic malcontents, disgruntled at Macbeth's rule: he says "chambers" in general. And was it not characteristic of the totalitarian regimes, imbued with an ideology, to which Solzhenitsyn refers, that citizens were not safe, even in the privacy of their own homes and bedrooms, to speak their own minds: in other words, that chambers were not safe? As Shakespeare knew, rule without consent entails terror, ideology or not.

Solzhenitsyn was quite right that Macbeth has no ideology. Macbeth is motivated in equal measure by ambition and by the fear of appearing weak and small in the eyes of his wife. By stripping him of any philosophical or political justification (real or imagined) for his acts—for example, by not having him assert that the king whom he supplants is a bad one deserving of overthrow; by not letting him pretend even for a moment that he acts for the good of his country and people—Shakespeare goes straight to the heart of human evil considered *sub specie aeternitatis*. Shakespeare is interested in the essentials of human nature, not the accidentals of human history, though of course he knows that every man must live at a particular time and place. Indeed, the play refers obliquely to the current historical situation: for example, Banquo was believed to have been an ancestor of James I, and therefore the scene in which the witches tell Banquo that he will be the progenitor of many kings, though no king himself, was a form of flattery of the reigning monarch. But such topical significance is of interest mainly to pedants. If *Macbeth* were but an elaborate attempt to legitimize Jacobean rule, it is hardly credible that it should have been translated into Zulu (in which language I once saw it performed) and that it should have meant a great deal to a Zulu audience. Macbeth stands witness to the universality of great literature.

It is characteristic of Shakespeare's genius that he should have emptied Macbeth not only of ideological reasons for his actions but also of psychological ones, apart from those that spring solely from universal human nature. Macbeth is no stage villain, if I may put it thus: he is no Richard III, "Deformed, unfinished, sent before my time / Into this breathing world scarce half made up," whose physical deformity parallels, indeed plausibly explains, his moral deformity. On the contrary, Macbeth is a hero, a valiant soldier in a good cause, bravely and loyally saving the realm of good king Duncan ("O valiant cousin, worthy gentleman," exclaims the king, when he hears of Macbeth's exploits on the battlefield against the forces of his enemies). He is no psychopath or sociopath. He is a normal man, endowed with a nature no worse than ours: which is why, of course, he stands as a chilling example to us all.

Nor is he the victim of injustice or ingratitude that might extenuate, though not excuse, his later crimes. He has nothing to complain of: quite the reverse, for he is fortunate in his aristocratic birth, and he is more than generously rewarded by the king for his military services. Greeting Macbeth for the first time after his victories, Duncan says:

> The sin of my ingratitude even now
> Was heavy on me. Thou art so far before,
> That swiftest wing of recompense is slow
> To overtake thee. Would thou hadst less deserved,
> That the proportion both of thanks and payment
> Might have been mine. Only I have left to say,
> More is thy due than more than all can pay.

Macbeth can hardly claim to be undervalued by Duncan—but he kills him nonetheless.

He cannot complain of his domestic or economic circumstances, either. When Duncan later arrives at Macbeth's castle, he remarks upon its beauty and tranquility:

> This castle hath a pleasant seat; the air
> Nimbly and sweetly recommends itself
> Unto our gentle senses.

What more than Macbeth already has when he starts on his road to ruin could a man want?

Macbeth says as much. He specifically recognizes that he has no motive for his future crimes but a lust for power that comes entirely from within:

> I have no spur
> To prick the side of my intent, but only
> Vaulting ambition which o'erleaps itself.

This motivation is in specific contrast with the two murderers whom he employs to kill Banquo. By the time they appear on stage, Macbeth has already poured poison in their ears, informing them (falsely, of course) that Banquo is the author of all their woes:

> This I made good to you in our last conference; passed in probation with you how you were borne in hand, how crossed, the instruments, who wrought with them, and all things else that might to half a soul and to a notion crazed say, "Thus did Banquo."

The two murderers are only too eager to hear that they have an enemy responsible for all their disappointments. They are resentment personified, archetypes of men with grudges against the world, who—unlike Macbeth—are thereby predisposed to evil. The Second Murderer says:

> I am one, my liege,
> Whom the vile blows and buffets of the world
> Hath so incensed that I am reckless what I do
> To spite the world.

The First Murderer then adds:

> And I another
> So weary with disasters, tugged with fortune,
> That I would set my life on any chance
> To mend it or be rid on't.

Superficially, then, they have a reason, if not a justification, for their heinous deeds. We do not know, of course, whether their disappointments and setbacks are real or imaginary, self-inflicted or undeserved, and it doesn't matter: Shakespeare gives us to understand that their self-pity—and by extension all self-pity, including our own—is dangerous, permitting evil in the name of restitution.

Macbeth, however, is not a resentful man; he never complains of ill-treatment. So while resentment is a cause of man's evil, it is not the sole or fundamental cause. Macbeth is led to evil by his ambition: and because we all live in society, in which jockeying for position and power is inevitable, we all understand him from within. Macbeth is us without the moral scruples.

By depriving Macbeth of any particular predilection for evil that is not common to all men, and by denying him every possible circumstance that might justify or occasion his actions, Shakespeare excavates down to the line between good and evil that runs through every human heart, to use a phrase from *The Gulag Archipelago* that contradicts Solzhenitsyn's faintly dismissive estimate of Shakespeare's evil characters. He writes: "Gradually it was disclosed to me [in the Gulag] that the line separating good from evil passes not through states, nor between classes, nor between political parties either—but right through every human heart—and through all human hearts." And it is Shakespeare who shows us this line.

But he does more. He shows us not only how easily that line is crossed, even by someone without an excuse or a special propensity to do so, but what the consequences are of crossing it. And in showing us that the line is always there, easily and disastrously crossed, Shakespeare destroys the utopian illusion that social arrangements can be made so perfect that men will no longer have to strive to be good. Original sin—that is to say, the sin of having

been born with human nature that contains within it the temptation to evil—will always make a mockery of attempts at perfection
based upon manipulation of the environment. The prevention of
evil will always require more than desirable social arrangements: it
will forever require personal self-control and the conscious limitation of appetites.

Macbeth is ambitious before the opening of the play. That is
why he is startled when the three witches greet him as Thane of
Cawdor and future king of Scotland: they echo his secret thoughts.
But he has so far kept his ambition under ethical control (as Lady
Macbeth puts it, "Thou wouldst be great / Art not without ambition, but without / The illness [malevolence] should attend it"),
and even after his meeting with the witches he ponders, like a
Marxist wondering whether or not the historical inevitability of
the triumph of the revolution requires his participation:

> If chance will have me king, why chance may crown me
> Without my stir.

As Russian Marxists needed their Lenin, so Macbeth needs his
Lady Macbeth. Decisive during the simplicities of battle, without
her he would forever be a waverer in the complexities of peace:
more Hamlet, indeed, than Macbeth.

The tool that Lady Macbeth uses to galvanize her husband
into action is humiliation. She humiliates him into doing what he
knows to be wrong, just as many of my patients who take heroin
started to take it because they were afraid to seem weak in the eyes
of their associates. Macbeth loves and respects his wife ("my dear-
est partner in greatness," he calls her), but Lady Macbeth perverts
his love—and his essential, ineradicable, and often laudable human desire to be respected and loved by the person one respects
and loves—to the purposes of evil. The lesson is that any powerful
emotion or desire, however virtuous in many circumstances, can
be turned to evil purposes if it escapes ethical control.

For Shakespeare, human nature has the potential for both
good and evil, depending upon the decisions we make. Macbeth
is ambitious, true: but not only is ambition, in the sense of a desire for the just approbation of one's fellow men, a good quality,

but Macbeth is not so ambitious that nothing else matters. His ambition for approbation sets bounds and limits to his ambition, so to speak. Lady Macbeth recognizes her husband's reflexive scrupulousness:

Yet I do fear thy nature,
It is too full o'th'milk of human kindness
To catch the nearest way.

She must curdle the milk, make Macbeth abjure his good qualities, if he is to act as she wishes.

But paradoxically she, who is usually taken to represent the acme of evil, is not by nature altogether evil herself but only evil potentially—in other words, evil by choice. She recognizes the need to suppress the potential for good in her own nature if she is to obey the promptings of ambition:

Come, you spirits
That tend on mortal thoughts, unsex me here
And fill me from the crown to the toe topfull
Of direst cruelty; make thick my blood,
Stop up th'access and passage to remorse
That no compunctious visitings of nature
Shake my fell purpose.

No more chilling evocation of the willing choice of evil exists in all literature than Lady Macbeth's famous renunciation of maternal feeling for the sake of power:

I have given suck and know
How tender 'tis to love the babe that milks me:
I would, while it was smiling in my face,
Have plucked the nipple from his boneless gums
And dashed the brains out, had I so sworn
As you have done to this.

And yet the point remains: the true psychopath has not in the first place the compunctious visitings whose passage needs to be stopped up. Most men and women must suppress the good within them to be evil; just as, to be good, they must suppress the evil. There is no final victory of one or the other.

Indeed, Lady Macbeth's tragedy is that she so gravely underestimates the strength of the good within her. Eventually it takes its revenge upon her, for she "by self and violent hands / Took off her life."

Her psychological error is to imagine that the good within her could simply be ignored without consequences. After she and Macbeth have covered themselves in blood by the murder of Duncan and the two chamberlains, she says: "Retire we to our chamber; / A little water clears us of this deed." How many of my patients think they can behave unscrupulously without a penalty to be paid!

The shallowness of Lady Macbeth's idea of exculpation stands revealed—completely and piercingly—in the sleepwalking scene, in which she acknowledges that "all the perfumes of Arabia will not sweeten this little hand." A little water will wash away the blood but not the sin and the guilt.

Macbeth succumbs to Lady Macbeth's taunting. One is reminded of the famous experiments that Stanley Milgram, the social psychologist, described in his book *Obedience to Authority*. In these experiments, researchers, using mere words, induced ordinary people—like Macbeth, without any special propensity to evil—to administer what they believed to be dangerous electric shocks to complete strangers.

But Shakespeare is not so crude as to believe that social pressure is always bad. On the contrary, our desire to see ourselves favorably reflected in the esteem of others is the source of honor and other worthy qualities. For example, when Macduff replies to Malcolm's suggestion that they simply bemoan their fate as victims of Macbeth, he says:

> Let us rather
> Hold fast the mortal sword and like good men
> Bestride our down-fall'n birthdom.

Good men, he suggests, are engaged upon a common enterprise, strengthened by values they hold in common. When Siward hears that his son has been killed in the final battle to overthrow Macbeth, he says:

> Why then, God's soldier be he;
> Had I as many sons as I have hairs
> I would not wish them a fairer death.

Without the social virtues of honor and obedience to duty, young Siward might have fled and saved his skin—as, indeed, would everyone else, leaving Macbeth still in power. And it is the fact of his death having been a worthwhile sacrifice that gives it meaning, and that meaning places a limit to the father's grief.

Macbeth is aware throughout the play that what he does is morally wrong: he never claims (as do so many modern relativists) that fair is foul and foul is fair. He thus single-handedly refutes the Platonic theory of evil as ignorance of the good. Unlike his wife, he never deceives himself that a little water can clear them of their deeds. On the contrary, as soon as he has murdered Duncan, he knows that he is irredeemably compromised:

> Will all great Neptune's ocean wash this blood
> Clean from my hand? No: this my hand will rather
> The multitudinous seas incarnadine,
> Making the green one red.

And so he at once regrets what he has done, as he says when he hears knocking at the outer gate after the murder: "Wake Duncan with thy knocking: I would thou couldst."

He knows that Macbeth shall sleep no more. He has committed himself to such a treadmill by his initial act of evil that he comes to envy his own victims:

> Better be with the dead
> Whom we, to gain our peace, have sent to peace,
> Than on the torture of the mind to lie
> In restless ecstasy.

Time's arrow flies in one direction only. On several occasions, Macbeth makes reference to the unchangeability of what has already been done: a disconcerting thought when incontinent public confession is all the rage, as if mere words automatically undid harm and made bad good. Evil, once committed, has an inescapable logic of its own, as Macbeth famously discovers:

> I am in blood
> Stepped in so far that should I wade no more,
> Returning were as tedious as to go o'er.

Macbeth utters the key line in the play, when his wife is taunting him into killing Duncan:

> Wouldst thou have that
> Which thou esteem'st the ornament of life,
> And live a coward in thine own esteem,
> Letting I dare not wait upon I would?

And he replies:

> Prithee, peace.
> I dare do all that may become a man;
> Who dares do more is none.

In other words, there is a boundary that, once crossed, deprives a man of his full humanity. Boundaries are what keep us human, and they are not lightly to be crossed. That is why the admiration of the transgressive in art is so deeply frivolous. And it is why Britain's most notorious murderess, Myra Hindley, who has just died, properly stayed in prison until the end. She and her associate, Ian Brady, tortured and murdered several children on a whim in the first half of the 1960s, and she devoted much of her life in prison to campaigning for her own release. She had changed, she insisted; she had paid her debt to society long ago.

But life is not a matter of double-entry bookkeeping. No number of years in prison can be equivalent to the torture and killing of children: if it were, the term could be served in advance and the person who served it would be entitled to commit his crimes on his release. Hindley's victims were dead and could not be resurrected; she could not undo what she had done.

Macbeth warns us to preserve our humanity by accepting limitations to our actions. As Macduff says to Malcolm, when the latter presents himself as a heartless libertine:

> Boundless intemperance
> In nature is a tyranny.

Only if we obey rules—the rules that count—can we be free.

2003

Sex and the
Shakespeare Reader

SHAKESPEARE'S PLAYS are subject to fashion, just like everything else. In a recent production of *Hamlet* at my local repertory theater, the prince raped Ophelia on stage, which fully explained her subsequent insanity to any politically correct audience. At last it understood why she chanted snatches of old tunes, as one incapable of her own distress. Shakespeare, it seems, can be made to serve almost any agenda.

For most of the four centuries since it was first performed, *Measure for Measure* found little favor, and was even despised. Dryden, Dr. Johnson, and Coleridge—acute critics, all—detested it. Dryden wrote that it was "grounded on impossibilities, or at least so meanly written, that the comedy neither caused your mirth, nor the serious part your concernment." Dr. Johnson thought that in this play, Shakespeare "makes no just distribution of good and evil . . . he carries his persons indifferently through right and wrong, and at the end dismisses them without further care." Coleridge called it "the most painful—say, rather, the only painful—part of his genuine works."

But suddenly, in the latter half of the twentieth century, it came to seem one of Shakespeare's most compelling and intriguing works. The questions it asks—to what extent does the state have the right or the duty to impose a sexual moral code upon its citizenry and, deeper still, how is sexual passion to be humanized?—seem more relevant to us now than at any time in the intervening years. In my everyday work as a doctor, for example, I see the results of ungoverned, and consequently ungovernable, passion: that is to say, murder, mayhem, and misery.

And, as usual, Shakespeare's answers to the questions he raises are subtle, far subtler than those of any ideologue or abstract theorist could ever be: for he is a realist without cynicism and an idealist without utopianism. He knows that the tension between men as they are and men as they ought to be will forever remain unresolved. Man's imperfectibility is no more an excuse for total permissiveness, however, than are man's imperfections a reason for inflexible intolerance.

Vincentio is Duke of Vienna, a sovereign with undisputed power and therefore much responsibility. Unfortunately, he has let things slide; he has allowed the laws against immorality to become a dead letter, and the Viennese to do very much as they please. He does not like the results:

> We have strict statutes and most biting laws,
> The needful bits and curbs to headstrong jades,
> Which for this fourteen years we have let slip;
> Even like an o'ergrown lion in a cage,
> That goes out not to prey.
> Now, as fond fathers,
> Having bound up the threatening twigs of birch
> Only to stick in their children's sight,
> For terror, not for use, in time the rod
> Becomes more mocked than feared . . .
> And liberty plucks justice by the nose;
> The baby beats the nurse, and quite athwart
> Goes all decorum.

The duke realizes that something must be done, but he is not the man to do it:

> Sith 'twas my fault to give the people scope,
> 'Twould be my tyranny to strike and gall them
> For what I bid them do. . . .

He therefore proposes to leave Vienna for a time, ostensibly to go on a long journey, but in reality to disguise himself as a friar to observe what happens in Vienna in his absence. As his deputy, he appoints Angelo, a man of inflexible moral principle, akin to the Puritans, who were increasingly influential in the Corporation of London at the time *Measure for Measure* was first performed. Viewing the drama and the playhouses as destructive of virtue and provocative of vice, the Puritans wished to close them down— a threat to Shakespeare's art and livelihood.

Angelo disdains human weakness. According to the duke:

> . . . Lord Angelo is precise,
> Stands at a guard with envy; scarce confesses
> That his blood flows, or that his appetite
> Is more to bread than stone.

Having been handed the duke's power, Angelo decrees that all the brothels in Vienna must be closed and pulled down, and he orders that Claudio, "a young gentleman," be arrested and condemned to death for having got his beloved Juliet, whom he has promised to marry, with child. This is in strict accordance with the law against fornication.

Isabella, Claudio's beautiful and chaste young sister, who has just entered a convent as a novice, goes to plead with Angelo for her brother's life. At first he refuses her suit; but then he finds that he is as other men are and comes strongly to desire her. "Ever till now," he soliloquizes, "When men were fond, I smiled and wondered how."

He offers to spare her brother's life if Isabella will sleep with him. Isabella is horrified; but after various machinations suggested by the duke disguised as a friar, it is arranged that Angelo should sleep with a former betrothed of his, Mariana, whom he has cruelly repudiated because her dowry was lost at sea. After he has done so, however, still believing that he has slept with Isabella, he goes back on his word and orders that Claudio be executed nonetheless. Further machinations of the duke prevent this mischance. The duke returns to Vienna, publicly exposes Angelo as a hypocritical villain, and condemns him to death—the *Measure for Measure* of the title. Angelo is spared, however, because of the pleas of Mariana and Isabella on his behalf. He marries Mariana, the duke marries Isabella, and Claudio marries his Juliet. Puritanism is soundly defeated, and all's well that ends well.

Measure for Measure was the first Shakespeare play I ever saw acted on the professional stage. It was in 1962, and my father took me to Stratford to see it during a school vacation. I don't suppose I understood much of its moral import at the time, and I certainly didn't realize that the questions it raises were to be so important in my later professional life. It must have been a somewhat uncomfortable experience for my father, an inveterate womanizer given to stern, universal, and almost puritanical moral pronouncements.

As it happens, the one individual performance I still remember is that of Angelo, who was played by Marius Goring, a distinguished stage and screen actor. When I read of his death in 1998, aged eighty-six, more than a third of a century after I had seen him on the stage, he was still clad in my imagination in the burgundy velvet tunic and tights of his costume as Angelo.

By strange coincidence, Goring's father, Charles Goring, was a prison doctor, as I was myself to become years later. Dr. Goring wrote a big volume called *The English Convict*, intended as a refutation of the predominant criminological theory of the time, Italian positivism, whose most famous proponent, Cesare Lombroso, argued that criminality was a biological trait recognizable by physical signs such as a sloping forehead or narrowness between the eyes. Dr. Goring measured hundreds of English prisoners from head to toe and administered batteries of tests to them, correlating each measure with every other, and concluding that, Measure for Measure, there was no such thing as the biological criminal type.

At the time, this argument decisively swept the field: criminals are made, not born. But no refutation of so broad a theory as Italian positivism is ever quite decisive, and since then biological theories of crime have made a spirited, if still wrongheaded, comeback. The heredity of criminality and the neurobiology of illicit acquisition and aggression are once again respectable subjects of research, though they can never explain the important question of why some eras or populations are more crime-ridden than others.

The relation between the biological and the social, between the animal and the human, is the principal theme of *Measure for Measure*, as it was of Dr. Goring's less inspired, but still important, work. And Shakespeare certainly gives biology its due. Not only is his play anti-puritanical but it recognizes without censoriousness the strength of the sexual urge and the intense pleasure it offers. The comic characters of the play (and *Measure for Measure* is counted among Shakespeare's comedies, though its theme could hardly be more serious, and a tragic outcome is only just averted) are almost innocent in their cheerful acceptance of fornication as a permanent and welcome feature of human existence. Certainly Mistress Overdone, the innkeeper whose hostelry is also a brothel of which she is the madam, Pompey her tapster, and Lucio, "a Fantastic," never sink anywhere near the depths of evil to which Angelo sinks, on account of the inevitable conflict between his unbending principles and his own human nature. Better a certain moral elasticity than complete moral rigidity. Moreover, an evening in their company would be very much more fun than an evening with Isabella, however morally perfect she might be. And if I had to guess what Shakespeare's personal attitude was to Mistress Overdone and her cronies, it would be affection, not outrage.

These comic characters are not without insight into human nature. When Mistress Overdone learns that Angelo has ordered that "All houses [brothels] in the suburbs of Vienna must be plucked down," Pompey consoles her:

> Come, fear not you; good counsellors lack no clients.
> Though you change your place, you need not change your trade.

The oldest profession will survive whatever the laws against it might be, for human nature will never change. Similarly, when Lucio, a libertine somewhat higher up the social ladder than Mistress Overdone and Pompey, speaks to the duke (at the time still disguised as a friar) about Lord Angelo, he suggests that "a little more lenity to lechery would do no harm in him." The duke replies, "It is too general a vice, and severity must cure it." With a shrewd realism, Lucio says something whose truth only a man deluded by his moral enthusiasm, such as Angelo is, would not recognize at once: "it is impossible to extirp it quite . . . till eating and drinking be put down." Lust really does spring eternal.

But Shakespeare most decidedly does not leave it at that. He does not say, or in any way imply, that because lust is eternal, because it can never be extirpated quite, any and all sexual relations are perfectly in order and morally equal. I do not think, for example, that Shakespeare would view the sexual free-for-all of contemporary Britain—with its harvest of child neglect and abuse, morbid jealousy, sexual violence, and egocentric savagery—with the complacent impassivity of today's British intelligentsia. On the contrary: he would loathe it, for its consequences are precisely what he sees lurking in human nature if civilizing restraint be removed. Shakespeare is not a partisan of the noble savage who lives by instinct alone: rather, it is the savage in man that he fears and detests. The service that Mistress Overdone provides is fine—indeed, needed—as a safety valve, but as a model of all intimate human relations it is the primrose path to earthly perdition.

In fact, none of the major characters in the play regards sex as merely a biological or animal function and therefore of no moral concern. Of course, to regard sex only as a moral problem, as an impulse to be repressed at all costs, as Angelo does, is as deforming as to regard it as having no moral importance. An excess of moral rigor leads to dehumanization as surely as its total absence: and because of his moral zeal, Angelo's relations with women are thus either coldly contractual, as in the breaking of his engagement to Mariana, or those of a rapist, when the natural impulse becomes too strong to be resisted.

Claudio, the first victim of Angelo's inhuman zeal, does not himself deny the moral content of sexual relations and extenuates his impregnation of Juliet thus:

. . . upon a true contract
I got possession of Julietta's bed:
You know the lady; She is fast my wife,
Save that we do denunciation lack
Of outward order.

47

His love of Juliet and his sincere promise to marry her, therefore, extenuate his conduct in his own eyes and, he hopes, in the eyes of others. But you only offer extenuation when you believe you have done wrong, or at least behaved less than ideally, in the first place. So Claudio is not claiming that he is innocent, only that his sin of not waiting for all the formalities to be completed is not a mortal one. And obviously we are intended to agree, for otherwise the disproportion between his action and Angelo's proposed punishment would not strike us so forcibly, and the tension would go out of the play. (Perhaps it is not coincidental that Ann Hathaway gave birth to Shakespeare's first child only six months after they were married.) If Angelo had merely fined Claudio and given him a stern lecture, the drama would have ended there and then.

But though Claudio accepts his guilt, he also points out that he is the victim of the zeitgeist of leniency in Vienna. When Lucio sees him being led off to jail, he asks Claudio "whence comes this restraint?"

> From too much liberty, my Lucio, liberty.
> As surfeit is father to much fast,
> So every scope by the immoderate use,
> Turns to restraint.

And, like everyone else in Vienna, Claudio has taken advantage of this liberty without much thought for the consequences:

> Our natures do pursue
> Like rats that ravin down their proper bane,
> A thirsty evil, and when we drink we die.

In other words, restraints upon our natural inclinations, which left to themselves do not automatically lead us to do what is good for us and often indeed lead us to evil, are not only necessary; they are the indispensable condition of civilized existence.

Of course Isabella, Claudio's sister, disapproves of sexual intercourse outside of marriage. When she goes to Angelo to plead for her brother's life, she begins by saying:

There is a vice that most I do abhor,
And most desire should meet the blow of justice,
For which I would not plead, but that I must. . . .

Later, when she goes to her brother in jail to tell him of Angelo's wicked proposition, she is horrified that Claudio, after a very brief resistance, suggests that, after all, his life is more important than her chastity, and therefore she should comply with Angelo. Outraged, she replies:

Mercy to thee would prove itself a bawd,
'Tis best that thou diest quickly.

These are the very last words she addresses to her brother in the play, and modern critics have found her fierce defense of her own chastity, even at the cost of her brother's life, puzzling and disproportionate, sententious and unattractive.

But this response shows a lack of historical understanding and imagination. Throughout most of history, chastity has been honored as an important virtue, precisely because it helps to control and civilize sexual relations. It has often been horribly overvalued, of course: for example, only last week a Kurdish Muslim refugee in Britain cut his own sixteen-year-old daughter's throat and left her to bleed to death because she was dressing in revealing Western clothes and having sex with her boyfriend. But Isabella knows that a society that places no value at all on chastity will not place much value on fidelity either: and then we are back to the free-for-all and all its attendant problems. She fears not only for her own soul if she sins, but for that of society.

But if virtues and ideals (all of which are impossible to achieve perfectly) are part of what makes us human, Shakespeare implies that they too must be proportionate. At the end of the play, Isabella abandons her chastity and marries the duke, suggesting that there is a time and place for such restraint, but it is not over the whole course of a human life. Carried to an extreme, chastity will cease to be a virtue and become, if not a vice, at least a stimulus to vice. If Angelo had not been so militantly chaste, he would have been far less likely to make his wicked attempt on Isabella.

Perhaps more surprisingly, Lucio, the rake and libertine, also sees the value of chastity. When he approaches Isabella to ask her to go to Angelo to plead for her brother's life, he says (and there is no suggestion that he is merely buttering her up):

I hold you as a thing enskied and sainted,
By your renouncement an immortal spirit
And to be talked with in sincerity,
As with a saint.

These are not the words of someone who thinks that sex is of no moral import. On the contrary, they are the words of someone who takes St. Paul's view of sex as a regrettable but inevitable snare, which most people, Lucio included, are too weak to avoid. His own conduct, however, is a living refutation of the impossibility of imposing the Pauline view by force, as Angelo tries to do.

A speech that the duke, disguised as a friar, addresses to Pompey, Mistress Overdone's tapster, provides the key to the play. The duke, remember, is responsible for the moral laxity of Vienna, but his previous reluctance to enforce the "strict statutes and most biting laws" does not spring from an ideological belief that everyone should be allowed to do whatever he wants, that anything goes, but rather from inattention, weakness, cowardice, and perhaps a desire for popularity. He is not himself licentious, being a studious and cultivated man, nor does he approve of licentiousness in others. He says to Pompey:

Fie, sirrah, a bawd, a wicked bawd!
The evil that thou causest to be done,
That is thy means to live. Do thou but think
What 'tis to cram a maw or clothe a back
From such a filthy vice. Say to thyself,
From their abominable and beastly touches
I drink, I eat, array myself and live.
Canst thou believe thy living is a life,
So stinkingly depending?

This is not just rhetoric: the duke, still disguised as a friar and acting, presumably, on religious authority, has Pompey carted off to jail.

The key word is "beastly": their beastly touches. By beastliness the duke means sexuality without the human qualities of love and commitment: for without love, sex is merely animal—beastly in the most literal sense. And, as the play's premise makes clear, the animal triumphs over the human when laws or institutions are too weak. The baby is not socialized by the nurse but beats her whenever it is thwarted in a desire, which in infancy can only be instinctive. It is only by having desire thwarted, and thereby learning to control it—in other words, by becoming civilized—that men become fully human.

So if Shakespeare is not a Puritan—he certainly does not think, because there is such a thing as virtue, that there shall be no more cakes and ale—he is not a complete latitudinarian in moral matters either. On the one hand, Angelo's utopian scheme to "extirp it quite" must founder on the rock of human nature, not least the human nature of the would-be extirpers themselves (as history attests); on the other, complete surrender to instinct leads to beastliness and therefore to a shallowing of the human personality. Shakespeare thus places himself between utopian totalitarians and libertarian fundamentalists. He provides us with no easy answers to the questions that confront us now and that will always confront us. His is a call neither to draconian severity and repression, nor to utter leniency and permissiveness, the two temptations of those who like to argue from first principles. He calls us to proportion, that is to say, to humanity. We must both recognize the limitations imposed upon us by our natures and at the same time not give up striving to control ourselves. If we fail to do either, we shall succumb to ideological or instinctual beastliness—or (the curious achievement of our own age) to both.

2003

What's Wrong with
Twinkling Buttocks?

◆ A CRUDE CULTURE makes a coarse people, and private refinement cannot long survive public excess. There is a Gresham's law of culture as well as of money: the bad drives out the good, unless the good is defended.

In no country has the process of vulgarization gone further than in Britain: in this, at least, we lead the world. A nation famed not so long ago for the restraint of its manners is now notorious for the coarseness of its appetites and its unbridled and anti-social attempts to satisfy them. The mass drunkenness seen on weekends in the center of every British town and city, rendering them unendurable to even minimally civilized people, goes hand in hand with the appallingly crude, violent, and shallow relations between the sexes. Britain's mass bastardy is not a sign of an increase in the authenticity of our human relations but a natural consequence of the unbridled hedonism that leads in short order to chaos and misery, especially among the poor. Take restraint away, and violent discord follows.

Curiously enough, the revolution in British manners did not come about through any volcanic eruption from below: on the contrary, it was the intellectual wing of the elite that kicked against the traces. It is still doing so, though there are very few traces left to kick against.

For example, the boundless prurience of the British press concerning the private lives of public figures, especially politicians, has an ideological aim: to subvert the very concept and deny the possibility of virtue, and therefore of the necessity for restraint. If every person who tries to defend virtue is revealed to have feet of clay (as which of us does not?) or to have indulged at some time in his life in the vice that is the opposite of the virtue he calls for, then virtue itself is exposed as nothing but hypocrisy: and we may therefore all behave exactly as we choose. The loss of the religious understanding of the human condition—that man is a fallen creature for whom virtue is necessary but never fully attainable—is a loss, not a gain, in true sophistication. The secular substitute—the belief in the perfection of life on earth by the endless extension of a choice of pleasures—is not merely callow by comparison but much less realistic in its understanding of human nature.

It is in the arts and literary pages of our newspapers that the elite's continuing demand for the erosion of restraint, and its unreflective antinomianism, is most clearly on view. Take for example the arts section of a recent *Observer*, Britain's most prestigious liberal Sunday paper. The section's two most important and eye-catching articles celebrated pop singer Marilyn Manson and writer Glen Duncan.

Of the pop singer, the *Observer*'s critic wrote: "Marilyn Manson's ability to shock has swung like a pendulum in a high wind. . . . He was really scary at first, when [he] burst out of [his] native Florida and declared war on all Middle America holds dear. Manson spun convincing tales of smoking exhumed bones for kicks. . . . But . . . Manson's autobiography revealed a smart, funny man—even if he did enjoy covering hearing-impaired groupies in raw meat for sexual sport. He turned into an artist, rather than the incarnation of evil. Church groups still picketed his gigs, which often echoed Nazi rallies (they still do). But any fool could see that Manson was making a valid point about rock 'n' roll gigs and mass behavior, as well as flirting with fascist style."

The author of this review—who fastidiously balks at using the word "deaf" for the hearing-impaired but appears not to mind too much if they are exploited for perverted sexual gratification—takes pains to let the reader know that she is not so unsophisticated, naive, and, well, Middle American as to find the whole spectacle disgusting: for example, by objecting to the adoption of the name of a sadistic multiple killer for trivial publicity purposes. To have responded in such a way would have been to lose caste, to side with the gawky, earnest Christians rather than with the secular devil worshipers—though the determination to be shocked by nothing, to object to nothing, is itself, of course, a convention. It seems beyond the critic's range of imagination or sympathy that people who actually fought against fascism and risked their lives and lost their compatriots in doing so, or who suffered under fascism's yoke, might find the concept of flirtation with fascist style not only offensive but a cause of real despair in the last years of their lives. Fascism is not fashion.

The "any fool" of the last sentence is a subtle form of intellectual snobbery and flattery, intended to suck the reader into the charmed circle of the sophisticated, disabused intellectual elite, the knowing and the cognoscenti who have moved beyond moral judgment and principles, who are not deceived by mere appearances, do not condemn according to outmoded ways of thought, and are therefore unmoved by such trifling (and oppressive) considerations as public decency. It does not occur to the writer—nor would it matter to her if it did—that in the audience in which fascism was flirted with there might not have been any fools but many fools, those who failed to see the ironically playful "valid" point behind the flirtation and would embrace fascism without irony. Not long ago a newspaper asked me to attend a "concert" to report on a group whose main selling point was that they urinated and vomited over their audience, as well as abused it constantly by calling every member of it "motherfucker" countless times. Thousands attended the "concert"—in fact, a reverberating wall of deafening, discordant electronic noise punctuated by the chanting of obscenities—among whom were hundreds of children as young as six. For these unfortunate children, this was not *nostalgie de la boue*; this was total immersion in the *boue* itself, the *boue* in which they lived and breathed and took their cultural being, the *boue* from which it is highly unlikely that they would now ever crawl. Any fool could see that this was not a suitable spectacle for children, but many fools—their parents—didn't.

What's Wrong with Twinkling Buttocks?

The *Observer*'s interview with the author Glen Duncan was entitled DARK, SATANIC THRILLS, and the interviewer found herself "pleasantly shocked" by the sadomasochism of Duncan's work—any other kind of shock than the pleasant being strictly infra dig for one of her caste, of course. "[He] has ventured even further into the dark wood of sexual violence and cruelty" than another author of sadomasochistic literature, Mary Gaitskill—praise indeed, since Gaitskill has been critically acclaimed for "her unflinching flirting with taboo" (oh, how flirtatious they are, our literati, drawn to taboo as flies to dung), "her clear-eyed use of seamy detail." There is nothing finer for extending human freedom, maturity, and self-knowledge than a bit of seamy detail, of course: though naturally, you can never be quite unflinching enough, nor the detail sufficiently seamy.

Not, of course, that Mr. Duncan's graphic depiction of sadomasochistic practices is prurient or sensationalist; heaven protect us from so "grossly reductive" a thought: "though"—let us be quite frank, for mature people can face any truth—"it is an excellent selling point for the publishers." The sexual scenes, "not for the fainthearted" (such as those who, for example, do not think that fascism is a fit subject for merely stylistic treatment), have a serious philosophical import and not a merely commercial one. As the author put it to the interviewer, no doubt to establish beyond doubt his reputation as a serious thinker: "Weird shit happens and I wanted the narrator to have to figure out how to live even in the light of that." The sexual scenes are not gratuitous, therefore, much less publicity stunts—nor of course are they the result of human choice (weird shit isn't chosen: it just happens; it is inevitable)—but they raise important metaphysical questions about the boundaries of the permissible.

When exactly did this downward cultural spiral begin, this loss of tact and refinement and understanding that some things should not be said or directly represented? When did we no longer appreciate that to dignify certain modes of behavior, manners, and ways of being with artistic representation was implicitly to glorify and promote them? There is, as Adam Smith said, a deal of ruin in a nation: and this truth applies as much to a nation's culture as to its

55

economy. The work of cultural destruction, while often swifter, easier, and more self-conscious than that of construction, is not the work of a moment. Rome wasn't destroyed in a day.

In 1914, for example, Bernard Shaw caused a sensation by giving Eliza Doolittle the words "Not bloody likely!" to utter on the London stage. Of course the sensation that this now innocuous, even innocent exclamation created depended wholly for its effect upon the convention that it flouted: but those who were outraged by it (and who have generally been regarded as ridiculous in subsequent accounts of the incident) instinctively understood that sensation doesn't strike in the same place twice, and that anyone wanting to create an equivalent in the future would have to go far beyond "Not bloody likely." A logic and a convention of convention-breaking was established, so that within a few decades it was difficult to produce any sensation at all except by the most extreme means.

If there was a single event in our recent cultural history that established literal-minded crudity as the ideal of artistic endeavor, however, it was the celebrated 1960 trial of Penguin Books for the publication of an obscene book, the unexpurgated version of D. H. Lawrence's *Lady Chatterley's Lover*. The trial posed the question of whether cultural tact and restraint would crumble in the absence of legal sanctions. For, as the much derided prosecutor in the case, Mervyn Griffith-Jones, understood only too well, and specifically advised the government of the day, if the publication of *Lady Chatterley's Lover* went legally unchallenged, or if the case were lost, it would in effect be the end of the law of obscenity. To adapt slightly Dostoevsky's famous dictum about the moral consequences of the nonexistence of God, if *Lady Chatterley's Lover* were published, everything could be published.

Penguin Books had long wanted to publish Lawrence's novel but decided to do so in 1960 because Parliament had changed the obscenity law the previous year. The law, whose stated purpose was to suppress pornography while protecting literature, retained more or less the preceding definition of obscenity, as that which, taken as a whole, tended to corrupt and deprave. But for the first time the law contained a provision according to which the interests of art, literature, or science could override the goal of preventing depravity and corruption. Furthermore the law allowed "expert" evidence to be called in defense of the artistic or literary merit of an allegedly obscene work. The timing of Penguin Books' proposed publication of *Lady Chatterley's Lover* clearly suggests that the company knew the book could not be defended against the charge of obscenity; publication had to wait until Penguin could rely for the book's defense upon the evidence of "expert," that is to say elite, opinion. Among the expert witnesses was Roy Jenkins, later a liberal home secretary, who was one of the framers of the new law, whose effect turned out to be more the protection of pornography and the suppression of literature than the other way around—an effect that, in view of Jenkins's later pronouncement that the permissive society was the civilized society, was exactly what the framers of the law desired but found inexpedient to acknowledge at the time.

The elite fell over itself to testify in the book's favor during the trial, and the defense was able to produce a star-studded list of experts, including E. M. Forster and Rebecca West. It was undoubtedly assisted in its task by the maladroitness of the prosecutor, who seemed not to have noticed that society had changed since his upper-class youth, and who opened the case with such consummate pomposity that he became a figure of fun ever afterward and is still remembered—and remembered only—for what he said in his opening remarks to the jury: "You may think that one of the ways in which you can test this book . . . is to ask yourselves the question . . . would you approve of your young sons, young daughters—because girls can read as well as boys—reading this book? Is it a book you would leave lying about your house? Is it a book you would even wish your wife and servants to read?" The court, not surprisingly, erupted in laughter; and later, after the "not guilty" verdict, in a debate in the House of Lords on an unsuccessful motion to strengthen the law of obscenity, one of the noble lords was reported to have replied to the question of whether he would mind if his daughter read *Lady Chatterley's Lover* that he wouldn't mind in the least, but he would mind very much if his gamekeeper read it.

Griffith-Jones was clumsily raising the possibility that what was harmless for some individuals might not be harmless for society as a whole, and that artists, writers, and intellectuals had a responsibility to consider what the effects of their work were likely to be: a debatable proposition, certainly, but not an inherently absurd one. But his case never recovered from his gaffe, and the fact that a mere gaffe could so have obscured the important question at issue illustrated the frivolity of mind that had already taken hold in British society.

In fact, the expert evidence was, in its way, just as absurd as Griffith-Jones's opening remarks, and vastly more destructive in its effects. For example, when Helen Gardner, the eminent, cultivated, and very proper Cambridge don who had spent much of her life studying the metaphysical poets, was asked about Lawrence's repeated if not incessant use of the word "fuck," she (as well as other witnesses) implied that Lawrence had somehow managed to render the word less obscene and more refined by depriving it of its smutty connotations. In his closing address to the jury, Griffith-Jones—absurd, maligned, pompous as he was—proved much more realistic than the expert witnesses about the likely social consequences of weakening the taboo against bad language: "Miss Gardner said . . . 'I think the very fact that this word is used so frequently in the book, with every subsequent use the original shock is diminished. . . .' I suppose that is put as mitigation for the use of this language. Is it? Or, if it be right, is it not a terrible thing to say, 'It is all right, if we forget about the shock of using this language, if we use it sufficient times, no one will be shocked, everybody will be using it and it will be all right?' Can you not apply the same test to everything? Filthy pictures, if you look at them a number of times, the shock, the effect will die out and so we can have everything flooded with filthy pictures!" Miss Gardner, but not Griffith-Jones, would have been surprised had she been present in my consulting room four decades later, to hear a three-year-old child say to his mother, when thwarted in his attempts to destroy my telephone, "Well, fuck you!"

The witnesses grossly, and I suspect dishonestly, inflated Lawrence's status as a writer to bolster the defense's case, which was, in effect, but a stalking horse in their campaign for the removal of artistic limits and the erosion of the irksome restraints of civilization. Helen Gardner stated in her testimony that in assessing the literary value of a work there were two considerations to be taken into account: what the author was trying to say, and his success in saying it. On both counts Lawrence fails, and fails dismally. No doubt it is remarkable that the son of a Nottinghamshire miner of that era should have written novels at all, which explains why he became the Bloomsbury group's pet proletarian: but the rarity of a thing should not cloud our judgment as to its intellectual or aesthetic value. For example, Lawrence's prose manages the difficult feat of being leaden and overwrought at the same time. I found the following passage by opening the book at random and pointing with my eyes shut to a place on the page: "She ran, and he saw nothing but the round wet head, the wet back leaning forward in flight, the rounded buttocks twinkling: a wonderful cowering female nakedness in flight." Polonius would have exclaimed, "That's good! 'Twinkling buttocks' is good."

The radical humorlessness of this passage (apart from being typical) is indicative of a profound moral defect, insofar as a sense of humor requires a sense of proportion. Of course, as Somerset Maugham once noted, only a very mediocre writer is always at his best: but only a very bad writer is so often at his very considerable worst, as is Lawrence. The following passage relates to a conversation that the gamekeeper, Mellors, has with Lady Chatterley's father, Sir Malcolm, after she has become pregnant by Mellors:

Only when coffee was served, and the waiter had gone, Sir Malcolm lit a cigar and said, heartily: "Well, young man, and what about my daughter?" The grin flickered on Mellors' face. "Well, Sir, and what about her?" "You've got a baby in her all right." "I have that honour!" grinned Mellors. "Honour, by God!", Sir Malcolm gave a little squirting laugh, and became Scotch and lewd. "Honour! How was the going, eh? Good, my boy, what!" "Good!" "I'll bet it was! Hah-ha! My daughter, chip off the old block, what! I never went back on a good bit of fucking, myself. Though her mother, oh Holy Saints!" He rolled his eyes up to heaven. "But warmed her up, oh, you warmed her up, I can see that. Hah-ha! My blood in her! You set fire to her haystack all right."

It would be difficult to find a worse, cruder, or more insensitive passage in the whole of English literature. It is startlingly unrealistic, of course (and Lawrence claims to be a realist): no father would speak of his own daughter in this men's-locker-room manner, nor any widower of his deceased wife. It reduces human relationships to the lowest possible denominator: humans become no more than farmyard animals. And Lawrence approves of Sir Malcolm, wanting us to accept his view that he is superior, because more earthy and biological, to others of his social class.

Lawrence was an earnest, but not a serious, writer—if by serious we mean one whose outlook on life is intellectually or morally worthy of our consideration. Lawrence put a lot of himself into Mellors, who at one point in the book enunciates the essence of Lawrence's philosophy, the summary of all his reflections on human existence, his final testament to the world: "I believe in something, I believe in being warm-hearted. I believe especially in being warm-hearted in love. I believe that if men could fuck with warm hearts and women took it warm-heartedly, everything would be all right." The idea that social perfection is to be achieved through wonderfully sensual sexual relations between men and women is a fantasy unworthy of prolonged intellectual consideration. To call it adolescent tripe is to be unfair to many intelligent adolescents. The fact that so many eminent persons were willing to testify in court that Lawrence was one of the greatest writers of the twentieth century, worthy to be compared, say, with Conrad, is an indication of the elite's loss of taste and judgment. Their imprimatur helped transform a bad writer and worse thinker into a major cultural influence: and his crude, egotistical literal-mindedness has been successively trumped ever since by yet cruder, more egotistical literal-mindedness.

Yet literal-mindedness is not honesty or fidelity to truth—far from it. For it is the whole experience of mankind that sexual life is always, and must always be, hidden by veils of varying degrees of opacity, if it is to be humanized into something beyond a mere animal function. What is inherently secretive, that is to say self-conscious and human, cannot be spoken of directly: the attempt leads only to crudity, not to truth. Bawdy is the tribute that our instinct pays to secrecy. If you go beyond bawdy and tear all the veils away, you get pornography and nothing else. In essence, therefore, Lawrence was a pornographer, though a dull one even in that dull genre.

There never was much demand, except from the elite, for relaxation of the law of censorship: indeed, until the law was relaxed, the public had shown a distinctly limited appetite for the works of D. H. Lawrence. But no sooner had the relaxation been legislated, and the book published, than one in four British households had acquired it. The genie was well and truly out of the bottle, the supply had created a demand, and the appetite grew with feeding.

It is, of course, a common prejudice that censorship is bad for art and therefore always unjustified: though, if this were so, mankind would have little in the way of an artistic heritage, and we should now be living in an artistic golden age. But if we cannot censor, we can censure: and we should be tireless in saying that D. H. Lawrence and his deplorable and hackneyed progeny down to Marilyn Manson and Glen Duncan, with his "dark, satanic thrills," darken the world rather than enlighten it.

2003

The Rage of Virginia Woolf

◈ IN 1938, the year my mother left Germany for good and never saw her parents again, Virginia Woolf published a book entitled *Three Guineas*. It was about how women could prevent war.

Virginia Woolf's name is not normally associated with great affairs of state, of course. Quite the reverse. She regarded them with a fastidious disgust, as a vulgar distraction from the true business of life: attendance to the finer nuances of one's own emotional state. Along with the other members of the Bloomsbury group—that influential and endlessly chronicled little band of British aesthetes of which she was a moving spirit—she was dedicated to the proposition that beings as sensitive as they to the music of life ought not to be bound by gross social conventions, and that it was their duty (as well as their pleasure) to act solely upon the promptings of the sympathetic vibrations of their souls. In a demotic age, however, their justification for personal license could not long be confined to socially superior types such as themselves. Before very long, what was permissible for the elite became mandatory for the *hoi polloi*; and when the predictable social disaster occurred, in the form of a growing underclass devoid of moral bearings, the elite that had absorbed (indeed, reveled in) Bloomsbury's influence took the growth of the underclass as evidence that their original grudge against society and its conventions had been justified all along. The philosophy brought about the disaster, and the disaster justified the philosophy.

The *Cambridge Guide to English Literature* describes *Three Guineas* as an established classic—but a classic of what genre exactly? Of political philosophy? Contemporary history? Sociological analysis? No: it is a *locus classicus* of self-pity and victimhood as a genre in itself. In this it was certainly ahead of its time, and it deserves to be on the syllabus of every department of women's studies at every third-rate establishment of higher education. Never were the personal and the political worse confounded.

The book is important because it is a naked statement of the worldview that is unstated and implicit in all of Virginia Woolf's novels, most of which have achieved an iconic status in the republic of letters and in the humanities departments of the English-speaking world, where they have influenced countless young people. The book, therefore, is truly a seminal text. In *Three Guineas*, Virginia Woolf lets us know without disguise what she really thinks: and what she thinks is by turns grandiose and trivial, resentful and fatuous. The book might be better titled: *How to Be Privileged and Yet Feel Extremely Aggrieved.*

The guineas of the title refer to a unit of currency: a pound and a shilling. Even in Woolf's day, no guinea coin or guinea banknote actually existed. It was purely a notional unit, used for transactions of superior social status, such as the purchase of art at auction, the payment of surgeons, or, as in this book, the giving of charitable contributions. Virginia Woolf writes of three requests made of her for donations of one guinea each: the first by an eminent lawyer for his society for the protection of intellectual freedom and the promotion of peace; the second by the head of a Cambridge University women's college to help rebuild and enlarge the college; and the third by the treasurer of a society for the aid of professional women, to enable them to buy the evening clothes necessary to their status in life.

Three Guineas tries to show how the threat of war is linked to the condition of women. War throughout the ages, Mrs. Woolf says, has been a male activity, and during those same ages men have suppressed women: ergo, if men cease to suppress women and treat them as equals, there will be no war. One might think that to descend from the aesthetic to the ideological plane would be distasteful for a woman of such languorous, highly strung, thoroughbred equine beauty as she; but under the influence of a general idea, Mrs. Woolf revealed herself to be a thoroughgoing philistine of the most revolutionary and destructive type, quite prepared to bring the temple crashing down about her ears, that her grudges might be paid back. Let my ego be satisfied, though civilization fall!

My copy of the book is a slightly battered first edition that was once in the library of Michel Leiris, the French writer and anthropologist who knew all the best-worst (or worst-best) people, such as Sartre and de Beauvoir. Leiris's annotations consist only of a list of three pages of special impact to him, written in the elegant hand of a bygone era, and small crosses on the top outside corners of the pages themselves—pages 62, 63, and 64.

And what do pages 62, 63, and 64 say? On the preceding page, page 61, Mrs. Woolf begins her discursive reply to a request for a contribution for the rebuilding and extension of a Cambridge women's college. Where education is concerned, Mrs. Woolf certainly does not want more of the same—the granting of the same opportunities to more women—having previously argued that all the education prior to the Great War did not prevent that cataclysm from happening but on the contrary actually provoked it by fostering a spirit of competition among those who underwent it. "Let us," she writes, ". . . discuss as quickly as we can the sort of education that is needed." Since the past has been nothing but a catalog of vice, folly, cruelty, and the suppression of women, the college of her dreams "must be an experimental college, an adventurous college. Let it be built on lines of its own."

And what might these lines be? "It must be built not of carved stone and stained glass, but of some cheap, easily combustible material which does not hoard dust and perpetrate traditions." This is surely an odd architectural position for an aesthete to take: a position whose baleful practical consequences are, alas, visible throughout the whole island of Great Britain, where hardly a townscape has escaped being ruined by it. The avoidance of dust (and therefore presumably of housework or other oppressive forms of maintenance) is elevated to the pantheon of life's highest goals: and Mrs. Woolf's use of the word "perpetrate" in connection with "traditions" is indicative of her revolutionary state of mind, since "perpetrate" generally takes as its object a heinous crime or a massacre or some other disaster. For Mrs. Woolf, tradition in general, not any particular tradition, is what needs to be eliminated.

What furnishings should the college of Mrs. Woolf's dreams contain? Certainly not a repository of the best that has been said and thought. "Do not have museums and libraries with chained books and first editions under glass cases," she advises. No: "Let the pictures and the books be new and always changing. Let it be decorated afresh by each generation with their own hands cheaply." (By now we have passed on to the pages bearing Michel Leiris's marks.) What is this but a manifesto for Cool Britannia *avant la lettre*, an expression of the shallow belief that the new is better than the old merely by virtue of its novelty?

And what, most important, would be taught in Mrs. Woolf's college of dreams? "Not the arts of dominating other people; not the arts of ruling, of killing, of acquiring land and capital." (Let us remind ourselves that she is talking of the university of Milton, Wordsworth, and Wittgenstein.) "The . . . college should teach only the arts that can be taught cheaply and practised by poor people; such as medicine, mathematics, music, painting and literature." The superior virtue of poverty and the poor is assumed; and Mrs. Woolf obviously conceives of medicine as a kind of Gandhian cottage industry (though she personally always availed herself of the best specialists available), carried out by bucolics and wise-women, gathering herbs by moonlight and operating, if at all, on kitchen tables. She continues: The college "should teach the arts of human intercourse; the art of understanding other people's lives and minds, and the little arts of talk, of dress, of cookery that are allied with them." Not being a systematic thinker, to put it kindly, Mrs. Woolf here fails to realize that she is proposing to enclose women in precisely the little domestic world from which she also claims to be rescuing them.

Mrs. Woolf's ideal college—the kind that would prevent rather than promote wars—would not be in any way elitist. It would "not [be] parcelled out into the miserable distinctions of rich and poor, of clever and stupid." It would, rather, be a place "where all the different degrees and kinds of mind, body and soul met and co-operated." It would be entirely nonjudgmental, even as to intellect. For her, the urge to compete does not inhere in man's nature, nor does it result in anything other than violent strife. Henceforth there is to be no testing oneself against the best, with the possibility, even the likelihood, of failure: instead, one is perpetually to immerse oneself in the tepid bath of self-esteem, mutual congratulation, and benevolence toward all.

Of course, it is a mistake to suppose that a hypothetical future state of perfect toleration means toleration in or of the present: far from it. Mrs. Woolf would not let her opponents, or those who think differently, live in peace: on the page after the last marked by Michel Leiris, she gives full expression to her slash-and-burn concept of cultural renewal: "No guinea of earned money should go to rebuilding the college on the old plan. . . . [T]herefore the guinea should be earmarked 'Rags. Petrol. Matches.' And this note should be attached to it. 'Take this guinea and with it burn the college to the ground. Set fire to the old hypocrisies. Let the light of the burning building scare the nightingales and incarnadine the willows. And let the daughters of educated men dance round the fire and heap armful upon armful of dead leaves upon the flames. And let their mothers lean from the upper windows [before, presumably, being burned to death] and cry "Let it blaze! Let it blaze! For we have done with this education!" ' "

This incendiary passage, Mrs. Woolf insists in her very next sentence, is not mere empty rhetoric, though she subsequently retreats a little from her incitement to arson by pointing out the self-defeating nature of that crime, insofar as the college she was proposing to burn down was necessary to train women to be able to earn the guinea of discretionary income with which to buy the materials to burn it down in the first place. What a dilemma! The passion, if not the logic, of her argument is clear and perhaps casts a new light on the deliberate destructiveness of the motives that lay behind her literary innovations. She was nothing if not a great hater of all that had gone before her.

What was the wellspring of this great hatred? No doubt some would say it was the sexual abuse that she was alleged to have suffered as a child at the hands of her two half-brothers, George and Gerald Duckworth; but the extent and gravity of that abuse is open to question and would in any case hardly explain (let alone justify) the desire of a famous and successful fifty-six-year-old novelist to destroy civilization in the name of preventing war. And if by any chance it *were* the explanation, it would certainly not redound to her credit: for the conclusion that an entire civilization needed to be destroyed because it permitted her sexual abuse is no better than the conclusion that the existence of *any* injustice demonstrates that all efforts to achieve justice are a sham. A self-pitying lack of proportion, far from alien to Mrs. Woolf, was in fact the very signature of her mind.

Mrs. Woolf belonged by birth not merely to the upper middle classes but to the elite of the intellectual elite. She was a Stephen, her father, Sir Leslie Stephen, being an eminent essayist, editor, and critic, the founding editor of the monumental and magnificent *Dictionary of National Biography* and at one time the publisher of Thomas Hardy. He knew everyone who was anyone in the literary and intellectual world. Mrs. Woolf's uncle, Sir James Fitzjames Stephen, was an eminent legal scholar and historian, jurist, judge, and political philosopher, who wrote a brilliant and still-classic riposte to John Stuart Mill's essay on liberty. She grew up in a rarefied intellectual atmosphere in which it would clearly be difficult to equal, let alone surpass, the achievements of her elders. One way to surpass her father and her uncle in achievement was, of course, to disparage and destroy all they had erected.

Her historiography was very modern: she scoured the records to justify the backward projection of her current resentments. For her there was no such thing as the human condition, with its inevitable discontent and limitations. She thought that all the things she desired were reconcilable, so that freedom and security, for example, or artistic effort and complete selflessness, might abide in perpetual harmony. As a female member of the British upper middle class and one of what she called "the daughters of educated men," she felt both socially superior to the rest of the world and peculiarly, indeed uniquely, put upon. The very locution, "the daughters of educated men," is an odd one, capturing her oscillation between grandiosity and self-pity: she meant by it that class of women who, by virtue of their gentle birth and hereditarily superior minds, could not be expected to perform physical labor of any kind, but who were prevented by the injustice of "the system" from participating fully in public and intellectual affairs.

In her descriptions of this class, self-pity vies with snobbery. Her reply to the philanthropist who requested a donation to buy evening clothes for professional women vibrates with outrage that the daughters of educated men should find themselves in financial difficulties (which, in her view, should properly belong only to social inferiors). "Not only are we incomparably weaker than the men of our own class," she writes to the eminent lawyer; "we are weaker than the women of the working class." "Economically, the educated man's daughter is much on a level with the farm labourer." "Society has been so kind to you [the educated men, one of whom is her interlocutor], so harsh to us [the daughters of educated men, of whom she is one]: it is an ill-fitting form that distorts the truth; deforms the mind; fetters the will." It must therefore be destroyed—presumably by those whose will has been fettered and whose minds have been deformed.

For those who actually know anything about the hardships endured by the British working class, male and female, during the years of the depression, statements that insinuate an equality, or even a superiority, of suffering on the part of the daughters of educated men are little short of nauseating; but they would clearly appeal to the pampered resentful, a class that was to grow exponentially in the postwar years of sustained prosperity.

According to Mrs. Woolf, women of her own class were so dependent upon men that for centuries they were incapable of having, much less expressing, opinions of their own. For her, "independent opinion" was indispensably based upon independent income, though later in the book she lays down criteria for the independence of income that are so stringent and esoteric that only heiresses could meet them. Poor struggling Mrs. Oliphant, for example, the Victorian novelist and biographer, came nowhere near meeting them, because she was obliged to earn money herself for the upkeep of her children. (Mrs. Woolf suggested as a solution that the daughters of educated women should be paid a government subsidy, so that they might create works of art—or do nothing at all—free of all sordid monetary conditions.) Her desire to have it all ways at once—to be utterly independent because unconditionally supported by the taxpayers—illustrates her kind of querulous and irresponsible sense of entitlement.

Her sole conclusion from the entire literature of the nineteenth century is that women were constantly ridiculed for "attempting to enter their solitary profession," marriage—as if that vast and magisterial literature accorded women no other role in life; as if it depicted relations between men and women as being nothing but domination and subordination. So grotesque is this as a reading of, say, Jane Austen that it amounts to an outright lie. And is Mrs. Micawber an object of contempt or of affection, even admiration?

As for the fabled influence of women on men, Mrs. Woolf will have none of it. She writes that it is so "beneath our contempt" that "many of us would prefer to call ourselves prostitutes simply and to take our stand openly under the lamps of Piccadilly Circus rather than use it." I confess that I find the idea of Mrs. Woolf as a streetwalker under the lamps of Piccadilly Circus irresistibly funny: but could there be a clearer case of the triumph of hyperbolic self-pity over honesty?

No interpretation of events, trends, or feelings is too silly or contradictory for Mrs. Woolf if it helps to fan her resentment. Explaining the evident enthusiasm of the daughters of educated men at the outbreak of the Great War, she writes, "So profound was [their] unconscious loathing for the education of the private house with its cruelty, its poverty, its hypocrisy, its inanity that [they] would undertake any task however menial [such as working in factories and hospitals], exercise any function however fatal that enabled [them] to escape. . . . [U]nconsciously [they] desired our splendid war." That they might have been actuated by the same patriotism as the men who volunteered for the slaughter was for her an impossibility, for she denies that the daughters of educated men were truly English: like the proletarians of Marx's imagination, they have no country. "The law of England," she writes, "denies us, and let us hope it will long continue to deny us, the full stigma of nationality." As ever wanting it both ways, she complains at one moment of exclusion and at the next, that inclusion is not worthwhile. She is like a humorless version of Groucho Marx, who did not want to be a member of any club that would accept him. What is a joke for Groucho Marx is serious political philosophy for Virginia Woolf.

She explains the falling birthrate among the daughters of educated men by their refusal any longer to provide cannon fodder for wars: thus ignoring the fact that the decline in fertility had been long and continuous, affecting all classes of society—even in Sweden, which had not had a war since Napoleonic times.

Not that one could entirely blame Mrs. Woolf for her lack of dialectical rigor, for, as she writes, "The daughters of educated men have always done their thinking from hand to mouth. . . . They have thought while they stirred the pot, while they rocked the cradle." This piece of self-pity drew the memorable riposte from the literary critic Q. D. Leavis, herself no unqualified admirer of the common man, that Mrs. Woolf wouldn't know which end of the cradle to stir.

Resentment playing so large a part in Mrs. Woolf's mental economy, much of her intellectual effort went into justifying it. She is thus a very modern figure indeed, even though she died sixty years ago. Her lack of recognition that anything had ever been achieved or created before her advent that was worthy of protection and preservation is all but absolute, along with her egotism. How, she asks, can we, the daughters of educated men, enter the professions and yet remain civilized human beings?—a question that implies that such professionals as Lister, Lord Birkenhead, or Marconi, working during Mrs. Woolf's lifetime, were neither civilized themselves nor contributed anything to civilization. By so contemptuously denying the achievements of the past, bought at so great a cost of thought and effort, she totally misunderstood the material and intellectual conditions that made possible her own life, with its languorous contemplation of the exquisite.

The only occasion in the book when Mrs. Woolf implicitly recognizes past achievement, she does so not to praise it but to denigrate the lack of it among her fellow countrymen. Suppose an outsider (as she far from truthfully calls herself) feels the temptation to patriotism: "Then she will compare English painting with French painting; English music with German music; English literature with Greek literature. . . . When all these comparisons have been faithfully made by the use of reason, the outsider will find herself in possession of very good reasons for her indifference." There is nothing here of Shakespeare or Newton, of Wren or Turner—an omission extraordinary in the daughter of the first editor of the *Dictionary of National Biography*. And it is extraordinary to believe that patriotism is justified only by supremacy in all the arts and sciences simultaneously—a doctrine that would be exceedingly hard on, say, a Norwegian or a Bolivian patriot.

Patriotism is for Mrs. Woolf only one of the many "unreal loyalties" against which she rails. Loyalty to school, to university, to church, to club, to family, to traditions or structures of any kind—even municipal pride—are to her the equivalent of Marx's false consciousness. The only clue that Mrs. Woolf offers as to what she considers real rather than unreal loyalties occurs in a brief discussion of the *Antigone* of Sophocles: "You want to know which are the unreal loyalties which we must despise, which are the real loyalties which we must honour? Consider Antigone's distinction between the laws and the Law. . . . Private judgement is still free in private; and that freedom is the essence of freedom." Louis XIV claimed only that he was the state: Mrs. Woolf claimed that she was the Law. For Mrs. Woolf, loyalty to herself was the only real, true loyalty.

It comes as no surprise that a thinker (or perhaps I should say a feeler) such as Mrs. Woolf, with her emotional and intellectual dishonesty, should collapse all relevant moral distinctions, a technique vital to all schools of resentment. Time and again we find her misappropriating the connotation of one thing and attaching it to another, by insinuating a false analogy: that since both the British policeman and the Nazi stormtrooper wore a uniform, the British policeman was a brute. It is one of the chief characteristics of modern rhetoric, designed not so much to find the truth as (in the words of former Australian prime minister Gough Whitlam) to "maintain your rage."

One would hardly guess from reading *Three Guineas* that it was written at a uniquely dangerous historical juncture, in the shadow of a barbaric threat. It would be unfair to blame Mrs. Woolf for lacking the prescience of the catastrophe to come that many other people lacked—though she had had the advantage of seeing the virulence of the Nazis firsthand when she toured Hitler's Germany with her Jewish husband, whom the Foreign Office had advised not to go, as his safety could not be assured. But all that the experience taught her was that English society—with its unfairness toward women, especially the daughters of the educated class—was proto-Nazi, if not worse. At least the Nazis had the courage of their brutality and were not hypocrites, like the English.

Thus when a man wrote to the newspaper to suggest that the employment of women was a cause of mass unemployment among men, and that the real place of women was in the home, Mrs. Woolf comments: "There we have in embryo the creature, Dictator as we call him when he is Italian or German, who believes he has the right, whether given by God, Nature, sex or race is immaterial, to dictate to other human beings how they live; what they shall do."

Comparing the letter writer's views on the subject with those of Hitler, she continues: "But where is the difference? Are they not both saying the same thing? Are they not both the voice of Dictators, whether they speak English or German, and are we not all agreed that the dictator when we meet him abroad is a very dangerous as well as a very ugly animal? And he is here among us, raising his ugly head, spitting his poison, small still, curled up like a caterpillar on a leaf, but in the heart of England. Is it not from this egg . . . to quote Mr. Wells . . . that 'the practical obliteration of [our] freedom will spring?' And is not the woman who has to breathe that poison and to fight that insect, secretly and without arms, in her office, fighting the Fascist or the Nazi as surely as those who fight him with arms in the limelight of publicity?"

Her inability to distinguish metaphor from the literal truth is unremitting. Discussing the struggle for female emancipation, she says: "It is true that the combatants did not inflict flesh wounds;

chivalry forbad; but you will agree that a battle that wastes time is as deadly as a battle that wastes blood."

As deadly? As *deadly*? It is small wonder that Mrs. Woolf finds it difficult to draw a distinction between the Church of England and the Nazi party. Citing a Church of England commission that recommended against the ordination of women, she writes: "The emphasis which both priests and dictators place upon the necessity for two worlds [the public for men and the domestic for women] is enough to prove that it is essential to their domination."

Over and over she lets her rage and resentment blind her. Discussing the need, in the name of peace and the avoidance of all competition between people, to eschew all ceremonial and public distinctions, she writes that right-minded people such as she "will dispense with personal distinctions—medals, ribbons, badges, hoods, gowns—not from any dislike of personal adornment, but because of the obvious effect of such distinctions to constrict, to stereotype and to destroy. Here, as so often, the example of the Fascist States is at hand to instruct us—for if we have no example of what we wish to be, we have, what is probably equally valuable, a daily and illuminating example of what we do not wish to be. With the example, then, that they give us of the power of medals, symbols, orders . . . to hypnotize the human mind, it must be our aim not to submit ourselves to such hypnotism." There is thus no real difference between a university degree convocation and a Nuremberg rally.

In reply to the lawyer who asks her for a contribution to promote peace, she writes: "The whole iniquity of dictatorship, whether in Oxford or Cambridge, in Whitehall or in Downing Street, against Jews or against women, in England or in Germany, in Italy or in Spain, is now apparent to you." In other words, there is no relevant difference between the defects of Britain and those of Germany, or between the Garrick Club (which still admits no women members) and Treblinka. Referring to the dictator Creon in Sophocles' *Antigone*, she writes, "And he shut [Antigone] not in Holloway [the women's prison to which suffragettes who broke the law were briefly sent] or in a concentration camp, but in a tomb." Holloway equals a concentration camp: Mrs. Woolf's signature mode of argument.

For Mrs. Woolf, the man in uniform is inherently evil, whether the uniform be that of the SS or the Great Western Railway, of the Gestapo or the Metropolitan Police. There is no difference; it all leads to the same calamity. Oddly enough, the one comparison that Mrs. Woolf does not make is that between the Nazis' book-burning and her own proposal to burn down colleges with libraries, replacing the old books with new ones. The Nazis, too, were all in favor of new books. Had they ever occupied Britain, she would have found common cause with them, since to her the culture and intellectual freedom that the eminent peace-loving lawyer wants her to protect are "rather abstract goddesses."

A person who believed that all the established institutions of her own country were tyrannical, as tyrannical as those of the worst tyrannies ever established in the history of the world, and who believed that all loyalty to country or to anything other than one's own inner freedom was false, that all uniforms were equally evil and therefore that there was nothing to choose between them, that war on all occasions was a manifestation of male psychopathology and the desire to dominate brought about by competitive education, and that therefore there could be no such thing as a just war, would have made a wonderful collaborator, ready with every sophistical excuse to hand. She was most unlikely to be a furious defender of her country against the foreign invader: Mrs. Woolf believed she had nothing to defend, her life as the daughter of an educated man being already so intolerable. When in 1936 a British Member of Parliament, Sir E. F. Fletcher, "urged the House of Commons to stand up to dictators," Mrs. Woolf saw not the desire to oppose radical evil but only "a desire for dominance," exactly analogous in her opinion (and here I can hardly refrain from pointing out that I am rendering the literal truth of what she wrote) to the demand of a husband, whose wife appeared in a Bristol court at the same time as Fletcher made his speech, applying for financial support after she left him because he had insisted that she address him as Sir and obey his every command without delay. It was not even Hitler, *nota bene*, who was analogous in

Mrs. Woolf's mind to the domineering husband, but the man who proposed to stand up to Hitler.

There was no more intellectual freedom in Britain than in Nazi Germany, as far as Mrs. Woolf was concerned, because "Mrs. Oliphant sold her brain, her very admirable brain, prostituted her culture and enslaved her intellectual liberty in order that she might earn her living," and all writers were more or less in the same position. She protests and complains as a woman and as a writer, but above all as a human being, who has discovered with bitterness that being born privileged does not alter the conditions and limitations of human existence.

So what, in Mrs. Woolf's opinion, should women actually do if war with Germany came? Since it was evidently a matter of indifference if the Nazis won (every British male being already a virtual Nazi), the answer was obvious to Mrs. Woolf: they should do nothing.

"Their first duty . . . would be not to fight with arms. . . . Next they would refuse . . . to make munitions or nurse the wounded [because the prospect of being nursed if wounded would give men a perverse incentive to fight]. . . . [T]he next duty to which they would pledge themselves [would be] not to incite their brothers to fight, or to dissuade them, but to maintain an attitude of complete indifference." And she commended as wise and courageous the mayoress of the London suburb of Woolwich, who made a speech in December 1937 in which she said that she "would not even so much as darn a sock to help in a war."

Well, war came—as it happens, not so very long after Mrs. Woolf wrote her book and my mother arrived in England. Strangely enough, my mother, who was seventeen at the time (about forty years younger than Mrs. Woolf) and who had been denied an education in a far more forceful manner than anything to which Mrs. Woolf and the daughters of educated men had been subjected, was able despite her disadvantages to spot at once the morally relevant difference between Britain and her erstwhile homeland. Had Mrs. Woolf's views prevailed, of course, my mother's life would have been a short one. Failing to notice the brutal dictatorship under which the daughters of educated men lived, she became a fire-watcher by night during the Blitz and a mechanic constructing tank engines by day. She did not refuse to knit socks.

Once the war started and the bombs began to fall (destroying the Woolfs' London house), even Mrs. Woolf began to think that a Nazi victory might not be such a good thing. Even more astonishing, she began to see virtues in the very people whom previously she had only disdained. Writing to the composer Ethel Smyth in 1940, she said: "What I'm finding odd and agreeable and unwonted is the admiration this war creates—for every sort of person: chars, shop-keepers, even more remarkably, for politicians—Winston at least—and the tweed-wearing, sterling dull women here . . . with their grim good sense."

Eventually Mrs. Woolf must have wondered from what deep source the virtues she noticed had arisen—or could they have been present all along and she had failed to notice them? Might the revelation by the war of the utter frivolity of her previous attitudinizing have contributed to her decision to commit suicide? If the good life is a matter of judgment, the war proved that all her adult life she had none. My mother, with her wrench by day and helmet by night, did more for civilization (a word that Mrs. Woolf enclosed in quotation marks in *Three Guineas*, as if it did not really exist) than Mrs. Woolf had ever done, with her jeweled prose disguising her narcissistic rage.

Had Mrs. Woolf survived to our time, however, she would at least have had the satisfaction of observing that her cast of mind—shallow, dishonest, resentful, envious, snobbish, self-absorbed, trivial, philistine, and ultimately brutal—had triumphed among the elites of the Western world.

2002

How—and How Not—
to Love Mankind

◈ ALMOST EVERY intellectual claims to have the welfare of
humanity, and particularly the welfare of the poor, at heart: but
since no mass murder takes place without its perpetrators alleging
that they are acting for the good of mankind, philanthropic sentiment can plainly take a multiplicity of forms.

Two great European writers of the nineteenth century, Ivan
Turgenev and Karl Marx, illustrate this diversity with vivid clarity.
Both were born in 1818 and died in 1883, and their lives paral-
leled each other almost preternaturally in many other respects as
well. They nevertheless came to view human life and suffering in
very different, indeed irreconcilable, ways—through different ends
of the telescope, as it were. Turgenev saw human beings as individuals always endowed with consciousness, character, feelings, and
moral strengths and weaknesses; Marx saw them always as
snowflakes in an avalanche, as instances of general forces, as not
yet fully human because utterly conditioned by their circumstances. Where Turgenev saw men, Marx saw classes of men;
where Turgenev saw people, Marx saw the People. These two
ways of looking at the world persist into our own time and profoundly affect, for better or for worse, the solutions we propose to
our social problems.

The resemblances between the careers of these men begin with
their attendance at Berlin University at overlapping times, where
both were deeply affected—even intoxicated—by the prevailing

Hegelianism. As a result, both considered careers as university teachers of philosophy, but neither ever held a university post. They had many acquaintances in common in Berlin, including Mikhail Bakunin, the Russian aristocrat who later became a revolutionary anarchist, the philosopher Bruno Bauer, and the radical poet Georg Herwegh. They shared a carelessness with money, perhaps because they were both born into easy circumstances and therefore assumed that money would never be a problem. Both started their writing careers as romantic poets, though more of Turgenev's poetry than Marx's was published.

Their literary influences and tastes were similar. Each read widely in the Greek and Latin classics; each could quote Shakespeare in the original. Both learned Spanish in order to read Calderón. (Turgenev, of course, also learned it to speak the native language of the great but unsatisfactory love of his life, the famous prima donna Pauline Viardot.) The two men were in Brussels at the outbreak of the 1848 revolution against the July monarchy in France, and both left to observe the events elsewhere. Turgenev's closest Russian friend, Pavel Annenkov, to whom he dedicated some of his work, knew Marx well in Brussels—and left an unflattering description of him.

The secret police spied upon both men, and both lived most of their adult lives, and died, in exile. Each fathered a child by a servant: a youthful indiscretion in Turgenev's case, a middle-aged one in Marx's. Unlike Marx, however, Turgenev acknowledged his child and paid for her upbringing.

Both men were known for their sympathy with the downtrodden and oppressed. But for all their similarities of education and experience, the quality of each man's compassion could not have been more different: for while one's, rooted in the suffering of individuals, was real, the other's, abstract and general, was not.

To see the difference, contrast Turgenev's 1852 story "Mumu" with Marx's *Communist Manifesto*, written four years earlier. Both works, almost exactly equal in length, took shape in difficult circumstances: Marx, expelled from France for revolutionary activity, was residing in Brussels, where he had no wish to be and no income, while Turgenev was under house arrest at Spasskoye, his isolated estate southwest of Moscow, for having written his *Sketches from a Hunter's Album*, an implicitly anti-serfdom—and therefore subversive—book. The censor who allowed it to be published was dismissed and stripped of his pension.

"Mumu" is set in Moscow in the days of serfdom. Gerasim is a deaf and dumb serf of enormous stature and strength, whose owner, an old and tyrannical feudal landowner, has had him brought to the city from the countryside. Unable to express himself in words, Gerasim clumsily woos a peasant girl called Tatyana, also owned by the landowner. On a whim, however, the landowner, a sour and embittered widow who is never named, decides to marry Tatyana off to another of her serfs, a drunken cobbler called Kapiton, thus dashing Gerasim's hopes.

Not long after, Gerasim finds a young puppy drowning in a muddy creek. He rescues her and looks after her until she is a healthy, full-grown dog. He calls her Mumu, the nearest he can come to articulating a word, and everyone in the landowner's Moscow establishment soon knows the dog by that name. Gerasim grows passionately fond of the dog, his only true friend, whom he allows to live with him in his little room, and who follows him everywhere. The dog adores Gerasim.

One day the landowner sees Mumu through the window and asks for the dog to be brought to her. But Mumu is afraid of the landowner and bares her teeth to her. The landowner instantly conceives a dislike of the dog and demands that she be gotten rid of. One of the landowner's servants takes the dog away and sells it to a stranger. Gerasim searches for Mumu frantically but fails to find her. However, Mumu finds her way back to him, to his overwhelming joy.

Unfortunately, Mumu barks on the following night and wakes the landowner, who believes herself to be sorely tried by this interruption of her sleep. She demands that the dog, this time, be destroyed. Her servants go to Gerasim and, by means of signs, pass on her demand. Gerasim, recognizing the inevitable, promises to destroy the dog himself.

There follow two passages of almost unbearable pathos. In the first, Gerasim takes Mumu to the local tavern: "In the tavern they knew Gerasim and understood his sign language. He ordered cabbage soup and meat and sat down with his arms on the table. Mumu stood beside his chair, looking at him calmly with her intelligent eyes. Her coat literally shone: clearly she had only recently been combed. They brought Gerasim his cabbage soup. He broke some bread into it, cut up the meat into small pieces and set the bowl down on the floor. Mumu started eating with her customary delicacy, her muzzle hardly touching the food. Gerasim studied her for a long time; two heavy tears rolled suddenly out of his eyes: one fell on the dog's forehead, the other into the soup. He covered his face with his hand. Mumu ate half the bowl and walked away licking herself. Gerasim stood up, paid for the soup and left."

He takes Mumu down to the river, picking up a couple of bricks en route. At the riverbank, he gets into a boat with Mumu and rows out some distance.

"Finally Gerasim sat up straight, hurriedly, with a look of sickly bitterness on his face, tied the bricks together with string, made a noose, placed it round Mumu's neck, lifted her over the river, looked at her for the last time. . . . Trustingly and without fear she looked at him and slightly wagged her tail. He turned away, grimaced and let go. . . . Gerasim heard nothing, neither the whining of the falling Mumu, nor the heavy splash in the water; for him the noisiest day was still and soundless, as not even the quietest night can be soundless for us; and when he again opened his eyes the little waves were as ever hurrying along the river's surface, as if racing after each other, as ever they rippled against the sides of the boat, and only far behind one or two broad rings rippled towards the bank."

We learn that after Mumu's death Gerasim runs away back to his village, where he works like a slave in the fields: but never again does he form a close attachment to man or dog.

When the cultivated, aristocratic, revolutionary Russian exile Alexander Herzen read the story, he trembled with rage. Thomas Carlyle said it was the most emotionally affecting story he had ever read. John Galsworthy said of it that "no more stirring protest against tyrannical cruelty was ever penned." And one of

Turgenev's relatives, to whom the author read "Mumu," wrote afterward, "What a humane and good man one must be to understand and give expression to the experience and torments of another's heart in that way!"

The story is autobiographical, and the tyrannical, captious, arbitrary, and selfish landowner is the author's mother, Varvara Petrovna Turgeneva. Widowed early, she was an absolute monarch on her estate. Many stories have come down to us of her cruelty, though not all have been authenticated: for example, that she had two serfs sent to Siberia for having failed to make their obeisances to her as she passed—because they did not see her. And the model for Gerasim was a deaf and dumb serf belonging to Varvara Petrovna called Andrei.

Clearly "Mumu" is an impassioned protest against the exercise of arbitrary power of one person over another, but it is not politically schematic. Though it is obviously directed against serfdom, the story does not suggest that cruelty is the prerogative of feudal landowners alone, and that if only serfdom were abolished, no vigilance against such cruelty would be necessary. If power is a permanent feature of human relationships—and surely only adolescents and certain kinds of intellectuals, Marx included, could imagine that it is not—then "Mumu" is a permanent call to compassion, restraint, and justice in its exercise. That is why "Mumu" does not lose its power to move 140 years after the abolition of serfdom in Russia; while it refers to a particular place at a particular time, it is also universal.

In making his general point, Turgenev does not suggest that his characters are anything but individuals, with their own personal characteristics. He does not see them just as members of a group or class, caused by oppression to act in predetermined ways like trams along their rails: and his careful observation of even the humblest of them is the most powerful testimony possible to his belief in their humanity. Grand aristocrat that he was, and acquainted with the greatest minds of Europe, he did not disdain to take seriously the humblest peasant, who could not hear or speak. Turgenev's oppressed peasants were fully human beings, endowed with free will and capable of moral choice.

He contrasts Gerasim's tenderness toward Mumu with the landowner's selfish fractiousness. "Why should that dumb man have a dog?" she asks, without the thought entering her head for a moment that "that dumb man" might have interests and feelings of his own. "Who allowed him to keep a dog out in my yard?"

Turgenev does not suggest that the landowning widow's quasi-absolute power is in any way enviable. Although religious in a superficial and sententious way, she regards God as a servant, not a master, and she acknowledges no limits, either God's or the law's, to the exercise of her will. The result for her is misery, a permanent state of irritation, dissatisfaction, and hypochondria. The satisfaction of her whims brings no pleasure, precisely because they are whims rather than true desires; and—used as she is to obedience, and deserving of it as she believes herself to be—she experiences all resistance, even that of time, as intolerable.

For example, when Mumu is brought in, the landowner talks to her in a syrupy, ingratiating manner; but when the dog fails to respond, she changes her tune. "Take her away! A disgusting little dog!" Unlike Gerasim, who has nurtured Mumu with tender devotion, the landowner wants the dog to love her immediately, just because she is who she is.

Her power renders her dishonest and incapable of introspection. When Gerasim disappears after drowning Mumu, "she flew into a temper, shed tears, ordered him to be found no matter what happened, avowed that she'd never ordered the dog to be destroyed and finally gave [her steward] a dressing down." Her denial of responsibility is breathtaking. Power corrupts, Turgenev knows; and the failure to accept any limitation to one's thoughtless wishes makes happiness impossible. But no set of social arrangements, he understands, will eliminate these dangers altogether.

Nor does Turgenev believe that the people who are subject to the power of the landowner are, by virtue of their oppression, noble. They are scheming and conniving and sometimes thoughtlessly cruel, too. Their mockery of Gerasim is limited only by their fear of his physical strength, and they do not sympathize in the least with his predicament. When Gavrila, the landowner's steward, goes at the head of a delegation of serfs to tell Gerasim that he must get rid of Mumu once and for all, he bangs on Gerasim's door and shouts "'Open up!' There came the sound of smothered barking; but no answer. 'I'm telling you to open up!' he repeated.

"'Gavrila Andreich,' remarked Stepan from below, 'he's deaf, he doesn't hear.' Everyone burst out laughing."

There is no compassion in their laughter, not then and not at any other time in the story. Cruelty is not the province only of the landowner, and the heartlessness of the serfs toward Gerasim always reminds me of a scene from my childhood, when I was about eleven years old. I had gone to line up for tickets to a soccer match—in those days, for reasons I can no longer recapture, I was enthusiastic about the game. The line was long, and there was at least a two-hour wait. An old blind man with an accordion passed along the line, singing "The Man Who Broke the Bank at Monte Carlo," while a companion held out a cap for alms. They passed some young working-class men who had a radio, and who turned the volume up to drown out his song. They laughed loudly at his bewilderment as his companion led him away, reduced to silence.

No one intervened or told the young men how abominably they had behaved; I was too cowardly to do so. But in that little scene, I saw man's permanent capacity for inhumanity to man, a capacity that transcends social condition, class, or education.

An incident when I practiced medicine many years later on an island in the Pacific Ocean reinforced this lesson. Next to the small psychiatric hospital, with its yard enclosed by a high wire fence, was the leper colony. Every afternoon the lepers would gather at the fence to mock the lunatics as they were let out for their exercise, performing their strange dances and shouting at unseen persecutors.

The victory over cruelty is never final, but, like the maintenance of freedom, requires eternal vigilance. And it requires, as in "Mumu," the exercise of the sympathetic imagination.

Turning from Turgenev to Marx (although the *Manifesto* appears under the names of both Marx and Engels, it was almost entirely Marx's work), we enter a world of infinite bile—of rancor, hatred, and contempt—rather than of sorrow or compassion. It is true that Marx, like Turgenev, is on the side of the underdog, of the man with nothing, but in a wholly disembodied way. Where Turgenev hopes to lead us to behave humanly, Marx aims to incite us to violence. Moreover, Marx brooked no competitors in the philanthropic market. He was notoriously scathing about all would-be practical reformers: if lower class, they lacked the philosophic training necessary to penetrate to the causes of misery; if upper class, they were hypocritically trying to preserve "the system." Only he knew the secret of turning the nightmare into a dream.

In fact, the hecatombs his followers piled up are—to the last million victims—implicit in the *Manifesto*. The intolerance and totalitarianism inhere in the beliefs expressed: "The Communists do not form a separate party opposed to other working-class parties. They have no interest separate and apart from those of the proletariat as a whole."

In other words, there is no need for other parties, let alone individuals with their own personal quirks: indeed, since the Communists so perfectly express the interests of the proletariat, anyone opposed to the Communists must, by definition, be opposed to the interests of the proletariat. Moreover, since the Communists "openly declare that their ends can be attained only by the forcible overthrow of all existing social conditions," it follows that Lenin and Stalin were perfectly right in eliminating their opponents by force. And since, according to Marx, the ideas that people have are determined by their position in the economic structure of society, it is not even necessary for people to declare their enmity: it can be known ex officio, as it were. The killing of the kulaks was the practical application of Marxist epistemology.

As you read the *Manifesto*, a ghostly procession of Marxist catastrophes seems to rise up from it, as from the witches' brew in *Macbeth*. Take for example points 8 and 9 of the Communist program (interestingly, as in God's program published on Mount Sinai, there were ten in all): "8. Equal liability to work. Establishment of industrial armies, especially for agriculture. 9. Combination of agriculture with industry, promotion of the gradual elimination of the contradictions between town and countryside." Those who experienced Pol Pot's regime, and Ceauşescu's "systematization," which demolished villages and replaced them with half-completed high-rise apartments in the middle of fields, will have no difficulty in recognizing the provenance of their misfortunes.

The *Manifesto* makes no mention of individual human life, except to deny its possibility under present conditions. True, Marx mentions a few authors by name, but only to pour heavily Teutonic scorn and contumely upon them. For him there are no individuals, or true humans, at all. "In bourgeois society capital is independent and has individuality, while the living person is dependent and has no individuality."

It is no wonder, then, that Marx speaks only in categories: the *bourgeois*, the *proletarian*. For him, individual men are but clones, their identity with vast numbers of others being caused not by the possession of the same genes but by that of the same relations to the economic system. Why study a man, when you know Men?

Nor is this the only generalization in the *Manifesto* that reduces the entire population of men to mere ciphers: "On what foundation is the present family, the bourgeois family, based? On capital, on private gain. . . . But this state of things finds its complement in the practical absence of the family among the proletarians, and in public prostitution. . . . The bourgeois claptrap about the family and education, about the hallowed co-relation of parent and child, becomes all the more disgusting, the more, by the action of modern industry, all family ties among the proletarians are torn asunder, and their children transformed into simple articles of commerce and instruments of labor. . . . The bourgeois sees in his wife a mere instrument of production. . . . Our bourgeois, not content with having the wives and daughters of their proletarians at their disposal, not to speak of common prostitutes, take the greatest pleasure in seducing each other's wives. Bourgeois marriage is in reality a system of wives in common and thus, at the most, what the Communists might possibly be reproached with, is that they desire to introduce, in substitution for a hypocritically concealed, an openly legalized community of women."

There is no mistaking the hatred and rage of these words; but anger, while a real and powerful emotion, is not necessarily an honest one, nor is it by any means always ungratifying. There is a permanent temptation, particularly for intellectuals, to suppose that one's virtue is proportional to one's hatred of vice, and that one's hatred of vice is in turn to be measured by one's vehemence of denunciation. But when Marx wrote these words he must surely have known that they were at best a savage caricature, at worst a deliberate distortion calculated to mislead and destroy.

As a family man, he himself was not an unqualified success. Although he lived a bourgeois existence, it was a disorderly, bohemian one, flamboyantly squalid. Two of his daughters, Laura and Eleanor, committed suicide, partly as a result of his interference in their lives. But not even his worst enemy could claim that he saw in his wife, Jenny von Westphalen, "a mere instrument of production," a spinning jenny, so to speak. Half his youthful poems were addressed to her in the most passionate and romantic terms only a few years before he wrote the *Manifesto*; and though their relations had later cooled, he was nevertheless deeply affected by her death and did not long survive her. Even he, whose information about people came mainly from books, must have known that the *Manifesto*'s depiction of the relations between men and women was grossly distorted. His rage was therefore—as is so much modern rage—entirely synthetic, perhaps an attempt to assume a generosity of spirit, or love of mankind, that he knew he did not have but felt he ought to have.

His lack of interest in the individual lives and fates of real human beings—what Mikhail Bakunin once called his lack of sympathy with the human race—shines out in his failure to recognize the often noble attempts by workingmen to maintain a respectable family life in the face of the greatest difficulties. Was it really true that they had no family ties, that their children were mere articles of commerce? For whom were they mere articles of commerce? It is typical of Marx's unrigorous mind that he should leave the answer ambiguous, as if commerce could exist independently of the people carrying it on. Only his outrage, like the grin of the Cheshire cat, is clear.

Marx's firm grasp of unreality is also evident in his failure to imagine what would happen when, through the implementation of the ideas of radical intellectuals influenced by his mode of thinking, the bourgeois family really would break down, when "the practical absence of the family" really would become an undeniable social fact. Surely the increased sexual jealousy, the widespread child neglect and abuse, and the increase in the interpersonal violence (all in conditions of unprecedented material prosperity) should have been utterly predictable to anybody with a deeper knowledge than his of the human heart.

Compare Marx's crudity with Turgenev's subtlety, alluded to by Henry James, who knew Turgenev in Paris and wrote an essay about him a year after his death: "Like all men of a large pattern, he was composed of many different pieces; and what was always striking in him was the mixture of simplicity with the fruit of the most various observation. . . . I had [once] been moved to say of him that he had the aristocratic temperament: a remark which in the light of further knowledge seemed singularly inane. He was not subject to any definition of that sort, and to say that he was democratic would be (though his political ideal was democracy) to give an equally superficial account of him. He felt and understood the opposite sides of life; he was imaginative, speculative, anything but literal. . . . Our Anglo-Saxon, Protestant, moralistic, conventional standards were far away from him, and he judged things with a freedom and spontaneity in which I found a perpetual refreshment. His sense of beauty, his love of truth and right, were the foundation of his nature; but half the charm of his conversation was that one breathed an air in which cant phrases and arbitrary measurements simply sounded ridiculous."

I don't think anyone could have said this of Marx. When he wrote that "the workingmen have no country. We cannot take from them what they have not got," he wrote as a man who, as far as is known, had never taken the trouble to canvass the living views of anyone but himself. His pronouncement of the death of nationalist feeling was premature, to say the least. And when he wrote that the bourgeois would lament the cultural loss that the proletarian revolution inevitably entailed, but that "that culture . . . is, for the enormous majority, a mere training to act as a machine," he failed to acknowledge the profoundly moving attempts of workingmen in Britain to acquire that very culture as a liberating and ennobling agency. It needs very little effort of the imagination to understand what fortitude it took to work in a Victorian factory by day and read Ruskin and Carlyle, Hume and Adam Smith by night, as so many workingmen did (volumes from their lending libraries and institutes are still to be found in British secondhand bookshops); but it was an effort that Marx was never prepared to make, because he did not consider it worthwhile to make it. One might ask whether he has not set a pattern for hordes of cultivated brutes in the academy, who have destroyed for others what they themselves have benefited from.

Very different from all this, the sympathy that Turgenev expressed for the downtrodden was for living, breathing human beings. Because he understood what Henry James called "the opposite sides of life," he understood that there was no denouement to history, no inevitable apocalypse, after which all contradictions would be resolved, all conflicts cease, when men would be good because arrangements were perfect, and when political and economic control would turn into mere administration for the benefit of everyone without distinction. Marx's eschatology, lacking all common sense, all knowledge of human nature, rested on abstractions that were to him more real than the actual people around him. Of course, Turgenev knew the value of generalizations and could criticize institutions such as serfdom, but without any silly utopian illusions: for he knew that man was a fallen creature, capable of improvement, perhaps, but not of perfection. There would therefore be no hecatombs associated with Turgenev's name.

Marx claimed to know man, but as for men other than his enemies—he knew them not. Despite being a Hegelian dialectician, he was not interested in the opposite sides of life. Neither kindness nor cruelty moved him: men were simply the eggs from which a glorious omelette would one day be made. And he would be instrumental in making it.

When we look at our social reformers—their language, their concerns, their style, the categories in which they think—do they resemble Marx or Turgenev more? Turgenev—who wrote a wonderful essay entitled "Hamlet and Don Quixote," a title that speaks for itself—would not have been surprised to discover that the Marxist style had triumphed.

By a curious twist of fate, the coldhearted Marxist utopians in Russia found a cynical use for Turgenev's story "Mumu," which they printed in tens of millions of copies, to justify their own murderous ruthlessness in destroying every trace of the former society. Could any more terrible and preposterous fate have befallen Turgenev's tale than that it should have been used to justify mass murder? Could there be any more eloquent example of the ability of intellectual abstraction to empty men's hearts and minds of a sense of shame and of true feeling for humanity?

Let us recall, however, one detail of Turgenev's and Marx's biographical trajectory in which they differed. When Marx was buried, hardly anyone came to his funeral (in poetic revenge, perhaps, for his failure to attend the funeral of his father, who adored and sacrificed much for him). When the remains of Turgenev returned to St. Petersburg from France, scores of thousands of people, including the humblest of the humble, turned out to pay their respects—and with very good reason.

2001

A Neglected Genius

ON FEBRUARY 22, 1942, two British nationals committed suicide by an overdose of barbiturates in their house in Petropolis, Brazil. The photograph of them on their deathbed is one of the most heartrending I know, the woman holding the man's hand and resting her head gently on his shoulder. The couple received a state funeral—in Brazil, not in Britain—attended by thousands of mourners. The man was Stefan Zweig, an Austrian Jew who for many years had been one of the most famous writers in German, his works translated into fifty languages. The woman was Lotte Altmann, his secretary and second wife.

Although Zweig had taken refuge in Britain and become a British passport holder, his work never won much appreciation in his adopted country, or for that matter in any English-speaking country, and such little fame as he achieved there has now evaporated. Even among highly literate English speakers, he stands nearly forgotten; even good bookstores in Britain, America, and Australia rarely stock his titles.

It is different in France. There his biographical, critical, and historical studies, as well as his novellas and novel, have stayed in print (except during the occupation); mass-market editions of them are on sale almost everywhere, even at airports. Biographical and literary-critical studies of him appear regularly, and he enjoys almost universal regard as one of the twentieth century's great writers. In this, at least, I think the French have it right.

Two main themes pervade Zweig's writings. The first is the part that passion plays in human life. If reason, as Hume says, is and should be the slave of the passions, how can we control and reconcile our passions so that we may live decently together in society? And if, as Zweig's work suggests, the need for control and the need for expression are in constant tension, there is no abstract or perfect solution to man's existential plight. Any attempt to resolve the contradictions of our existence by dogmatic reference to a simple doctrine (and, compared with life, all doctrines are simple) will thus end in monomania and barbarism. And that reality informs Zweig's second preoccupation: the destruction of civilization by political dogma—as exemplified by the two world wars that destroyed Zweig's world and led him ultimately to commit suicide.

Zweig was born in 1881 into a rich bourgeois Viennese Jewish family, completely assimilated to Austro-German culture. His life charted a long descent from bliss to torment. In his memoir (*The World of Yesterday*), written at sixty, when he was an exile in Brazil without documentation to aid his recollections, Zweig describes the happiness of living in a cultivated and tolerant cosmopolitan society in which politics were secondary, any wars (like government itself) were small, limited, distant, and unimportant, personal freedom reached its apogee, and everything had the appearance—delusory, of course—of solidity and permanence. People felt they could plan for the future because money would always retain its value and interest rates would never change. The joy of material progress, evident year after year, was unclouded by the realization that man remained a wolf to man: moral progress seemed as natural as material progress.

Hapsburg Vienna, in Zweig's view, was deeply civilized because it was politically and militarily impotent:

There was hardly a city in Europe where the aspiration to culture was more passionate than in Vienna. It was precisely because, after so many centuries, the monarchy, Austria itself, no longer knew either political ambition or military success, that patriotic pride was so strongly attached to the achievement of artistic supremacy. The Habsburg Empire, which had once dominated Europe, had long been despoiled of its most important and prosperous Provinces,

German and Italian, Flemish and Wallonian; but the capital remained intact in its ancient splendour, the seat of the court, preserver of a millennial tradition.

The contrast between Vienna's cultural and intellectual splendor and its political decadence no doubt inspired Zweig's lifelong pacifism. He contrasted the Viennese ideal with the aggressive German or Wilhelmine one:

> [O]ne lived an easy and carefree life in this old city of Vienna, and our neighbours to the north, the Germans, looked down with something of spite and envy, and something of disdain, on us Danubians who, instead of showing ourselves to be hardworking and serious, and obedient to a rigid order, peacefully enjoyed our lives, eating well, taking pleasure in festivals and the theatre, and moreover making excellent music. Instead of those German "values" that eventually spoiled and envenomed the life of all other peoples, instead of that avidity to dominate others, instead of always being in the lead, in Vienna we liked to chat amicably, took pleasure in family reunions, and let everyone take part, without envy, in a spirit of friendly complaisance, that was perhaps even a little too loose. "Live and let live," said the old Viennese proverb, a maxim that even today seems more human to me than any categorical imperative. . . .

Such, in Zweig's experience, was the prelapsarian Vienna of Emperor Franz Josef, a man with little culture but also with little ambition other than keeping intact his ramshackle, polyglot empire (which existed with no justification beyond its immemorial existence). The emperor had no desire to intrude into the daily life of his subjects, which had not yet become deeply politicized, as it would during the twentieth century.

Yet the personal freedom of Hapsburg Vienna, great as it was—perhaps greater than any we know today—rested upon no deep philosophical basis but instead upon informal psychological and cultural traits that had developed organically over time. In the crucible of cataclysm, these proved weak protections. Here was a contradiction that Zweig preferred not to think about, let alone resolve: true freedom, he believed, required informality, yet informality offered no protection against the enemies of freedom. Like all pacifists, Zweig evaded the question of how to protect the peaceful sheep from the ravening wolves, no doubt in the unrealistic hope that the wolves would one day discover the advantages of vegetarianism.

In Zweig's Edenic Vienna, informal rules and conventions governed people's lives far more deeply than laws or rights conferred by legislators: Zweig recounts, for example, that his father, though a multimillionaire mill owner easily able to afford it, refused to dine at the Hotel Sacher, since it was the traditional haunt of the empire's upper aristocracy. He would have felt it tactless to obtrude where he was not really wanted; and (an almost inconceivable attitude today) he felt no bitterness at not being wanted. His actual freedoms were more than enough for his appetites. What more could a man reasonably desire?

Zweig became a close friend of Freud's and published a study of him in a three-part book entitled *The Healers* (the other parts focusing on Franz Anton Mesmer and Mary Baker Eddy, a slightly ironic juxtaposition that Freud didn't find appealing). But Zweig admired his father in a completely pre-Freudian way and even modeled himself after him. A self-made man, Zweig's father was always modest, dignified, and unhurried, able to succeed so brilliantly because he lived in times propitious to men of his (good) character:

[His] prudence in the expansion of his business, maintained in spite of the temptations offered by favourable opportunities, was entirely in keeping with the spirit of the times. It corresponded, moreover, with my father's natural reserve, his lack of greed. He had adopted the credo of his epoch: "safety first"; it appeared to him more important to have a "solid" business—still a favoured expression in those days—supplied with its own capital, than to expand it vastly by resorting to bank credits or mortgages. It was a matter of pride for him that, in all his life, no one had ever seen his name on a letter of credit or a loan, and that he had always been in credit at his bank—naturally the most solid of all banks, Rothschild.

The key to Zweig's own character reveals itself in a passage in which he extols his father and then describes himself:

> Although he was infinitely superior to the majority of his colleagues, in his manners, social graces and culture—he played the piano very well, wrote with elegance and clarity, spoke French and English—he refused all public distinctions and honorary posts, and . . . never sought or accepted any title or honour, although, as a great industrialist, he was often offered them. Never having asked for anything, never having had to say "please" or "thank you," his secret pride was more to him than any outward sign of distinction. . . . Because of the same secret pride, I have myself always declined any honorific distinction, I have accepted no decoration, title, or presidency of an association, I have never belonged to an academy, a committee, or a prize-giving jury; the simple fact of sitting at an official table is to me a torture, and the thought alone of having to ask for something, even on behalf of someone else, is enough to dry my mouth out before I have said a single word . . . it is my father in me and his secret pride that make me shrink [from the limelight] . . . for it is to my father that I owe the only good of which I feel certain, the feeling of inner freedom.

Zweig never suggested that his personal ideal was a social one: that no one should ever sit at an official table or accept membership in an academy. But having grown up in a world where it was possible to live happily as so free an agent, he found himself plunged into a world where it became impossible, where men had to organize to resist evil so that any freedom at all might be enjoyed. In such a world, Zweig's refusal to commit to any collective institution or endeavor appeared feeble and parasitic.

That said, however, his very lack of commitment, the very indefinition of his own personality, allowed him to enter the worlds of others in his fiction from the inside, and even more important, to convey those worlds to his readers so that they could enter them too. If he had been other than he was, his work would have lacked its peculiarly empathic quality.

Literature and high culture obsessed Zweig from an early age. At nineteen, he published his first serious article, in the literary supplement of the *Neue Freie Presse*, Vienna's newspaper of record (then edited by the founder of modern Zionism, Theodor Herzl), as well as his first collection of poems. But he soon realized that he was too young to have anything to say, and he traveled to Berlin and Paris in search of experience. In his travels he met many of the young men who would become the most important writers of their age. And by cultivating the acquaintance of prostitutes, pimps, and others on the margins of society, he learned about the lower depths, from whose ugly reality his status as a child of the *haute bourgeoisie* had sheltered him. He spent several years translating into German the modernist Belgian poet Emile Verhaeren, self-effacing literary work of the kind that he recommended to any young person aspiring to become a writer but not yet mature enough to create anything original.

The Great War, of course, smashed to smithereens the old world that Zweig so esteemed. But Zweig clung fast to his prewar ideals, in a climate increasingly hostile to them. Repeatedly his work extols the worth of personal freedom and denies that abstract ideas can guide a man through life's dilemmas. Zweig retained his fear of joining any association or group, however laudable its ends; he never wanted to face the choice of upholding a "party line" against the dictates of his conscience. He was not devoid of general principles, of course: no man other than a psychopath could be. But a preference for kindness over cruelty, say, does not get anyone very far in considering particular cases, which requires reflection as to what kindness actually consists of in concrete situations. Sometimes accused of sentimentality, he was both explicitly anti-sentimental and an anti-rigorist in morals.

His one full-length novel, *Beware of Pity*, explores the disastrous consequences that flow from sentimental and insincere pity. In this novel, set immediately before World War I, a handsome young cavalryman (the narrator) is posted to a provincial Hungarian town. There he meets the crippled daughter of Herr von Kekesfalva, an ennobled Jewish peddler who has made an immense fortune. By his well-meaning but shallow expressions of sympathy for her, the cavalryman arouses hopes of a different kind of relationship, false hopes that he does nothing to dispel until too late, and disappointment leads the young woman to suicide. With brilliant clarity, Zweig traces the consequences of well-meaning emotional dishonesty—consequences far worse than what would have followed an initial callousness.

Zweig was master of the novella (which helps explain his lack of success in the Anglophone world: English-language publishers assumed that this literary form was uneconomic to print, despite its profitability in other countries, where Zweig sold by the millions). He could capture huge historical shifts in a short compass, in plain yet evocative language. In *Buchmendel*, for example, he indicates symbolically, and with great force, the destruction of cosmopolitan tolerance by the nationalist madness of World War I in the fate of a single person.

Buchmendel is a Jewish peddler of antiquarian books in Vienna. For many years before the outbreak of the war, he carried out his business in a Viennese café. Buchmendel lives for books; he has no other life. He is astonishingly learned, in the offbeat way of secondhand book dealers; every scholar in Vienna (the Vienna, recall, of Brahms, Freud, and Breuer, of Mahler and Klimt, of Schnitzler, Rilke, and Hofmannsthal) consults him on bibliographical matters. (Zweig himself possessed one of the world's greatest private collections of literary and musical manuscripts until the coming of the Nazis forced him to dispose of it.)

Buchmendel is otherworldly. His wants are few, his interest in money minimal. The café owner is happy to have as a customer a man consulted by so many eminent men, even though he consumes little and occupies a table all day. The café owner understands, as does everyone else, that Buchmendel is a contributor to, because he is a conservator of, civilization, and being a civilized man himself, he is honored to welcome him. But then the war supervenes. Buchmendel does not notice it; he carries on as if nothing has happened. He is arrested because he has written to both London and Paris, the capitals of the enemy countries, asking why he has not received copies of bibliographical reviews. The military censors assume that this correspondence is a code for espionage: they can't conceive that a man could concern himself with bibliography at such a time.

The government authorities discover that Buchmendel, born in Russian Galicia, is not even an Austrian citizen. Interned in a camp for enemy aliens, he waits two years before the authorities realize that he is only what he seems, a book peddler.

On his release, Vienna has changed. No longer the center of an empire, it has become the impoverished capital of a monoglot rump state. Buchmendel's café has changed hands; the new owner does not understand or welcome Buchmendel and ejects him. Buchmendel's life has fallen apart, as has the civilization to which he was a valuable contributor; now homeless, he soon dies of pneumonia.

Zweig makes it clear that though Buchmendel was eccentric and his life one-dimensional, even stunted, he could offer his unique contribution to Viennese civilization because no one cared about his nationality. His work and knowledge were vastly more important to his cosmopolitan customers than his membership in a collectivity. No man was more sensitive than Zweig to the destructive effects upon individual liberty of the demands of large or strident collectivities. He would have viewed with horror the cacophony of monomanias—sexual, racial, social, egalitarian—that marks the intellectual life of our societies, each monomaniac demanding legislative restriction on the freedom of others in the name of a supposed greater, collective good. His work was a prolonged (though muted and polite) protest at the balkanization of our minds and sympathies.

In the realm of personal morality, Zweig appealed for subtlety and sympathy rather than for the unbending application of simple moral rules. He recognized the claims both of social convention and of personal inclination, and no man better evoked the power of passion to overwhelm the scruples of even the most highly principled person. In other words, he accepted the religious view (without himself being religious) that man is a fallen creature who cannot perfect himself but ought to try to do so. For example, in his novella *Twenty-four Hours in the Life of a Woman*, he tells the story of a woman so swept up by passion that for twenty-four hours she lives more intensely than in the rest of her life put together.

The book opens with a quotation from William Blake's "Auguries of Innocence" (though "Auguries of Imperfectibility" might be more apt):

Every night & every Morn
Some to Misery are Born.
Every Morn & every Night
Some are Born to sweet Delight.

The story takes place in a pension on the Riviera, just before the First World War. Suddenly, an untoward event shatters the little society's calm:

Madame Henriette, whose husband [a rich bourgeois French manufacturer] had been playing dominoes with his friend from Namur as usual, had not come back from her evening walk on the terrace by the beach, and it was feared she had suffered an accident. The normally ponderous, slow-moving manufacturer kept charging down the beach like a bull, and when he called "Henriette! Henriette!" into the night, his voice breaking with fear, the sound conveyed something of the terror and the primaeval nature of a gigantic animal wounded to death. The waiters and pageboys ran up and down the stairs in agitation, all the guests were woken and the police were called. The fat man, however, trampled and stumbled his way through all this, waistcoat unbuttoned, sobbing and shrieking as he pointlessly shouted the name "Henriette! Henriette!" into the darkness. By now the children were awake upstairs, and stood at the window in their night dresses, calling down for their mother. Their father hurried upstairs to comfort them. And then something so terrible happened that it almost defies retelling. . . . Suddenly the big, heavy man came down the creaking stairs with a changed look on his face, very weary. . . . He had a letter in his hand. "Call them all back!" he told the hotel major-domo, in a barely audible voice. "Call everyone in again. There's no need. My wife has left me."

A little later, "we heard the sound of his ponderous massive body dropping heavily into an armchair, and then a wild, animal sobbing, the weeping of a man who had never wept before. . . . Suddenly, one by one, as if put to shame by so shattering an emotional outburst, we crept back to our rooms, while that stricken specimen of mankind shook and sobbed alone . . . in the dark as the building slowly laid itself to rest, whispering, muttering, murmuring and sighing."

Zweig's sympathy for the deserted husband is palpable, and he makes us feel it. The novella is by no means an ideological anti-marriage, anti-bourgeois tract. But Zweig's sympathy also extends to Henriette, the man's wife. The following day, the guests of the pension have a vigorous debate about Henriette's conduct. The narrator opines that Henriette, who acted foolishly, will almost certainly soon regret her action bitterly and be miserable. She is therefore worthy of compassion as well as condemnation: after all, if her marriage were happy, if there had not been hidden depths, she wouldn't have behaved as she did.

The narrator's understanding of Henriette's conduct attracts the attention of Mrs. C., an aristocratic Englishwoman of perfect manners, now approaching old age. She takes him aside and tells him her own story, explaining why she too is unwilling to condemn Henriette in conventional terms, though she does not suggest that the adulteress has behaved well. Many years before, Mrs. C. says, after the death of her husband, to whom she had been happily married, she had traveled to Monte Carlo, where, in the casino, she had noticed a handsome young Polish nobleman, an inveterate gambler, who evidently gambled the last of his money away and left the casino with the aim of committing suicide. She followed him, to rescue him; one thing led to another, and she found herself, uncharacteristically, spending a passionate night with him in a hotel.

The following day, she and her young nobleman take an exhilarating drive in the country, where they enter a little Catholic chapel. He swears that he will give up gambling forever (it is a beautiful moment), and Mrs. C., now passionately in love, gives him a sum of money equal to what he has stolen from his own family to gamble with—a theft that, if discovered, will disgrace him forever. Instead of taking the train back to Poland, however, he returns to the casino, where that night she sees him gamble the money away again, in the process insulting his benefactress.

Mrs. C. has lavished her passion on a worthless man, and Zweig is certainly not suggesting that she behaved well or is a model that others should imitate. But the heart has its reasons that reason knows not of; and never to acknowledge that fact, never to make allowances for it, would be inhuman, just as always giving in to passion also makes us inhuman.

Zweig implies that only the reticent and self-controlled can feel genuine passion and emotion. Mrs. C.'s passion is so great precisely because she is normally a self-contained Englishwoman who had "that peculiarly English ability to end a conversation firmly but without brusque discourtesy." The nearer emotional life approaches to hysteria, to continual outward show, the less genuine it becomes. Feeling becomes equated with vehemence of expression, so that insincerity becomes permanent. Zweig would have dismissed our modern emotional incontinence as a sign not of honesty but of an increasing inability or unwillingness truly to feel.

Zweig saw the storm clouds gathering over his native Austria earlier than many. He bought a flat in London in 1934, realizing that the Nazis would not leave Austria in peace. By 1936 he accepted that he was a permanent exile. But other German exiles criticized him for being insufficiently vociferous in denouncing the Nazis. Some even accused him of trying to reach an accommodation with them to preserve his German income intact—a nonsensical charge: his books were among the first that the Nazis burned.

But it is true that he joined no anti-Nazi groups and hardly raised his voice against the Nazi horror. As a free man, he did not want the Nazis to be able to dictate his mode of expression—even if it were in opposition to them. The insufficiency of this fastidiousness at such a conjuncture needs little emphasis. But Zweig felt—in his own case, since he did not speak for others—that strident denunciation would grant the Nazis a victory of sorts. And—like many intellectuals who overestimate the importance that the intellect plays in history and in life—Zweig viewed the Nazis as beneath contempt. Their doctrine and world outlook being so obviously ridiculous and morally odious, why waste time refuting them?

The nearest he came to denouncing the Nazis was in one of his brilliant historical studies (his accuracy always won praise from professional historians), published in 1936: *The Right to Heresy: Castellio Against Calvin*. Castellio was a French humanist and scholar, more or less forgotten until Zweig resurrected his memory. In a book entitled *Treatise of Heretics*, Castellio denounced Calvin's totalitarian suppression of free opinion in sixteenth-century Geneva in the name of a theological doctrine. In the book, the parallels between Calvin's Geneva and Hitler's Germany are unmistakable, though Zweig, true to his literary method, lets the reader draw them for himself. For example, Calvin not only burned books but drew strength from his initial expulsion from Geneva after his first, failed, attempt to dominate the city, just as Hitler drew strength from his imprisonment after the beer-hall putsch, his first, failed, attempt to reach power in Germany.

Zweig saw himself in the role of Castellio:

> In wars of ideas, the best combatants are not those who thrust themselves lightly but passionately into battle, but those who hesitate a long time before committing themselves, and whose decision matures slowly. It is only once all possibilities of understanding have been exhausted, and the struggle is unavoidable, that they enter the fight with a heavy heart. But it is precisely they who are then the firmest, the most resolute. Such was the case with Castellio. As a real humanist, he wasn't a born fighter. Conciliation suited his peaceful and profoundly religious temperament better. Like his predecessor, Erasmus, he knew the extent to which all earthly and divine truth was multiple, susceptible to many interpretations. . . . But if his prudence taught him tolerance of all opinions, and he preferred to remain silent than involve himself too quickly in quarrels that did not concern him, his ability to doubt and his constant questioning did not make him a cold sceptic.

Of course, it was not so easy to dismiss the Nazis. The contempt of a fastidious aesthete would not defeat them: far sterner measures were necessary. But Zweig, born in the pre-ideological age, did not want to live in a world where the only alternative to one ideology was what he thought would be a counter-ideology. When Zweig committed suicide in Brazil, in despair at the news from Europe, and cut off from all he valued or any hope of ever again having an audience in his native language, Thomas Mann, among others, criticized him sharply. Zweig's suicide, Mann said, was "a dereliction of his duty, an egotistical disdain of his contemporaries," that would give comfort to "the enemy."

That Zweig's death would give much comfort to the Nazis seems doubtful to me, but Mann was alluding to every man's duty to do whatever he could, be it ever so little, to defeat the barbarism that threatened civilization. That Zweig was egotistical was true (though an odd accusation, coming from Mann): he did not want to live in a world where the price of freedom was submergence in a vast collective effort whose outcome he regarded, in the event wrongly, as uncertain.

We can find the key to Zweig's suicide, I think, in the life of Castellio. True, Castellio's belief in free inquiry triumphed over Calvin's narrow theocratic ideas long after his death (more than two centuries, in fact), but during their lifetimes Calvin won all along the line, and Castellio escaped execution only because illness "snatched him from Calvin's claws." Suicide was the illness that snatched Zweig from Hitler's claws, or the claws of the world that Hitler made. He thought that Nazism would win—not forever, but for long enough, and that he would never again have, or be allowed, an audience for his books. He thus no longer had a *raison d'être*.

In the event, Hitler was defeated, only three years after Zweig's death. Freedom returned, at least to the West. But I doubt that the modern world would have pleased Zweig very much. The shrillness of our ideological debates, the emotional shallowness, the vulgarity of our culture, would have appalled him. To read Zweig is to learn what, through stupidity and evil, we progressively lost in the twentieth century. What we have gained, of course, we take for granted.

2004

The Dystopian Imagination

◈ WHY DID the twentieth century produce so many—and such vivid—dystopias, works of fiction depicting not an ideal future but a future as terrible as could be imagined? After all, never had material progress been greater; never should man have felt himself freer of the anxieties that, with good reason, had beset him in the past. Famine had all but disappeared, except in civil wars or where regimes deliberately engineered it; and for the first time in history, the biblical span—or longer—was a reasonable hope for many. Medicine had conquered the dread infectious diseases that once cut swaths through entire populations. Not to enjoy luxuries that Louis XIV couldn't have imagined now was evidence of intolerable poverty.

Yet even as technology liberated us from want (though not, of course, from desire), political schemes of secular salvation—communism and Nazism—unleashed a barbarism that, if not unique in its ferocity, was certainly so in the determination, efficiency, and thoroughness with which it was practiced. The attempts to put utopian ideals into practice invariably resulted in the effort to eliminate whole classes or races of people. Many, especially intellectuals, came to regard the utopian condition, in which earth is fair and all men glad and wise, as man's natural state; only the existence of ill-intentioned classes or races could explain the fall from grace. Where hopes are unrealistic, fears often become exaggerated; where dreams alone are blueprints, nightmares result.

It is hardly surprising that a century of utopian dreams and coercive social engineering to achieve them should have been a century rich in imaginative dystopias. Indeed, from *The Time Machine* to *Blade Runner*, the dystopia became a distinct literary and cinematic genre, and Aldous Huxley's *Brave New World* and George Orwell's *1984* became so much a part of Western man's mental furniture that even unliterary people invoke them to criticize the present.

The dystopians look to the future not with the optimism of those who believe that man's increasing mastery of nature will bring greater happiness but with the pessimism of those who believe that the more man controls nature, the less he controls himself. The benefits of technological advance will be as nothing, they say, by comparison with the evil ends to which man will put it.

The great dystopias do not still command our interest because of their technological prescience. The contrivances they describe are often from today's standpoint laughably naive. H. G. Wells's time machine is hardly more than an elaborate bicycle made of ivory, nickel, and quartz. The radio reporter's aluminum hat, filled with transmitting equipment, in *Brave New World*, strikes us today as ridiculous, despite Huxley's reputation for scientific foresight. In *1984*, Orwell imagines a computer as being full of nuts and bolts, with oil lubricating its operations—more steam engine than motherboard.

Yet this technological naiveté finally does not matter, for the dystopians' purpose is moral and political. They are not crystal gazing but anxiously—despairingly—commenting on the present. The dystopias—depicting journeys to imaginary worlds, removed more in time than in space, whose most salient characteristics are exaggerations of what their authors take to be significant social trends—are the *reductio ad absurdum* (or *ad nauseam*) of received ideas of progress and sensitive indicators of the anxieties of their age, which is still so close to our own.

Some of these anxieties now seem unnecessary to us or based upon false premises. Reading about them today is salutary, however, for it encourages us to step back from our current worries and wonder whether they too might not be chimeras. Wells's *Time Machine*, for example, is virtually a tract on the social-medical fears of his time, most of which, in light of subsequent experience, proved unfounded.

Wells's hero travels 800,000 years into the future. Mankind, he discovers, has divided into two species: the diurnal Eloi; and the nocturnal, subterranean Morlocks. The Eloi are soft, weak creatures, small in stature and effete in gesture and conduct, who devote their time to the simple pleasures of erotic play and eating delicious fruit. The Morlocks, toiling in their underground factories, make everything the Elois need for their easeful existence. But like human spiders, the Morlocks emerge after dark to prey upon the Elois, who are meat for them.

Wells's outdated social Darwinian and eugenic preoccupations are clear enough from his fantasy. Society, Wells thought, was splitting into two castes that eventually would evolve into separate species because of their different conditions of existence. On the one hand were the owners of capital, doomed to mental and physical enfeeblement because they never had to struggle to survive; on the other were the workers, made increasingly stunted, amoral, and angry by the harshness of their labor. Wells's future dystopia showed what he thought would happen when this division reached its end.

Four years after *The Time Machine* first appeared, the Boer War broke out, and British army recruitment centers seemed to bear out Wells's worst fears. An astonishing number of British working-class men failed to measure up to the army's undemanding physical requirements—so much so that recruiters had to lower their standards. Eton adolescents stood six inches taller than slum-school pupils of the same age: here were two nations indeed, and a division into two species might have seemed imminent to someone as steeped in Darwin as Wells.

Yet a mere half-century after Wells's death, his countrymen's average height had increased by an inch per decade: both the Eloi and the Morlocks grew larger as the struggle for existence grew less desperate and survival more assured.

The division of society into separate castes also preoccupied Jack London's dystopia, *The Iron Heel*, published in 1907. London foresees an America in which the plutocracy of the Gilded Age, with hired mercenaries, confronts an immiserated proletariat. Determined to protect their wealth, the plutocrats mobilize their fascistic organization, the Iron Heel, to destroy U.S. constitutional liberties so thoroughly that mass terror ensues and Latin American–style disappearances (which London describes with frightening prescience) become commonplace. London accepts *in toto* Marx's theory of the ever-widening disparity between the owners of capital and those with only their labor to sell, with one important exception: he believes that the proletarian revolution lies in the distant future. In the meantime, man will squirm under the Iron Heel, like a worm under a boot.

Like all dystopians who favor the common man, London does not stoop to flatter. He hates the Iron Heel, but that does not mean he loves the proletariat as anything but an abstraction. When London portrays it in revolt, you begin, despite the author's intentions, to side with the Iron Heel:

> It was not a column but a mob, an awful river that filled the street, the people of the abyss, mad with drink and wrong, up at last and roaring for the blood of their masters. I had seen the people of the abyss before, gone through its ghettos, and thought I knew it; but I found that I was now looking on it for the first time. Dumb apathy had vanished. It was now dynamic—a fascinating spectacle of dread. It surged past my vision in concrete waves of wrath, drunk with hatred, drunk with lust for blood—men, women and children, in rags and tatters, dim ferocious intelligences with all the godlike blotted from their features and all the fiendlike stamped in, apes and tigers, anemic consumptives and great hairy beasts of burden, wan faces from which vampire society had sucked the juice of life, bloated forms swollen with physical grossness and corruption, withered hags and death's-heads bearded like patriarchs, festering youth and festering age, faces of fiends, crooked, twisted, misshapen monsters blasted with the ravages of disease and all the horrors of chronic innutrition—the refuse and the scum of life, a raging screaming, screeching demoniacal horde.

And this, to London, is the last—the only—hope of humanity. Even the Morlocks seem preferable.

It is not surprising that the two greatest literary dystopians, Huxley and Orwell, were English. For to be English in the twentieth century was to breathe in a climate of unrelieved pessimism. It was a period of continuous national decline. Starting from a position of world power and influence, England ended up a mere province, struggling to keep pace with the likes of Belgium or Holland. True, its people were much better off in material terms at the end of the century than at its outset, but man's sense of well-being depends upon comparison with others as well as upon his absolute condition. Material progress and despair went hand in hand in England: a nourishing brew for the dystopian imagination.

Huxley's *Brave New World* was published in 1932; Orwell's *1984* appeared in 1949. Huxley feared the growing Americanization of English life (though soon after publishing the book, he emigrated to California, America's *ne plus ultra*); Orwell feared the growing Sovietization of English life that had taken place during World War II. It seemed to both men that their native land no longer had sufficient intellectual, cultural, or moral energy to chart its own course through history and was caught in the grip of forces that the individual could struggle against only in vain.

Both dystopias retain their power to alarm because they are prophetic, almost in a biblical sense: they issue permanent calls to resist trends that, irrespective of the political regime we happen to find ourselves under, will impoverish human life.

Huxley's *Brave New World* is set in an indefinitely distant future: it will not be possible for many years to say that his apprehensions have not proved justified. It is unlikely that populations will undergo genetic and environmental manipulation in the exact way that Huxley foresaw: there will never be a fixed number of predetermined strata, from Alpha Plus to Epsilon Minus Semi-Morons. But as an Italian scientist prepares to clone humans, and as reproduction grows as divorced from sex as sex is from reproduction, it is increasingly hard to regard Huxley's vision as entirely far-fetched.

Brave New World describes a sexual regime that increasingly resembles the one that rules today. A little boy, younger than ten, must visit a psychologist because he does not want to indulge in erotic play with a little girl, as his teachers demand: a situation we seem to be fast approaching. Not only does sex education start earlier and earlier in our schools, but publications, films, and television programs for ever-younger age groups grow more and more eroticized. It used to be that guilt would accompany the first sexual experiences of young people; now shame accompanies the *lack* of such experiences.

In Huxley's dystopia, as among liberals today, enlightenment and permissiveness are synonymous. The Director of Hatcheries and Conditioning tells his students how it was in the old, unenlightened times:

> "What I'm going to tell you now," he said, "may sound incredible. But then, when you're not accustomed to history, most facts about the past do sound incredible."
>
> He let out the amazing truths. For a very long period . . . erotic play between children had been regarded as abnormal (there was a roar of laughter); and not only abnormal, actually immoral (no!): and therefore had been rigorously suppressed. A look of astonished incredulity appeared on the faces of his listeners. Poor little kids not allowed to amuse themselves? They could not believe it. . . .
>
> "But what happened?" they asked. "What were the results?"
> "The results were terrible . . . Terrible," he repeated.

Later the director's superior, Mustapha Mond, one of the ten World Controllers, notes: "Freud had been the first to reveal the appalling dangers of family life. The world was full of fathers—was therefore full of misery; full of mothers—therefore full of every kind of perversion from sadism to chastity; full of brothers, sisters, uncles, aunts—therefore full of madness and suicide." As for home— "a few small rooms, stiflingly over-inhabited by a man, by a periodically teeming woman, by a rabble of boys and girls of all ages. No air, no space; an understerilized prison; darkness, disease, and smells." In *Brave New World*, the word "mother" is smutty, in the same way that it is indelicate in the area of the city where I work to ask about the identity of a child's father. As in *Brave New World*, the word "father" is "not so much obscene as . . . merely gross, a scatological rather than a pornographic impropriety." In the matter of human relations, we are halfway to Huxley's dystopia.

Huxley himself was highly ambivalent about the family as an institution. He not only felt that it would, but that it should, disintegrate. His powers of imagination, however, overwhelmed his ratiocination, so he was able to convey the horror of a world in which "everyone belongs to everyone," a world in which no one formed any deep attachment to anyone else.

The ultimate target of Huxley's dystopia was the idea of the good life as the instant gratification of sensory desires. Mustapha Mond tries to prove to his students their good fortune to live in the Brave New World:

> "Consider your own lives," said Mustapha Mond. "Has any of you ever encountered an insurmountable obstacle?"
>
> The question was answered by a negative silence.
>
> "Has any of you been compelled to live through a long time-interval between the consciousness of a desire and its fulfillment?"
>
> "Well," began one of the boys, and hesitated.
>
> "Speak up," said the Director of Hatcheries and Conditioning. . . .
>
> "I once had to wait nearly four weeks before a girl I wanted would let me have her."
>
> "And you felt a strong emotion in consequence?"
>
> "Horrible!"
>
> "Horrible; precisely," said the Controller.

This passage reminds me of the advertising slogan of a credit card launched in Britain about thirty years ago: it "takes the waiting out of wanting." The advertisement showed no recognition that immediate gratification usually presents a bill, with extortionate interest.

Huxley surmised that life lived as the satisfaction of one desire after another would result in shallow and egotistical people. True, he had a poor opinion of mankind to start with: "About 99.5% of the entire population of the planet are as stupid," he once wrote, "as the great masses of the English." But after gratifying their desires instantly throughout their lives, people would cease to carry the divine spark that distinguished man from the rest of creation. They would seek entertainment unto death: at *Brave New World*'s

Park Lane Hospital for the Dying, "at the foot of every bed, confronting its moribund occupant, was a television box." I think of my own hospital, where the dying usually depart this world to the sight and sound of driveling television soap operas.

Those who live lives of immediate gratification, Huxley thought, would not be able to bear solitude of any kind. As Mustapha Mond explains, "people are never alone now. We make them hate solitude; and we arrange their lives so that it's almost impossible for them to ever have it." A life devoted to instant gratification produces permanent infantilization: "at sixty-four . . . tastes are what they were at seventeen." In our society, the telescoping of the generations is already happening: the knowledge, tastes, and social accomplishments of thirteen-year-olds are often the same as those of twenty-eight-year-olds. Adolescents are precociously adult; adults are permanently adolescent.

Orwell's *1984* refers more directly to contemporary events than does Huxley's book: the narrative takes place in the near rather than the distant future and obviously sets its sights on Stalinism. When I traveled in the Communist world before the fall of the Berlin Wall, I found that everyone I met who had read the book (clandestinely, of course) expressed immeasurable admiration for it and marveled that a man who had never set foot inside a Communist country could not only describe the physical environment so well—the universal smell of cabbage, the greyness of the dilapidated buildings—but also its mental and moral atmosphere.

It was almost as if the Communist regimes had taken *1984* as a blueprint rather than as a warning. How could one watch North Korea's "Great Leader" Kim Il Sung enter a vast stadium in Pyongyang, as I did in 1989, without recalling the "hymn to the wisdom and majesty of Big Brother"—"an act," Orwell writes, "of self-hypnosis, a deliberate drowning of consciousness by means of rhythmic noise," during which "to dissemble your feelings, to control your face, to do what everyone else was doing, was an instinctive reaction": instinctive because self-preserving. The Great Leader stood there impassively for minutes on end as 150,000 people threw up their arms in organized spontaneity, worshiping him, exactly as Orwell described. It was forty years, more or less to the day, after the publication of *1984*.

In Romania under Ceaușescu, the television reported in mind-numbing detail the figures from the annual harvest while everyone stood in line for hours to obtain a few miserable potatoes: just as the telescreen in Big Brother's Oceana tormented the population with news of the overfulfillment of the Three Year Plan while there was never a sufficiency of anything. Often I washed with precisely the same kind of soap that Orwell's "hero," Winston Smith, had to use; and when Smith reflects upon the quality of life in Oceana, I hear the voices of Albanians or Romanians under communism: "was it not a sign that this was not the natural order of things, if one's heart sickened at the discomfort and dirt and scarcity, the interminable winters, the stickiness of one's socks, the lifts that never worked, the cold water, the gritty soap, the cigarettes that came to pieces, the food with its strange evil tastes?"

People with no experience of life except under Communist regimes would tell me they knew—though they were unsure how—that their life was not "natural," just as Winston Smith concludes that life in Airstrip One (the new name for England in *1984*) was unnatural. Other ways of life might have their problems, my Albanian and Romanian friends would say, but theirs was unique in its violation of human nature. Orwell's imaginative grasp of what it was like to live under communism seemed to them, as it does to me, to amount to genius.

The totalitarian world Orwell describes in *1984* is thankfully today more a historical curiosity than a serious threat, except in an Islamist version. Yet many of Orwell's ideas, like those of Huxley, remain pertinent, even though the threat of Stalinism has passed, for Orwell warned us about undesirable trends that arose from the condition of modernity as much as from Stalinism. His fears arose not just from his intuitive grasp of Stalinist states and his knowledge of Communist conduct during the Spanish Civil War but from his experiences with the BBC's bureaucracy during World War II, where he witnessed firsthand the potential of the modern mass media to mislead and manipulate.

Consider his treatment of the family. In *1984*, parents fear their children, whom the Spies, the Party's youth organization, have indoctrinated. The Spies encourage and reward the denunciation of every political unorthodoxy, even in the nooks and crannies of private life, the very possibility of which is lost as a result. In modern England, parents fear their uncontrollable children, whom their peers, saturated with the violent and selfish values of a degraded popular culture, have indoctrinated. In both cases, parents are no longer the source of moral authority. Orwell forces us to confront imaginatively this overthrow of the natural order.

Doublethink—the ability to hold two contradictory ideas and assent to both—is with us too, and will remain so as long as we have large bureaucracies that claim to act for our own good while pursuing their own institutional interests. And what is political correctness but Newspeak, the attempt to make certain thoughts inexpressible through the reform of language?

Orwell's book also offers a prophetic view of modern politicized history. Winston Smith copies a passage from a child's history textbook:

In the old days, before the glorious Revolution, London was not the beautiful city that we know today. It was a dark, dirty, miserable place where hardly anybody had enough to eat and where hundreds and thousands of poor people had no boots on their feet and not even a roof to sleep under. Children no older than you are had to work twelve hours a day for cruel masters, who flogged them with whips if they worked too slowly and fed them on nothing but stale breadcrusts and water. But in among all this terrible poverty there were just a few great big beautiful houses that were lived in by rich men who had as many as thirty servants to look after them. These rich men were called capitalists. They were fat, ugly men with wicked faces, like the one in the picture on the opposite page. You can see that he is dressed in a long black coat that was called a frock coat, and a queer shiny hat shaped like a stovepipe, which was called a top hat. This was the uniform of the capitalists and no one else was allowed to wear it. The capitalists owned everything in the world, and everyone else was their slave.

They owned all the land, all the houses, all the factories, and all the money. If anyone disobeyed them, they could throw him into prison, or they could starve him to death. When any ordinary person spoke to a capitalist he had to cringe and bow to him, and take off his cap and address him as "Sir."

The kind of historiography expressed in this satirical passage has become virtually standard in the various branches (feminist, black, gay, and so on) of academic resentment studies, in which history is nothing but the backward projection of current grievances, real or imagined, used to justify and inflame resentment.

The object of such historiography is to disconnect everyone from a real sense of a living past and a living culture. Indeed, the underlying theme uniting the two great dystopias of the twentieth century is the need to preserve a sense of history and cultural tradition if life is to be bearable. This theme is all the more powerful because both Huxley and Orwell were by nature radicals: Huxley was a socialist at Oxford, flirted with fascism in the 1930s, and then became a West Coast guru; Orwell was a socialist from an early age and a lifelong enemy of the status quo. Both implicitly realized as they contemplated the future that preservation was as important as change in human life: that the past was as important as the present and the future.

In both dystopias, people find themselves cut off from the past as a matter of deliberate policy. The revolution that brought about the Brave New World, says Mustapha Mond, was "accompanied by a campaign against the Past"—the closing of museums, the blowing up of historical monuments (as in the Taliban's Afghanistan), the banning of old books. In *1984* "the past has been abolished." "History has stopped. Nothing exists except an endless present in which the Party is always right."

Such dystopian engineering is at work in my own country. By the deliberate decision of pedagogues, hundreds of thousands of children now leave school without knowing a single historical fact about their own country. The historical principles that museums have traditionally used to display art have given way to ahistorical thematic displays—portraits of women from a jumble of eras, say.

A meaningless glass box now sits on a pediment in London's Trafalgar Square as a "corrective" to the historical associations of that famous urban space. A population is being deliberately created with no sense of history.

For both Huxley and Orwell, one man symbolized resistance to the dehumanizing disconnection of man from his past: Shakespeare. In both writers, he stands for the highest pinnacle of human self-understanding, without which human life loses its depth and its possibility of transcendence. In *Brave New World*, possessing an old volume of Shakespeare that has mysteriously survived protects a man from the enfeebling effects of a purely hedonistic life. A few lines are sufficient to make him realize the superficiality of the Brave New World:

Is there no pity sitting in the clouds,
That sees into the bottom of my grief?
O, sweet my mother, cast me not away!

And when Winston Smith wakes in *1984* from a dream about a time before the Revolution, when people were still human, a single word rises to his lips, for reasons that he does not understand: Shakespeare.

This scene takes me back to Pyongyang. I was in the enormous and almost deserted square in front of the Great People's Study House—all open spaces in Pyongyang remain deserted unless filled with parades of hundreds of thousands of human automata—when a young Korean slid surreptitiously up to me and asked, "Do you speak English?"

An electric moment: for in North Korea, unsupervised contact between a Korean and a foreigner is utterly unthinkable, as unthinkable as shouting, "Down with Big Brother!"

"Yes," I replied.

"I am a student at the Foreign Languages Institute. Reading Dickens and Shakespeare is the greatest, the only pleasure of my life."

It was the most searing communication I have ever received in my life. We parted immediately afterward and of course will never meet again. For him, Dickens and Shakespeare (which the regime permitted him to read with quite other ends in view) guaranteed the possibility not just of freedom but of truly human life itself.

Orwell and Huxley had the imagination to understand why—unlike me, who had to go to Pyongyang to find out.

2001

A Lost Art

◈ RECENTLY a short stroll between two New York art galleries offered a textbook demonstration of the revolution that transformed aesthetic sensibility in the twentieth century. On view at the Adelson Galleries on East Seventy-seventh Street were prints and drawings by Mary Cassatt, part of a hitherto unexhibited cache from her own studio. Two blocks away, hanging at the Salander-O'Reilly Galleries on East Seventy-ninth Street, were sixteen of Joan Miró's "later masterworks" from the Fundacio Pilar I Joan Miró in Majorca. Produced only eighty years after the Cassatt works, the Miró paintings seemed artifacts from an entirely different universe. Seeing the two shows on the same day, I couldn't but wonder whether the upheaval in sensibility really was inevitable. As to whether it was desirable—that is an easier question.

Miró was one of the greatest painters of the twentieth century, a man of the most prodigious talent, so my first thought was that perhaps the descent into chaos and anarchy these late works represent was just a failing of old age. All these paintings date from 1973, when he was eighty, or later. But after all, such artists as Michelangelo, Titian, Tintoretto, and Chardin painted brilliantly into old age; and there is no evidence that Miró was anything other than extremely fit and alert when he painted his "late masterworks." The aesthetic impoverishment of these canvases, the degeneration they manifest, was not that of an individual alone but of an artistic epoch.

Miró was born in 1893, thirty-one years before Mary Cassatt's death in 1924. Though by the time Miró started to paint, blindness had forced Mary Cassatt into retirement, it is nevertheless a mark of the speed and suddenness of the destruction of an immemorial tradition that the lives of these two artists should have overlapped by so many years. While Cassatt's pictures demonstrate an intense, constructive love of the world, Miró's "late masterworks" demonstrate a strangely adolescent, deeply destructive attitude toward it.

Everyone knows Mary Cassatt as an artist of mothers and children: the first book about her, published in 1913, bore the unsurprising subtitle *Un peintre des enfants et des mères*. But it would be quite wrong to conclude from her subject matter that she was a soft-centered, weak sentimentalist. The difference between her and Miró was certainly not a matter of personal moral courage, for such courage Mary Cassatt had in full.

She defied the wishes of her upper-middle-class American parents in becoming a painter at all. To be sure, girls of her class were expected to paint and draw, but as a social accomplishment, not a life's passion; and they were certainly not expected to go off to Paris on their own, as she did, to sit at the feet of the morally dubious master painters of that city. She reminds me of a British contemporary, Mary Kingsley, who nursed her dear father until he died and then went off to the rivers, creeks, and mangrove swamps of West Africa to deal in trade goods and eventually to write a charming, informative, and still classic account of her tropical activities. No one could accuse such women of unthinking conformity.

Nor was Cassatt a conformist in politics. She was a firm believer in women's suffrage, and the exhibition of her work in New York in 1915 staged by her friend and collector, Louisine Havemeyer, was explicitly planned to raise funds for the suffragette cause.

But Cassatt's attitude toward the past was not that of the vandal (her study of the art of her predecessors was thorough and profound), nor did she see innovation as a virtue in itself. The idea that originality, divorced from any other quality or purpose, might be praiseworthy in itself would have been utterly alien to her. It would have struck her—rightly—as uncivilized.

Her quiet pictures of mothers and children, or of women alone in the privacy of their rooms, are deeply moving. They have that strange elusive quality of a Schubert song or a Vermeer painting, of capturing precisely the bittersweet fleeting moment that makes life, for all its disappointments, travails, and hardships, so worth living. Such moments are melancholy as well as joyful precisely because they are fleeting: transcendently beautiful but so brief as to be immeasurable. When we look at the milkmaid pouring milk in Vermeer's painting in the Rijksmuseum, we see—as for the first time—how beautiful is a humble stream of milk that pours from a jug, how supremely elegant is its trajectory, how subtle is the play of light upon it; but we understand simultaneously that the moment cannot last, indeed that part of its beauty is its very transience. Though not for long, perfection is indeed of this world. And this perception reconciles us to our existence, full of ugliness as it might otherwise be. If there are Vermeerian moments in our life—as there will be, if only we pay close enough attention—we shall reach serenity, at least intermittently. And that is enough.

Mary Cassatt is the Vermeer of mother and child. She depicts—even better in her prints than in her oils—the precise moment at which a mother's tenderness for her child is most poignant, in an elegant visual language. There is nothing sentimental or prettifying about this: it is perfectly realistic. Mothers, after all, really do love their children tenderly; and with a few very simple lines (the result of much practice, study, and weariness of flesh, one suspects), Cassatt conveys the physical gestures that express the emotional bond. She observed mothers' hands, for example, with a closeness usually reserved for the face, so that in her depiction of them, which is scrupulously accurate, one sees the physical correlate of fathomless love. She does not subscribe to the doctrine that only the ugly is truly real, and that all else in life is illusion.

Cassatt innovated, and yet her subject matter was not unprecedented, except perhaps in the degree of her concentration upon it. There is no doubt that she reacted strongly against much that was dreadful in Victorian painting, especially in its depiction of childhood: its falsity and sentimentality, its Little-Nellism, so to speak.

Well into her career, painters like Sir Lawrence Alma-Tadema or Léon Frédéric were still churning out the most dreadful pictures of childhood. Such artists strained after emotions not that they felt, but that they felt they ought to feel. This, of course, is one of the sources of sentimentality: it is the tribute that vanity pays to compassion. And thus Alma-Tadema and Frédéric could paint nothing that was truthful either to the world or to themselves.

Cassatt's repudiation of such painters was as much a return to tradition as a break with it. As I looked at her prints in the Adelson, I recalled a painting that I have loved ever since I first saw it over forty years ago, and that I revisit whenever I can. It was painted more than two centuries before Cassatt's work by Pieter de Hooch, who was second only to Vermeer in his ability to make us see beauty in the ordinary. The painting, *A Woman Peeling Apples for Her Daughter*, hangs in the Wallace Collection in London. A seated woman in a Dutch interior peels an apple for her solemn child, who is standing before her, with intense concentration on what her mother is doing. Neither mother nor daughter is beautiful in the conventional sense: in fact, both are decidedly plain. The beauty is in the moment and in the relationship between mother and daughter, not in the purely physical features of their faces. In this undramatic scene we see not merely a moment of an era gone by but the expression of a much deeper, enduring human verity that lies beyond appearance.

Stylistically, Mary Cassatt was strongly influenced by Japanese printmakers, whose work, widely exhibited in Paris in the second half of the nineteenth century, impressed so many painters of the period. The shades of color she used, the tone of flesh, the sharp graphic outlines, the very dimensions of the prints, register her creative response to Japanese art. Some of Cassatt's figures of women on their own—for example, *The Coiffure* or *Woman Bathing*— could almost have been by the eighteenth-century Japanese artist Utamaro Kitagawa.

Curiously, after Mary Cassatt's time, Western and Japanese art went in widely divergent directions. Never again did Western artists—at least, those who wanted to be considered serious— express the kind of straightforward, unaffected tenderness toward the world and human life that is expressed, say, in her drypoint etching, *Feeding the Ducks*, where we see two women in a rowboat solicitously supervising a young child engaged in the solemn delight of throwing bread to a duck. After Mary Cassatt, a disenchantment with the world, real or assumed, seems to have overcome Western artists, so that they would have considered a subject like feeding the ducks inherently sentimentalizing, trivial, and unworthy of their attention. By contrast, the Japanese printmakers—the early-twentieth-century Hasui Kawase and Yoshida Hiroshi, for example—continued unself-consciously to portray and celebrate the beauty of the world. Only after 1945 did Japanese artists undergo the disenchantment that led them to fear direct portrayals of beauty.

The contrast is instructive. The fact that Japanese artists felt able to continue and develop their tradition of woodblock printing—they were followers of their great forebears, not mere imitators of them—suggests that the change in sensibility that occurred among Western artists and eventually among the Japanese as well wasn't merely an aesthetic matter. It didn't take place because artists ran out of ideas and techniques for depicting the beauty of the world and the grandeur or tenderness of life. The reasons for the transformation lay elsewhere.

This isn't to say that the artists who broke with their immemorial tradition did so all at once, or that, having done so, they created nothing beautiful. Not at all: Miró himself was an artist whose utterly distinctive early work had great beauty of form and color, and whose fecund imagery delights and amuses. In his *Peinture* of June 1933, for example, now in the Kunstmuseum of Bern, the background's brilliant colors shimmer and change as in a tropical sunset, while before them takes place an absorbing drama of infinitely suggestive and elegantly drawn forms, one of them insistently female, whose black-booted or stockinged white leg stretches out almost in a goosestep. Miró was never quite figurative (at least, after his artistic adolescence) or quite abstract. His 1935 *Portrait of a Young Girl*, for example, manages to convey, with astonishing economy, all the dizzy frivolity and vanity of youth, with uncensorious affection for it into the bargain.

Nevertheless, talented and brilliant men such as Miró started a downward spiral that ended in artistic anarchy. The Duchamp of the famous urinal was himself a considerable draftsman; but before long, unsurprisingly, we got the urinals without the draftsmanship. Miró's talent, his sense of form and color, are still just visible in the "late masterworks" at the Salander-O'Reilly show, but his method of hurling paint at the canvas and letting it drip indicates a loss of faith in the value or purpose of artistic control. From now on, anything would go. He wanted chance to do his work for him. He burned holes in canvas in the hope that pleasing shapes might emerge; but only a predictable aesthetic and symbolic impoverishment resulted. The logic of an arms race came to rule in art: and legions of untalented hacks who came after Miró devoted themselves to thinking about what had never been done before rather than about what they wanted to express. Miró's later work is an assault on the very possibility of artistic meaning: if chance and destruction are as good as, or better than, direction and control, what sense can there be in sense itself?

This unfolding anarchism in Western art has two sources. First, a new sensibility became dominant among the artistic and intellectual elite after World War I. How was it possible to depict the world lyrically after that great cataclysm? To have done so would have been frivolous and unfeeling: or so it appeared to intellectuals, amongst whom the need to feel things more deeply and earnestly than others is an occupational hazard. (The Japanese, less involved than the Europeans in the First World War, had to wait for the Second World War for the cataclysm that delegitimated their traditional lyricism.)

The social and cultural critic Theodor Adorno eloquently voiced this cast of mind when he proclaimed the final death of art after the Second World War. After Auschwitz, he said, it was no longer possible to produce fine art. The world had become too horrible. "There is nothing innocuous left," he declared. "The little pleasures, expressions of life that seemed exempt from the responsibilities of thought, not only have an element of defiant silliness, of callous refusal to see, but directly serve their diametrical opposite. Even the blossoming of a tree lies the moment its bloom is seen without the shadow of terror; even the innocent 'How lovely!' becomes an excuse for an existence outrageously unlovely, and there is no longer beauty or consolation except in the gaze falling on horror. . . ."

As it happens, there is a kind of sour consolation in thinking that we live in the worst of times, that the horrors we have endured—or at least have heard and read about—are of a nature unprecedented in human history. But is it really true that the two world wars, the terror-famines, the Gulag, and the extermination camps of the twentieth century were of an order so completely different from all other horrors in history that they made traditional artistic endeavor not merely redundant but a positive betrayal of humanity? Should we not remember that Vermeer was born less than halfway through the Thirty Years' War, a war that resulted in the death of a third of the population of Germany, when corpses rotted by the roadside, fields were abandoned, villages destroyed, whole towns put to the sword, and looting was the only form of accumulation? Should we not remember that the treaty that ended this terrible war was signed but a relative handful of miles from where he was living? Does the Thirty Years' War mean that Vermeer was guilty of a callous refusal to see? And did the Great War really mean that henceforth mothers would love their children less than they did in Cassatt's prewar France?

Let us grant, however, that there was something peculiarly dreadful about the cataclysms of the twentieth century. They were appalling in themselves, of course: but an additional source of despair lay in the disjunction between what was technically possible—a decent living for the majority of mankind, for the first time in history—and the uses to which those technical possibilities were actually put. Man had finally freed himself from the burden of religious and other superstitions in order to reach the sunny uplands of rational thought and organization, only to discover the heart of his own darkness, the allegorical truth of the doctrine of original sin.

But does it follow from the special dreadfulness of the events of the twentieth century that the blossoming of a tree can no longer be seen by a decent, sensitive person without the shadow of terror falling upon it? Some of my patients say that they would never hit a woman because they saw their father hit their mother, while others say that they hit women because they saw their father hit their mother. In like fashion, it could just as well be argued that, in the face of catastrophe, the lyrical appreciation of the beauty of life becomes even more important. Sir Ernst Gombrich, the art historian, tells the story of some friends of his in his native Vienna who, after the *Anschluss*, expected to be arrested immediately by the Gestapo. They spent what they thought would be their last hours of freedom together, and possibly their last hours alive, playing late Beethoven quartets.

The idea that, after an event such as the Great War, an artistic celebration of the world is no longer possible is nonsense, compounded of strangely twisted romanticism and inverted sentimentality. The artist strikes an Adorno-like pose to establish that he feels the events more deeply than other people, so deeply that the tree in blossom is no longer for him just the tree in blossom but the hangman's tree in blossom, or the tree soon to be blasted to a charred skeleton of a tree in a nuclear explosion. What counts is depth of feeling. But this is simply a pose: supposing an Adorno-like figure had said, "After the war, sexual pleasure is no longer possible" or "Good cuisine is no longer possible"—the humbug of it all would have stood immediately revealed. Art is precisely the means by which man makes sense of, and transcends, his own limitations and flaws. Without art—or the arts—there is only flux.

Miró's writings and pronouncements are, in fact, a mine of sentimental humbug. It is perhaps unfair to stress too much what an artist says—he is, after all, an artist rather than an author or a journalist—and there can be no doubt of Miró's devotion to his artistic calling. But what he said must have had some connection with his practice, and—like so many intellectuals of his era—he was profoundly dishonest in his views.

I take his use of two words—"bourgeois" and "revolutionary"—as symptomatic. There are no prizes for guessing what value he places on each: bourgeois is always a term of abuse, revolutionary almost always a term of approbation. By bourgeois he always meant a fat, complacent, bellicose, porcine quality: a kind of *Der Stürmer* view of the class, with the anti-Semitism removed. By revolutionary, he meant something thrusting, inventive, and tending to ultimate justice and freedom, bringing about peace by the forcible abolition of everything that prevented peace.

To whom, then, did he actually sell his paintings? Again, no prizes for guessing. It turned out that no one appreciated his "slaps in the face of the bourgeois," as he called them, as much as the rich bourgeois himself. As to real revolutions, there is no evidence that Miró ever considered very deeply their effects upon the lives of artists or upon the freedom of artistic endeavor that he so strenuously demanded.

The second great cause of the ultimate dissolution of the artistic tradition is closely allied to the kind of political humbug Miró affected: the romantic cult of the original artist, divorced from his predecessors, "like stout Cortez . . . with eagle eyes . . . Silent, upon a peak in Darien." Since it was progressively more difficult to say anything new within a realist tradition, the tradition had to be abandoned.

Or worse than abandoned. Here are the first words of the director of the Fundacio Pilar I Joan Miró in the catalog of Miró's "late masterworks":

> Miró, who from the very beginning understood creation as an act which destroyed everything that came before, brought this attitude to its ultimate conclusion when, aging in body but young in spirit, he attacked his own pictorial universe. He returned to painting naive paintings and collages, flinging paint on the canvas, which he tore and burned, possessed by a fit of creative destructiveness. This attitude was the consummation of his old desire to "assassinate painting," so that, following the same law that governs nature itself, new life, new and vibrant forms could be born out of destruction.

Could one imagine anyone saying that of Mary Cassatt, for all her radicalism? Indeed, could anyone, other than a brute, mean those words sincerely, in any literal sense? Who but a barbarian could fail to believe that a man cannot stand alone if he wishes to create, that tradition is actually the precondition of creation, not its antithesis? The problem with uttering such high-sounding rubbish is that a thousand—no, a million—fools can always be found to believe it.

Miró did indeed say that he wished to "assassinate painting" (whatever that might mean) and to strip it of all representational elements. In 1924 he wrote, "I am moving away from all pictorial conventions (that poison!)." In an interview in *Ahora* in 1931, he said, "The only thing that's clear to me is that I intend to destroy, destroy everything that exists in painting. I have an utter contempt for painting. . . . Painting revolts me." Nearly half a century later, an interviewer from the Parisian magazine *L'Express* said of his art that its "audience laughs, and sometimes gives the impression of having been hit in the face." Miró replied, "So much the better! You should hit hard. Violence is liberating."

This is no better than, and not much different from, the fascist General Millan Astray's famous outburst in his dispute with Miguel de Unamuno in 1936 at the University of Salamanca: "*Muera la inteligencia! Viva la muerte!*" (Death to intelligence! Long live death!) And so a sensibility that starts out so horrified by modern warfare that it revolts against the lyrical depiction of the external world ends up by endorsing the worldview of the Baader-Meinhof gang, with its abolition of pity, mercy, and ordinary human affection. One is reminded of Lenin, who denied himself the pleasures of listening to Beethoven because it so reconciled him to the world that he wanted afterward to pat children on the head: a terrible weakness in a man who wanted to hit hard, who believed in the liberating powers of violence.

Miró also subscribed to the view—a natural enough corollary of the artist as lone creator—that change was progress. Probably he was dazzled, as many artists were, by the scientific and technological progress of his time. But just as the analogy between the laws of nature and the laws of artistic creation (an analogy drawn in the catalog of the exhibition of his "late masterworks" by the director of his foundation) is false, so the analogy between progress in the sciences and progress in the arts is false. Art, in its highest expression, explains our existence to us, both the particularities of the artist's own time and the universals of all time, or at least of all human history. It transcends transience and therefore reconciles us to the most fundamental condition of our existence. In the history of art, unlike that of science, what comes after is not necessarily better than what came before.

Miró's "late masterworks" lost almost all contact with human existence, not succeeding even as decoration, a failure all the more evident by comparison with the nearby works of Cassatt. In the transition of late Cassatt to late Miró, one sees the slide from the universally human to the merely egotistical.

2001

Gillray's Ungloomy Morality

THOSE WHO admire and wish to propagate the bourgeois virtues—prudence, thrift, industry, honesty, moderation, politeness, self-restraint, and so forth—are sometimes haunted by an uncomfortable question: how would the world be if, as is not very likely, everyone were to adopt these virtues as his own? Would not the world be a duller (though of course a much better ordered) place—a kind of giant Lucerne or Vevey? It is surely not a coincidence that the iconography of hell is so much more vivid and interesting than that of heaven, a location that induces a deadly boredom even as one strains to imagine what its attractions might be. Vice is like suffering: each individual instance of it is regrettable, but what sensible person would wish to eliminate it altogether? Indeed, life without the possibility of vice, and therefore without its actual practice, would be deprived of all moral meaning. And once the world is made virtuous, will there be no more cakes and ale?

The problem of upholding virtue and denouncing vice without appearing priggish, killjoy, bigoted, and narrow-minded has become so acute that intellectuals are now inclined either to deny that there is a distinction between the two or to invert their value. There is no higher word of praise in an art critic's vocabulary, for example, than "transgressive," as if transgression were in itself good, regardless of what is being transgressed. Likewise, to break a taboo is to be a hero, irrespective of the content of the taboo.

Who is more contemned than he who clings stubbornly to old moral insights?

A recent magnificent exhibition of the work of the great British caricaturist James Gillray (1756–1815) at the Tate Gallery in London demonstrates that the criticism of morals and manners was not always associated in Britain with puritanism, bigotry, and small-mindedness but on the contrary was once vigorous, joyful, and uproariously funny. Few of the spectators at the exhibition laughed, however: an art gallery being a temple of culture, the nearest thing a modern city has to a functioning cathedral, it would have been sacrilege to have smiled, let alone to have emitted a sound indicating amusement. I noticed the same strenuously poker-faced deportment at the exhibition of the work of Honoré Daumier in the Musée d'Orsay in Paris shortly before, a deportment that, in the light of the wonderfully funny material, can only be described as heroic.

As soon as you entered the Tate's rooms whose walls were covered with Gillray's astonishing output of work, you realized—however much you thought you already knew about Gillray—that he did not so much depict or satirize as create and people a world. It is the same kind of achievement as Dickens's, fecund, imaginative, and throbbing with life. Gillray's work, like that of Dickens, uplifts even as it pours scorn on what it criticizes or derides. It is the expression of an uninhibited and fearless freedom of spirit such as one rarely encounters anywhere today and that is possible only in a free society that contests neither individuality nor individualism. You left the exhibition thinking not that human weakness, folly, and vice were any the less weakness, folly, and vice—on the contrary, you left with a heightened awareness of them all around you—but that life is a rich and splendid experience, if only you viewed it aright. You can have both fun and a moral standpoint: they are not mutually exclusive.

Gillray, like Swift before him and Dickens after him, saw everything through a lens that clarified even as it distorted. It highlighted and distilled the salient moral characteristics of everyone and everything upon whom and upon which he turned it, and left the inessential out. This way of seeing is a mark (not *the* mark, of course) of original genius. It became second nature to Gillray, just as it was to Dickens, who, answering the accusation that his characters were mere caricatures, wrote in the preface to *Martin Chuzzlewit* that what were caricatures to his critics were to him straightforward representations of people who were easily to be found by those with eyes to see and ears to hear: the fault was not in his writing but in his critics' restricted and unimaginative powers of perception.

Remarkably little is known about Gillray's life, considering that his work was so celebrated in his own lifetime. He was born in humble circumstances to a father who had lost an arm as a dragoon at the Battle of Fontenoy in 1745—a fact that might explain why one of the only unequivocal expressions of pity in Gillray's generally pitiless oeuvre is for an ex-serviceman with two wooden legs and both arms amputated, who sits, unsuccessfully imploring alms, at the bottom left-hand corner of the print "A New Way to Pay the National Debt," in which George III emerges from the Treasury with bags of gold while being offered yet more by the prime minister, William Pitt, who has already filled his own pockets with gold.

After his enforced retirement from the army, Gillray's father became a sexton for the Moravians, a fundamentalist Christian sect of Bohemian origin. The Moravians were such puritanical naysayers that, when ill, they prayed for death rather than for recovery, to leave behind this irredeemably corrupt world for the purity of heaven. James's eldest brother, John, begged when he was grievously ill at the age of seven to have his coffin brought near him. His dying words soon afterward were, "Pray don't keep me. O let me go, I must go!" Such prayers were often answered in Georgian London: at the time of Gillray's birth, half of all children in London died before the age of five, and he himself was the only one of his parents' six children who survived into adulthood.

It is not unusual for the children of religious enthusiasts to reject the doctrines of their upbringing, though some emotional trace of them usually remains behind. In Gillray the residue of the belief that human life on this earth is a negligible and despicable thing conflicted with an exuberant love of that life, the result being an evenhanded ridicule of the human race that combined considerable ferocity with profound affection.

For the rest, Gillray as a person remains enigmatic. He preferred the company of tradesmen in a tavern (the shopkeepers of Napoleon's contemptuous remark) to that of the *beau monde* that he became so famous for depicting, and whose members he sketched in the street and in the Houses of Parliament. It is said that those who associated with him in taverns had no idea that he was so distinguished and famous a man: his modesty was unselfconscious, and the company of the tradesmen no doubt served to preserve the earthiness of his outlook and his ability to puncture pretension wherever he found it.

No doubt also the early loss of so many siblings taught him a certain detachment: and the only self-portrait of him, a miniature in the National Portrait Gallery, is curious in its greyness—literally the predominant color of the portrait—and its blandness. The only thing it tells us about him was that he was self-effacing, without easily definable personality traits, which makes it all the more likely that the graphic world he created, unequaled in its energy and vibrancy, full of immensely fat or preternaturally thin people, where vanity, greed, naïveté, duplicity, and chicanery rule, was what was most important to him: and that the theater of the world was of more significance to him than his own internal drama.

It is likely that there was considerable internal drama, however, for Gillray is never known to have had intimate relations with anyone. For most of his adult life he lived in Mrs. Humphreys's house, above her print shop on St. James Street. She was his publisher and business partner, and though they lived amicably together, their relationship was probably not a sexual one (Mrs. Humphreys was a spinster considerably older than he). Gillray probably had a problem with sex: he inevitably portrays contact between the sexes as gross, ridiculous, or both. His scatological disgust is almost of Swiftian intensity. And when he designed a print publicizing the excesses of the French Revolution, he lingered a little too lovingly on the whipping of the nuns by the Jacobins. Indeed, whenever he portrays whipping (as in a print depicting what would happen if the French Revolution crossed the Channel, in which Prime Minister

Pitt is tied bare-chested to a post and whipped by his radical opponent Charles James Fox), one detects in the artist a more than average attraction to the subject. And when finally Gillray lost control of his inner demons, when portrayal of the external world no longer sufficed to satisfy him, he went mad. He spent his last few years being looked after by Mrs. Humphreys, believing himself to be Rubens.

Gillray's draftsmanship was as elegant as his subject matter was inelegant (he received training at the recently established Royal Academy of Arts), and his composition was sure: he worked at such a speed that he could afford no errors. He was master both of baroque detail and of classical simplicity, crowding some of his prints with so many contemporary allusions that it took many pages for the correspondent of the Prussian monthly journal, *Paris und London*, to explain them all to the readers. (Gillray was very popular in Prussia, where his prints were often reproduced, and his uninhibited commentary on the political and social affairs of his time aroused both wonder and envy, raising the subversive question in militarized Prussia of how a society that permitted such commentary not only failed to fall apart immediately but actually flourished.) Despite the fact that his formal schooling lasted only a few years at most, Gillray frequently used quotations from Milton and Shakespeare, quotations that the Prussian commentator claimed that "every Englishman knows," thus implying the existence of a culture that was both widely diffused and of high quality. And certainly Gillray imbued whatever he drew with a sophisticated and subtle outlook on life such as a deep acquaintance with literature is likely to confer.

For example, one of his most famous (and simplest) prints, a masterpiece of emblematic distillation, was called "Fashionable Contrasts, or the Duchess's little shoe yielding to the Magnitude of the Duke's Foot." Two delicate little female feet in dainty, jewel-encrusted leather slippers pointing sideways are separated by two enormous male feet in buckled shoes, face downward on the bed. The sexual act has never been more suggestively portrayed (and Gillray's disgust is made evident by the physical inequality of the couple, suggesting violation rather than consent).

This elegantly drawn print is a devastating satire on the obsequious public commentary that followed the marriage of George III's second son, the Duke of York, to Frederica, a short and plain Prussian princess. In the attempt to find something flattering to say about her, the press widely remarked upon the smallness and delicacy of her feet and the beauty of her footwear. A writer in the *Morning Post* wrote that a foreigner might suppose from this commentary that most British newspapers were "conducted by shoemakers . . . so much have they said about the Duchess of York's slipper."

It was Gillray's print that put paid once and for all to this ridiculous and fulsome praise. Gillray was implicitly arguing against flattery and in favor of sincerity, without embracing the brutal and dehumanizing notion that every truth must be told. Showing a certain delicacy of feeling, he did not intend his print to wound the princess—whose plainness and public prominence were neither her own fault nor her own desire—but rather the lickspittles who had made themselves ridiculous in praising her. No one could have done a better job of criticizing the flatterers without insulting the flattered.

Gillray appealed, of course, to public opinion and was a pioneer in doing so: for he knew that his exposure of abuses and follies (and not merely political ones) would help, if not to end, then to limit them. Public criticism was thus essential to public progress, and Gillray knew its power. He had, for example, more or less single-handedly ruined the career of Benjamin Perkins, an American quack who had settled in London, by publishing a hilarious print of Perkins applying his "metallic tractors" to the rubicund nose of an obvious tippler. On the table next to the credulous patient (thoroughly "electrified" by the metal prongs that Perkins points at him) is a newspaper with an advertisement for the Perkinsian method: "a certain Cure for all Disorders, Red Noses, Gouty Toes, Windy Bowels, Broken Legs, Hump Backs." There is no better preserver of common sense than ridicule, and no one who had once seen Gillray's print could continue to credit Perkins's false promises of a panacea. Like all the other caricaturists of the age, Gillray exhibited a great interest in medicine, and his print of the gout—the Georgian disease *par excellence*—as a little blue devil sinking its sharp fangs into the inflamed joint of the sufferer's big toe is the sharpest pictorial representation of a disease ever drawn.

But it is for his political caricature that Gillray is most remembered, and it is doubtful whether he has ever been surpassed in this field, of which he was one of the first practitioners. George Orwell once said that he wanted to turn political writing into an art: Gillray had done that for political caricature a century and a half earlier.

Gillray's sincerity and integrity have sometimes been questioned, since for a number of years he took a grant from the government, and he also remarked that he had gone over to the government side because the opposition had no money to pay him or to buy his prints. At a distance of two centuries, however, it would not be altogether easy for the uninformed to distinguish the politicians whom he supported from those whom he attacked, and certainly his caricatures of the prime minister, his sometime paymaster, were never flattering: Pitt always appeared in the prints as gangling, awkward, cold, not altogether honest, and perpetually taken by surprise. Only Napoleon, whom Gillray depicts as Little Boney, a grandiose Lilliputian, appears more physically ridiculous.

Gillray's political evolution was determined not so much by his personal financial interest as by the stupendous events of the era in which he lived: the French Revolution, the birth of ideological politics, the expansion of democracy, and the dawn of romanticism. He began as a moderate admirer of the French Revolution but soon turned against it (well before he accepted government money) because of its evident excesses. As the struggle first with revolutionary and then with Napoleonic France grew ever more desperate, ever more like total war, so his attitude to George III relented. Originally depicting the king as contemptibly hypocritical and miserly—in refusing, for example, to put sugar in his tea, ostensibly out of sympathy for the poor slaves on the West Indian plantations but really for reasons of economy, to save a trifling sum of money—Gillray became more indulgent, seeing him as the symbol of British national resistance to the universalizing pretensions of Napoleonic France. Gillray was a patriot, who defended as vigorously as any pen has ever done the freedom of his country without ever losing sight of the defects of its inhabitants.

In remaining staunchly patriotic while retaining a clear-eyed and humorously critical view of his own society, Gillray performed a feat that was to prove beyond the majority of intellectuals during a later titanic struggle, the cold war. Gillray never lost sight of the greater and lesser evils: though the Britain of his day was corrupt, ridden with snobbery and other vices that he had no hesitation in exposing and lampooning, he did not conclude that there was nothing to choose between it and French revolutionary excess or Napoleonic domination of the world. The choice for Gillray, as for all persons of good sense, was never between perfection and hell on earth, but always between better and worse. He chose the better without believing it was the best possible, and he would never have believed that the time would come when the services of critics such as himself were redundant.

What were the values Gillray cherished? Despite the almost hallucinatory, chaotic pullulation of so many of his prints, he believed in a constitutional order that reduces, if it does not eliminate entirely, the exercise of arbitrary power, and that rests upon equality before the law. In "A March to the Bank," he mocks the arrogance of those who believe themselves to be unaccountable, and who therefore think they have the right to trample roughshod (in this case, quite literally) over the lesser fry by whom they are surrounded. Here we see a brigade of the militia that marched every day to guard the Bank of England after the anti-Catholic Gordon Riots of 1780, led by a self-important and preposterous popinjay officer goose-stepping with narcissistic satisfaction over the sprawled bodies of the common people in the street, convinced of his own warrant to behave as he likes. Gillray so lovingly renders the popinjay, and we laugh so deeply at his pretensions, that the savagery of the social criticism, though devastating, is somewhat mitigated. In making such arrogance ridiculous as well as bad, Gillray helps to keep the guillotine at bay. His criticism, while fierce, is good-humored and measured.

For Gillray, the essential difference between the Britain of his day and post-revolutionary and Napoleonic France was that between a nation of self-directed free men, pursuing their own interests under a law that permitted what it did not forbid, and a nation of servitors, living under a law that forbade what it did not require. Among the freedoms that Gillray extolled was that of commerce, the freedom of Napoleon's despised shopkeepers, whom Gillray knew well and counted as his friends. It is therefore no coincidence that his archetypal common Englishman, John Bull, is fat and robustly prosperous, more inclined to labor under "the horror of digestion" (to quote the title of one of Gillray's unflattering depictions of the disreputable prince regent, later George IV) than under the rigors of starvation, unlike his French counterpart, who, lacking John Bull's commercial freedom, is always thin, ragged, and sickly.

But Gillray is not insensible to the ironies of human existence, and if he is patriotically attached to the values that he believes make his country the superior of its enemies, he is certainly no xenophobe. Very occasionally, indeed, he gives in to the temptations of moral equivalence: for example, in one of the most famous political cartoons ever published, "The Plum-Pudding in Danger—or State Epicures Taking *un petit souper*," he shows Prime Minister Pitt sitting at a table with Napoleon, carving a world in the form of a plum pudding into slices with their swords, Pitt taking the ocean, and Napoleon Europe, without the faintest indication of any moral difference between them.

Even when he contrasts the fortunate state of John Bull with that of the French commoner, Gillray introduces a note of irony. John Bull is never an attractive figure for Gillray. In one print, entitled "French Liberty, British Slavery," for example, he shows a bald John Bull so fat that he bursts at the seams—the very epitome of today's British football hooligan—preparing to overeat from a huge roast beef, declaiming: "Ah! this cursed Ministry! They'll ruin us, with their damn'd Taxes—why, Zounds! They're making Slaves of us all, & Starving us to Death!" Opposite him is his French counterpart, thin and in rags, sitting on a stool before a wretched fire in a dilapidated room, gnawing hungrily on scallions, saying: "O! Sacre Dieu! Vat blessing be de Liberté. Vive le Assemble!—no more Tax! No more Slavery!—all Free Citizen!—ha! hah!—by Gar, how ve live! Ve svim in de Milk and Honey!"

In the absurd satisfaction of the Frenchman with his wretched lot, Gillray points to a new and powerful source of human self-delusion that was not to reach its apogee until more than a century later and that is still with us: political ideology. Political abstractions, he realized, can disguise or change the meaning of the most elementary realities. Meanwhile, John Bull indulges in the natural human propensity to grumble and not to count blessings, a propensity that is far from harmless during a confrontation with a ruthless ideological enemy.

Gillray's relations with the greatest political philosopher of the age, Edmund Burke, were also of an ironical nature. As a cultured man and avid reader, Gillray had likely read Burke and absorbed the lessons of his philosophy. Indeed, "The Tree of Liberty—with the Devil tempting John Bull" could be seen as a succinct graphic illustration of that philosophy. Of two trees, the one in the background, called Justice, has abundant green foliage; its two main branches, labeled Laws and Religion, bear healthy fruit called Happiness, Freedom, and Security. The tree in the foreground, called Opposition, is dead and without foliage, as if blasted by lightning; its two main branches are Rights of Man and Profligacy. From its lesser branches hang rotten, reddish-golden apples, each with a bite taken out of it, labeled with such temptations as Democracy, Conspiracy, and Revolution. Down the tree slithers a green snake ending in the jowly head, with its Nixonian stubble, of the radical Whig leader, Charles James Fox, holding out to the figure of John Bull an apple labeled Reform. "Nice apple, Johnny—nice apple!" says Fox. But the real meaning of the temptation is evident from the red revolutionary bonnet of liberty, from which the Fox-serpent's tail emerges, and from the difference in the roots of the two trees: those of the Tree of Justice being the Commons, King, and Lords of the established British constitution, those of the Tree of Opposition being Envy, Ambition, and Disappointment, the discreditable emotions that are, by implication, the true motives behind French revolutionary radicalism, rather than supposed love of the beautiful abstractions with which the rotten fruit of the Tree of Opposition is marked.

John Bull is a fat and slow-witted country bumpkin, with a certain shrewdness nonetheless: he is wise enough to resist the siren song of beautiful abstractions. "Very nice N'apple indeeed!" he replies to Fox, in the kind of rural dialect that is still to be heard in Norfolk and Gloucestershire. "But my Pokes [pockets] are all full of Pippins from off t'other Tree: and besides, I hates Medlars, they're so damn'd rotten that I'se afraid they'll gee me Guts-ach for all their vine looks!" The flashy intellectual brilliance of Fox is no match for the wisdom of ages, the common sense of the freeborn Englishman. I was reminded of an encounter I had with a Salvadoran peasant during the guerrilla insurgency there in the 1980s. He acknowledged that, man for man, the insurgents were probably better people than their opponents on the government side: but still he did not want them to win, for he saw in their abstractions not promises but threats. His house and farm might have been poor things, but they were his own.

No message could be more Burkean than that in Gillray's "The Tree of Liberty": yet Edmund Burke, like John Bull, never appears in Gillray in a flattering light. On the contrary, Gillray portrayed him a lean and hungry Jesuit (or jesuitical) dissembler, a dangerous man with a hidden agenda—actuated by malice, for example, when attacking Warren Hastings, the governor-general of British India, whom he attempted for seven years to impeach for corruption. Burke appears in one print absurdly caparisoned in a suit of armor and wearing a biretta, brandishing a ridiculous blunderbuss, ambushing Warren Hastings on an elephant. In another, Burke is seen—while he was still a Whig—as a rank political incompetent, driving the coach and horses of the opposition party arrogantly through the Slough of Despond of unelectability. After his resignation from the government in 1782, he is portrayed ironically as "Cincinnatus in Retirement" (the dictator who retired to rural life after saving Rome), dressed in a Jesuit's robe and sitting down to a chamber pot full of potatoes, one of which he lugubriously peels, in an Irish hovel.

In yet another print, he grovels avariciously for a pittance at the feet of Prime Minister Pitt as the latter grinds John Bull through a mincing machine to produce gold coins. Most famously, he appears simply as a sharp, elongated nose, a pair of spectacles, and a pair of hands holding aloft the British crown and a priest's crucifix, all emerging as an apparition from a cloud, to frighten Dr. Richard Price, a radical dissenting clergyman who preached in approval of the French Revolution and sent a congratulatory message to the National Assembly. The title of this print—"Smelling out a Rat—or—The Atheistical-Revolutionist disturbed in his Midnight Calculations"—suggests that the anti-ideological Burke has himself become an ideologue and is in danger of becoming a Grand Inquisitor.

Burke, brilliant but humorless, was one of the very few of Gillray's celebrated targets who did not laugh at himself. Even Benjamin Perkins is said to have laughed at the print that destroyed his reputation as a healer. One of the most truly admirable qualities of the society from which Gillray emerged, and which he depicted with such verve, was its ability to laugh at itself. Even the king, a man who took himself sufficiently seriously, laughed heartily at Gillray's lampoons of him; the prince regent, whom Gillray never depicts as other than the fat, unscrupulous voluptuary that he was, bought Gillray prints by the dozen and was one of Mrs. Humphreys's best customers. Rising politicians wanted to be caricatured by Gillray, though he was certain to cast them in an unflattering light and expose them to ridicule: for to be caricatured by him was a public certificate of importance. George Canning, later foreign secretary and briefly prime minister, went to considerable trouble to get himself into a Gillray print and was very pleased when he made his first appearance in one, albeit as one of the politicians hanged in the "Promis'd Horrors of the French Invasion—or—Forcible Reasons for Negotiating a Regicide Peace."

Gillray's contemporaries—not only in Britain—recognized him as a great artist. That recognition faded even before his death, and the exhibition at the Tate has now restored it. But Gillray's greatness was more than artistic: he proved by example that public opinion could be mobilized for the betterment of society, and that social criticism could be fierce and uncompromising yet good-natured, measured, and loyal. He proved that the popular could be subtle, learned, and philosophically intelligent. He proved what many have doubted: that having a moral standpoint does not entail solemnity and joylessness.

In a Blairite age, one feels like exclaiming:

Gillray, thou shouldst be living at this hour.
England hath need of thee.

2002

Trash, Violence, and Versace: But Is It Art?

◈ THE ENGLISH are not, on the whole, interested in modern art or indeed art of any description. They can't tell a constructivist from an abstract expressionist and are content to remain in their ignorance. So it's surprising that for several weeks this fall an exhibition of modern British art at the Royal Academy of Art in London, called "Sensation," should have captured their attention and become the talking point of the day.

The exhibition embodied fully that quintessential characteristic of modern British culture: extreme vulgarity. Its celebration of this quality helped "Sensation" break all records for attendance at a modern art exhibition in London, with queues to get in stretching around the block, while a mile away, at the National Portrait Gallery, an exhibition of Sir Henry Raeburn's exquisite portraiture, elegant and psychologically profound, went almost unattended—a perfect symbolic enactment of our desire to jettison our past in favor of our brave and vacuous new present. Mr. Blair—he of the rebranding of Britain—must have been proud of us.

As the Marxists used to say in their days of respectability, *it was no accident* that the "Sensation" exhibition was a selection of works owned by the advertising magnate Charles Saatchi, or that an advertising magnate should be by far the most openhanded patron of modern British art. In an interview in the *Daily Telegraph*, Mr. Saatchi said that, as an advertising man, he was drawn to immediate visual impacts, and he thought that his taste would appeal to a generation of young Britons who had been brought up on advertisements. Quite so: but what I took as a confession of deep shallowness (if I may be allowed an apparently paradoxical expression), he took to be a commendation. We all make God in our own image.

The exhibition attracted unprecedented controversy at home and wide publicity abroad. Television cameras from around the world whirred at the press preview. As for the British press, it divided into two camps, the exhilarated and the disgusted. The exhilarated camp—composed of the self-appointed guardians of freedom of expression and artistic license—exulted that at last Britain, so long a provincial backwater, was now the mainstream of artistic innovation. Young British artists were in the vanguard, bravely battling the forces of artistic reaction, though no one specified the precise destination of the artistic army whose advance they were supposedly leading. The disgusted press camp, by contrast, bemoaned this further, almost definitive, degradation of taste. There is no such thing as bad publicity, however; indeed, in an age of perversity, bad publicity isn't bad—it's the best. "Filthy," "disgusting," "pornographic," "sordid," "perverted," "vicious": no words could have been better calculated to attract the British to the Royal Academy.

Much of the original controversy surrounded a portrait of Myra Hindley. Should it have been shown in public or not?

The name Myra Hindley still stirs the deepest passions in Britain. In 1965 she received a life sentence for the murder of several small children, whom, in conjunction with her lover, Ian Brady, she tortured to death in pursuance of an absurd "pagan" ritual Brady dreamed up. They killed them in Manchester and buried them on the Yorkshire moors.

A tape recording they made while they tortured one of their young victims was played in court and seemed to usher in a new age of British brutishness. George Orwell had already lamented the decline of the English murder, of course, from its Victorian heyday of arsenic and strychnine, when it seemed to possess a certain Byzantine elegance; but this was something new, a fault line in the culture that had opened up to reveal an abyss. Here, for the first time, was multiple murder as self-expression, as self-indulgence, as recreation.

Ever since her conviction, Myra Hindley has divided British opinion into a small liberal camp, which calls regularly for her release, and a large conservative one, calling for her perpetual incarceration (unlike Hindley, Brady has never demanded release). The liberals say that she was young at the time of her offenses, being not yet twenty, that she was in psychological thrall to her lover, that she has since repented her crimes, and that she constitutes no further danger to children. The conservatives say that everyone knows well before the age of twenty that torturing children to death is wrong; that Hindley committed her crimes over a period of two years, so that they sprang from no sudden rush of blood to the head; that by doing so she put herself beyond the pale of normal human society once and for all; and that her repentance was, and is, bogus, inasmuch as she failed for more than twenty years to admit that she knew anything about the disappearance of two other children from Manchester whose bodies were not found but of whose murders she and Brady were certainly guilty.

The police mug shot taken at the time of her arrest has since become one of the most instantly recognizable photographic images in Britain. No newspaper in the country has not reproduced it countless times. She appears agelessly as a square-jawed, peroxided blonde, staring emotionlessly into the camera, the personification of heartless evil. It is this image that an artist called Marcus Harvey chose to magnify to the gigantic proportions of thirteen feet by ten (and Charles Saatchi chose to buy), the artist compounding the insult—in the eyes of the picture's detractors—by using the handprint of a small child in place of the dots by which the photograph is built up in newspaper reproductions of it.

The impact of the picture is enormous, especially on those who recognize Hindley instantaneously, as 99 percent of the British population does. Within the first few days of its exhibition, a spectator threw ink at it, after which it was removed, cleaned, and returned with a protective transparent sheet before it. (Naturally enough, the artistic fraternity took the attack as a tribute to the power of art: for no one attacks what is of no importance to him.)

Outside the academy's entrance, by the statue of its great and civilized first president, Sir Joshua Reynolds, mothers of murdered children, including some Myra Hindley murdered, implored the public not to enter. Members of MAMAA (Mothers Against Murder and Aggression), an organization the mothers founded, handed out a heartfelt photocopied plea from the mother of one of the missing children with whose murder neither Hindley nor Brady was ever charged, though they were almost certainly guilty of it.

"Myself and the parents of the other victims," it reads, "have had to live for over thirty years knowing that our children died a terrible death at the hands of that evil pair. Hindley is due to have her case heard at the [European] Court of Human Rights. What about our rights? There is no such thing as a normal life after your child has been murdered. We live a life sentence too but there is no appeal or reprieve for us, our suffering goes on and on and is only made worse every time something like this comes up. We are the forgotten victims. Hindley has never been charged with the murder of my Keith. . . . I would like to take out a private prosecution but I cannot afford it and cannot get Legal Aid. I still do not know where my son is and all I want is to have him home and give him a decent burial."

The raw sincerity of this appeal cries to heaven and is in marked contrast to the simpering prose of the academy's catalog and press releases, which talk, among other things, of the exhibiting artists' concern about the unjust British class system and of their deep sympathies for and with the working class. But the only members of the working class to visit, or to express an opinion of, the exhibition were precisely the Mothers Against Murder and Aggression, who called unequivocally for the destruction of the painting and the closure of the whole show. It goes without saying that the artists sympathized not with the actual working classes but with their own idea of the working classes, rather as Marie Antoinette wished to live not as a real shepherdess but as her romanticized conception of a shepherdess.

The member of MAMAA to whom I spoke said that Marcus Harvey would never have painted Myra Hindley had she not murdered her child and others. She objected strongly to the transformation of the murderer of her child into an icon to titillate the public for a moment or two, before it moved on to its next, equally momentary, preoccupation or amusement.

There is nothing intrinsically wrong with painting a murderer, even one as depraved as Hindley. But there was undoubtedly something profoundly distasteful about the public display of the painting in this exhibition. The very title of the exhibition as a whole suggested titillation or voyeurism; and this is how the catalog describes the work of Marcus Harvey, two of whose other paintings, both of nude women, were also exhibited, one of them leeringly entitled, *Dudley, Like What You See? Then Call Me:* "Marcus Harvey makes disquieting, tension-filled paintings that simultaneously contain and exceed their salacious imagery. Through the superimposition of pornographic female nudes onto a wildly expressionistic ground, form and content resist and comply with each other uneasily." What is a working-class mother from Manchester, who has had her child expressionistically, salaciously, and pornographically murdered, supposed to make of this?

I asked the Royal Academy's chief of exhibitions, Norman Rosenthal. A man much reviled by some academicians (a few of whom resigned from the academy over the exhibition), he is clearly very good at his job. Somewhat grubby and unwashed, he has the charismatic capacity to antagonize at a hundred yards; and when he speaks—hundreds of words to the minute—one feels one is listening to Mephistopheles.

"All art is moral," he said. "Anything that is immoral is not art."

There is no such thing, wrote Oscar Wilde, as a moral or an immoral book. Books are well written, or badly written. Presumably, then, *Mein Kampf* would have been all right had it been better written.

"The picture raises interesting questions," continued Rosenthal.

"What interesting questions does it raise?" I asked. "Because it must be possible to formulate them in words."

"It raises a question, for instance, about the exploitation of children in our society," said Rosenthal.

"Some might say that the use of a child's palm to produce a picture of a child murderer, when the child could not possibly appreciate the significance of the use to which its palm was being put, was itself a form of exploitation," I replied.

"If so, it is very minor by comparison with what goes on in the rest of society."

"But why must we judge everything by the lowest possible standard?" I asked.

Rosenthal simply couldn't see what the mothers were objecting to. It seems that a life spent in the cultivation of the plastic arts can desiccate a man to the point where he has little sympathy with people whose existence is on a less rarefied plane.

The Hindley picture was far from the only work of art at the exhibition to arouse comment. Indeed, at the exhibition's entrance a notice proclaimed: "There are works of art on display . . . which some people may find distasteful. Parents should exercise their judgement in bringing their children to the exhibition. One gallery will not be open to those under the age of 18." The academy had, in fact, retained an eminent lawyer to advise on which works to withhold from the prurient gaze of youth—more from a fear of prosecution, doubtless, than from a fear of corrupting the young. In the event, a visit from the vice squad of London's Metropolitan Police passed off without mishap: the boys in blue found nothing to object to in the newly refurbished galleries and left without arresting anyone.

Indeed, the eminent lawyer's choice of works to set aside from the young was highly idiosyncratic. One entered the adults-only gallery through a screen arrangement like those in every adult bookshop in every seedy urban area of England. The principal proscribed work was a fiberglass sculpture of several conjoined girls, some with anuses for mouths and semi-erect penises for noses, all naked except for sneakers on their feet, entitled *Zygotic acceleration, biogenetic, de-sublimated libidinal model.* I could understand why the academy's lawyer had thought children should not see it.

But on the wall was also a totally innocuous—indeed, vacuous—painting of a young man recumbent in his room, listening to his

Walkman. Try as I might, I could think of no reason (other than aesthetic) that children should be prevented from seeing it. The only explanation I could think of for this strange sequestration of both the pornographic and the innocuous was that the lawyer was trying to subvert the very idea of protecting children from pornography by making it appear ridiculous: which, in a sense, it was, since any child could have bought the catalog, with its no-obscenity-spared pictures of all the exhibits.

In any case, the part of the show open to children of all ages contained vastly more disturbing exhibits. But for the new art criticism, "disturbing" is an automatic term of approbation. "It has always been the job of artists to conquer territory that has been taboo," writes Norman Rosenthal in his grossly disingenuous essay, ambiguously entitled "The Blood Must Continue to Flow," which introduces the catalog. It would be difficult to formulate a less truthful, more willfully distorted summary of art history, of which a small part—and by no means the most glorious—is mistaken for the whole, that the unjustifiable may be justified.

"Artists must continue the conquest of new territory and new taboos," Rosenthal continues, in prescriptivist mood. He admits no other purpose of art: to break taboos is thus not a possible function of art but its only function. Small wonder, then, that if all art is the breaking of taboos, all breaking of taboos soon comes to be regarded as art.

Of course, he doesn't really mean what he says; but then, for intellectuals like him, words are not to express propositions or truth but to distinguish the writer socially from the common herd, too artistically unenlightened and unsophisticated to advocate the abandonment of all restraint and standards. It is unlikely, however, that even Rosenthal would find, say, a video of young hooligans raping his sister (to invoke Oscar Wilde again) to be merely the conquest of new territory and taboo. Thus, while he may not actually mean what he says, his promotion of this idea in the current exhibition will return to haunt not only him but the rest of society. For why should artists alone be permitted to break taboos? Why not the rest of us? A taboo exists only if it is a taboo for everyone: and what is broken symbolically in art will soon enough be broken in reality.

That civilized life cannot be lived without taboos—that some of them may indeed be justified, and that therefore taboo is not in itself an evil to be vanquished—is a thought too subtle for the aesthetes of nihilism. How ironic that a high official of the Royal Academy should have espoused this destructive doctrine, when the academy's first president, a greater and better man by far, wrote in his *Seventh Discourse on Art:* "A man who thinks he is guarding himself against prejudices [by which he means inherited moral standards and taboos] by resisting the authority of others, leaves open every avenue to singularity, vanity, self-conceit, obstinacy, and many other vices, all tending to warp the judgment." As Sir Joshua also pointed out—in urbane, witty, and civilized prose, of a kind impossible to imagine Norman Rosenthal writing—the intelligent and wise man examines his prejudices, not to reject them all because they are prejudices but to see which should be retained and which not.

I was less taken aback by the main exhibition than many because its atmosphere was oddly familiar to me. It transported me back to my days as a medical student: to the dissection room, the pathology museum, and the mortuary. For there were on display flayed corpses, sliced animals in formalin, a close-up photograph of a gunshot wound to the scalp, and even a work called *Dead Dad*, a scaled-down but hyperrealistic model in silicone and acrylic of a naked corpse. As the nonmedical visitors to the exhibition walked around, I recalled my student days, when my nonmedical-student friends would go through my pathology texts in fascinated horror, turning over the pages half in fear and half in hope of finding something worse overleaf.

I listened to the sculptor of *Dead Dad* give an interview to a European television station while he crouched by the shrunken corpse of his own creation, a huge technical advance over the headshrinkers of New Guinea. "Nothing in this exhibition offends my sensibility," he said, in a tone of evident self-satisfaction. What he omitted to mention, of course, was that modern sophistication demands a sensibility that nothing can offend or even surprise, that is ironclad against shock or moral objection. To be a man of artistic taste now requires that you have no standards at all to be violated: which, as Ortega y Gasset said, is the beginning of barbarism.

I asked the sculptor whether *Dead Dad* was his own father, and of course it was. He clearly regarded the sculpture as a work of filial piety, but it was precisely his sincerity in doing so that appalled me. If he had said that he had made his sculpture to exact revenge upon his father, who had led him a terrible life in his childhood, and who had abused him physically and sexually when he was six years old, his motives in producing it would at least have been clear. When respect, hatred, love, loathing, and contempt can call forth the same artistic product, then our sensibility, our power of discrimination, has been eroded out of existence. When filial piety displays a father's unclothed corpse, down to the last pubic hair, to the idle gaze of hundreds of thousands of strangers, then honoring one's father and one's mother becomes indistinguishable from dishonoring them.

A flippantly intellectualized coarseness is the hallmark of the exhibition, as it is of most modern British culture. The titles of many of the exhibits display this. Damien Hirst—he of the sliced cows and pigs, the bottled sheep and sharks—is a painter as well as a bottler of dead animals. He titles one of his two paintings in the exhibition *beautiful, kiss my fucking ass painting*. A canvas by Gary Hume bears the title *Begging for It*, where It, of course, can mean only one thing. Sarah Lucas calls her exhibit *Sod You Gits*. A painting by Chris Ofili, an artist of Nigerian extraction born in England, is entitled *Spaceshit*. According to the brief account of his life in the catalog, "It was in Zimbabwe that Ofili experienced what some might call 'a moment of clarity'—struck by the limits of his paintings, and in an effort to ground them physically in a cultural as well as natural landscape, he hit upon the idea of sticking elephant shit on them." This was evidently a commercial success. "Soon after, in 1993, Ofili held two 'Shit Sales,' one in Berlin and the other in . . . London, exhibiting several balls of elephant shit in the context of the market." The notes prepared by the academy for schoolteachers who bring their pupils to the exhibition suggest that the teacher discuss with the pupils how a conservator might react to deterioration in the dung of Ofili's pictures, though an answer is suggested by the information that, where he once used only free-range elephant excrement from the African bush, comparatively difficult of access, he now uses the cultivated variety from the London Zoo.

A work by Peter Davies called *Text Painting* consists of 6-1/2 by 7 feet of childish multi-colored lettering (not joined up), from whose unutterably contemptible text the following is but a selection: "Art I like is . . . Bruce Nash and all that aggressive white male stuff, Mike Kolley he does everything so trashy but we love it . . . Picasso he just did whatever the fuck he wanted . . . Lily Van der Stoker Mutha Fucka . . . Antony Caro now he really is one mean badass M.F. S.O.B., Velasquez he's Versace for art lovers . . . Matisse he had no problem with some fucker telling him his work looked decorative . . . Charles Ray like a fucking spoilt brat with his giant dolls + trucks . . ." etc. etc., *ad nauseam*.

Trash, violence, and Versace: a fair summary of the aesthetic of the exhibition.

The coarseness runs through not just the titles or even the subject matter of the exhibits but through every aspect of the show. Even the photographs of the artists in the catalog depict them as members of the underclass. Damien Hirst, for example, takes care to present himself as indistinguishable in appearance from the average British football hooligan. Sheer financial necessity cannot explain this, since many of the artists are by now extremely rich. They appear dirty and disheveled because they want to, because it appears to them virtuous to do so.

The artists are said to evince an interest in, indeed a fascination with, *punk* and *grunge*—the deliberate adoption of ugliness and bad taste that characterizes British popular culture. There is nothing wrong with an artistic interest in demotic coarseness and the underside of common life, of course: this is, after all, the land of Hogarth and Rowlandson. But those great artists remained aloof from the phenomena they were depicting and criticized them even as they laughed at them. They combined social commentary with humor and aesthetic grace. They had both an aesthetic and a moral standpoint (without which satire is impossible) and would have deplored the deep aesthetic and moral nihilism of the current exhibition. They would have been puzzled and appalled by the automatic equation of morality with narrow-mindedness and bigotry, so evident in Norman Rosenthal's essay. And when Hogarth and Rowlandson depicted the ugly, as they did frequently, they did so by comparison with an implicit standard of beauty, embodied in the very elegance of their execution.

The artists of "Sensation," however, have not so much expressed an interest in punk and grunge as surrendered to them. With Milton's Satan, they have exclaimed, "Evil, be thou my good"; and they have added, "Ugliness, be thou my beauty."

They are not alone in this, of course. Surrender on all fronts is the order of the day. Recently the Midland Bank announced that it was withdrawing its $1.6 million subsidy of the Royal Opera House, Covent Garden, because it was an elitist institution; instead, to prove that it was a democratic, caring bank, it would use the money to fund a pop music festival, which most of its customers would find "sexier." The cultural surrender of the better to the worse goes further and deeper. Recently, too, *The Lancet,* one of the world's two most important medical journals, carried a brief interview with Professor Sir Raymond Hoffenberg, former president of the Royal College of Physicians (in existence since the reign of Henry VIII). He was asked for his favorite word—itself a fatuous question, worthy of a women's-magazine interview with a soap-opera starlet—and he replied, "arsehole." Would any president of that august institution proudly have used such a word in public until the last few years?

What accounts for this extraordinary, and very rapid, coarsening of British culture, of which the "Sensation" exhibition is such a striking instance?

The coarsening is international, alas: Damien Hirst is celebrated wherever people have tens of thousands to spend on sliced and bottled animals. The same meretriciousness, the same overvaluation of the same Sensationalism, rules everywhere. The romantic conceit that originality is an artistic virtue in itself is everywhere accepted uncritically: which is why an artist called Marc Quinn, a Cambridge graduate, can be praised for withdrawing eight pints of his own blood over several months, freezing and storing it, and then using it to sculpt a permanently refrigerated self-portrait. It is good and worthwhile because no one has ever done such a thing before. When Damien Hirst was taxed with the fact that anybody could bottle a sheep in formalin, he replied, "But no one did it before, did they?" And if originality necessitates coarseness, then so be it.

The authentic man, in the romantic conception, is he who has cut himself free of all convention, who acknowledges no restriction on the free exercise of his will. This applies as much to morals as to aesthetics: and artistic genius becomes synonymous with waywardness. But a being as dependent on his cultural inheritance as man cannot escape convention so easily: and the desire to do so has itself become a cliché. Thus, for all its crudity and coarseness, "Sensation" is deeply conventional, but it obeys a wicked and socially destructive convention.

The crudity of which I complain results from the poisonous combination of an ideologically inspired (and therefore insincere) admiration for all that is demotic, on the one hand, and intellectual snobbery, on the other. In a democratic age, *vox populi, vox dei:* the multitude can do no wrong; and to suggest that there is or ought to be cultural activity from which large numbers of people might be excluded by virtue of their lack of mental cultivation is deemed elitist and, by definition, reprehensible. Coarseness is the tribute that intellectuals pay, if not to the proletariat exactly, then to their own schematic, inaccurate, and condescending idea of the proletariat. Intellectuals prove the purity of their political sentiment by the foulness of their productions.

As for snobbery, the intellectual raises himself above ordinary folk—who still cling quixotically to standards, prejudices, and taboos—by his thorough rejection of them. Unlike others, he is not a prisoner of his upbringing and cultural inheritance; and thus he proves the freedom of his spirit by the amorality of his conceptions.

Not surprisingly, artists in this mental atmosphere feel obliged to dwell only upon the visually revolting: for how else, in a world of violence, injustice, and squalor, does one prove one's democratic *bona fides* than by dwelling on the violent, the unjust, and the squalid? Any return to the conventionally beautiful would be an elitist evasion, and therefore:

Come let us mock at the great
That had such burdens on the mind
And toiled so hard and late
To leave some monument behind,
Nor thought of the levelling wind.

Among those great, of course, was Sir Joshua Reynolds, president of the Royal Academy, friend and confidante of Edmund Burke, of Oliver Goldsmith, of Edward Gibbon, of David Garrick, of James Boswell (who dedicated his *Life of Johnson* to him), and of Dr. Johnson himself, who said of Reynolds that he was "the man with whom if you should quarrel, you should find the most difficulty how to abuse." What would he have made of these young artists who, *inter alia*, have abused the Royal Academy itself in the coarsest and most vulgar language, these young barbarians who think that art, like the sexual intercourse of Larkin's famous poem, began in 1963? In the first *Discourse* (and with what relief one turns to his elegant way of expressing himself without the aid of a single expletive, as one takes a shower after immersion in dirt), Reynolds wrote: "But young men have not only this frivolous ambition of being thought masters of execution, inciting them on the one hand, but also their natural sloth tempting them on the other. They are terrified at the prospect before them, of the toil required to attain exactness. The impetuosity of youth is disgusted at the slow approaches of a regular siege, and desires, from mere impatience of labour, to take the citadel by storm. They wish to find some shorter path to excellence, and hope to obtain the reward of eminence by other means, than those which the indispensable rules of art have prescribed."

Yes; but what kind of culture is it that confers the reward of eminence on those who use self-advertisement and vulgarity, mere Sensation, as their means to obtain it?

1998

SOCIETY AND POLITICS

What We Have to Lose

WHENEVER WE LEARN of events of world-shaking significance, of catastrophes or massacres, we are inclined not only to
feel ashamed (all too briefly) of our querulous preoccupation with
our own minor tribulations but also to question the wider value of
all our activities. I do not know whether people who are faced by
death in a few seconds' time see their lives flash before them, as
they are said to do, and pass final judgment upon them; but whenever I read something about the Khmer Rouge, for example, or the
genocide in Rwanda, I reflect for a time upon my own life and
dwell a little on the insignificance of my efforts, the selfishness of
my concerns, the narrowness of my sympathies.

So it was when I first learned of the destruction of the two
towers of the World Trade Center. I was settling down to write a
book review: not of a great work, but of a competent, conscien-
tious, slightly dull biography of a minor historical figure. Could
any activity have been less important when set beside the horrible
fate of thousands of people trapped in the then flaming—and soon
collapsing—buildings? A book review, compared to the deaths of
more than three hundred firemen killed in the course of their duty,
to say nothing of the thousands of others? What was the point of
finishing so laboriously insignificant a task as mine?

In my work as a doctor in a prison, I save a few lives a year.
When I retire, I shall not in my whole career have saved as many
lives as were lost in New York in those few terrible moments,
even counting the time I spent in Africa, where it was only too
easy to save human life by the simplest of medical means. As for

my writing, it is hardly dust in the balance: my work amuses a few, enrages some, and is unknown to the vast majority of people in my immediate vicinity, let alone to wider circles. Impotence and futility are the two words that spring to mind.

Yet even as I think such self-regarding thoughts, an image recurs in my mind: that of the pianist Myra Hess playing Mozart in London's National Gallery even as the bombs were falling during the Second World War. I was born after the war ended, but the quiet heroism of those concerts and recitals, broadcast to the nation, was still a potent symbol during my childhood. It was all the more potent, of course, because Myra Hess was Jewish, and the enemy's anti-Semitism was central to its depraved view of the world; and because the music she played, one of the highest peaks of human achievement, emanated from the very same land as the enemy's leader, who represented the depths of barbarism.

No one asked, "What are these concerts for?" or "What is the point of playing Mozart when the world is ablaze?" No one thought, "How many divisions has Myra Hess?" or "What is the firepower of a Mozart rondo?" Everyone understood that these concerts, of no account in the material or military sense, were a defiant gesture of humanity and culture in the face of unprecedented brutality. They were what the war was about. They were a statement of the belief that nothing could or ever can vitiate the value of civilization; and no historical revisionism, however cynical, will ever subvert this noble message.

I recall as well a story told by the philosopher Sir Karl Popper, an Austrian refugee who made his home in Britain. Four cultivated men in Berlin, as they awaited their expected arrest by the Gestapo, spent their last night together—possibly their last night on earth—playing a Beethoven quartet. In the event, they were not arrested; but they too had expressed by their action their faith that civilization transcends barbarism, that notwithstanding the apparent inability of civilization at the time to resist the onslaught of the barbarians, civilization was still worth defending. Indeed, it is the only thing worth defending, because it is what gives, or should give, meaning to our lives.

Of course, civilization is not only an attachment to the highest peaks of human achievement. It relies for its maintenance upon an infinitely complex and delicate tissue of relations and activities, some humble and others grand. The man who sweeps the streets plays his part as surely as the great artist or thinker. Civilization is the sum total of all those activities that allow men to transcend mere biological existence and reach for a richer mental, aesthetic, material, and spiritual life.

An attachment to high cultural achievement is thus a necessary but not sufficient condition of civilization—for it is said that concentration-camp commandants wept in the evening over Schubert *lieder* after a hard day's mass murder—and no one would call such men civilized. On the contrary, they were more like ancient barbarians who, having overrun and sacked a civilized city, lived in the ruins, because they were still far better than anything they could build themselves. The first requirement of civilization is that men should be willing to repress their basest instincts and appetites: failure to do which makes them, on account of their intelligence, far worse than mere beasts.

I grew up in secure and comfortable circumstances, give or take an emotional problem or two; but an awareness of the fragility of civilization was instilled early, though subliminally, by the presence in London during my childhood of large numbers of unreconstructed bomb sites that were like the gaps between the rotting teeth in an old man's mouth. Often I played in small urban wildernesses of weeds and rubble, and rather regretted their gradual disappearance; but even so, I could hardly fail to see, in the broken fragments of human artifacts and in the plasterwork with wallpaper still attached, the meaning of the destruction that had been wrought before I was born.

Then there were the bomb shelters, in which I passed a surprising number of childhood hours. They were ubiquitous in my little world: in the school playgrounds and the parks, for example. That entry to them was forbidden made them irresistibly attractive, of course. Their darkness and fungal dampness added to their attraction: they were pleasantly frightening; one never quite knew who or what one might find in them. Had I been inclined to smoke, instead of being instantly sickened by nicotine, that is where—like so many of my friends—I would have learned to do so. And many a first sexual exploration took place in those inauspicious surroundings.

Despite the uses to which we put them, however, we were always aware of the purpose for which they had been built. Somehow the shades of those who had sheltered in them, not so very long before, were still present. The Blitz was within every adult's living memory: my mother's apartment building had been bombed, and she woke one morning with half of it gone, one of her rooms now open directly to the air. In my house, as in many other households, there was a multi-volume pictorial history of the war, over which I pored for entire mornings or afternoons, until I knew every picture by heart. One of them was ever present in my mind when I entered a bomb shelter with my friends: that of two young children, both blind, in just such a shelter, their sightless eyes turned upward to the sound of the explosions above them, a heartrending look of incomprehension on their faces.

More than anything else, however, the fact that my mother was herself a refugee from Nazi Germany contributed to my awareness that security—the feeling that nothing could change seriously for the worse, and that the life that you had was invulnerable—was illusory and even dangerous. She showed us, my brother and me, photographs (some of them sepia) of her life in pre-Nazi Germany: a prosperously bourgeois existence of that time, from the look of it, with chauffeurs and large cars, patriarchs in winged collars conspicuously smoking cigars, women in feather boas, picnics by lakes, winter in the mountains, and so forth. There were photos of my grandfather, a doctor decorated for his military service during the Great War, in his military uniform, a loyal subject of the kaiser. And then—suddenly—nothing: a prolonged pictorial silence, until my mother emerged into a new, less luxurious but more ordinary (because familiar) life.

She had left Germany when she was seventeen and never saw her parents again. If it could happen to her, why not to me or indeed to anyone? I didn't believe it would, but then neither had she or anyone else. The world, or that little part of it that I inhabited, that appeared so stable, calm, solid, and dependable—dull even— had shakier foundations than most people most of the time were willing to suppose.

As soon as I was able, I began to travel. Boredom, curiosity, dissatisfaction, a taste for the exotic and for philosophical inquiry drove me. It seemed to me that comparison was the only way to know the value of things, including political arrangements. But travel is like good fortune in the famous remark of Louis Pasteur: it favors only the mind prepared. To an extent, one brings back from it only what one takes to it: and I chose my countries with unconscious care and thereby received many object lessons in the fragility of the human order, especially when it is undermined in the abstract name of justice. It is often much easier to bring about total disaster than modest improvement.

Many of the countries I visited—Afghanistan, Mozambique, Iran—soon descended into the most terrible chaos. Their peace had always been flawed, of course: as which is not? I learned that the passion to destroy, far from being "also" a constructive one, as the famous but foolish remark of the Russian anarchist Bakunin would have it, soon becomes autonomous, unattached to any other purpose but indulged in purely for the pleasure that destruction itself brings. I remember watching rioters in Panama, for example, smashing shop windows, allegedly in the name of freedom and democracy, but laughing as they did so, searching for new fields of glass to conquer. Many of the rioters were obviously bourgeois, the scions of privileged families, as have been the leaders of so many destructive movements in modern history. That same evening I dined in an expensive restaurant and saw there a fellow diner whom I had observed a few hours before joyfully heaving a brick through a window. How much destruction did he think his country could bear before his own life might be affected, his own existence compromised?

As I watched the rioters at play, I remembered an episode from my childhood. My brother and I took a radio out onto the lawn and there smashed it into a thousand pieces with croquet mallets. With a pleasantly vengeful fury, as if performing a valuable task, we pursued every last component with our mallets until we had pulverized it into unrecognizability. The joy we felt was indescribable; but where it came from or what it meant, we knew not. Within our small souls, civilization struggled with barbarism: and had we suffered no retribution, I suspect that barbarism's temporary victory would have been more lasting.

But why did we feel the need to revolt in this fashion? At such a remove in time, I cannot reconstruct my own thoughts or feelings with any certainty: but I suspect that we rebelled against our own powerlessness and lack of freedom, which we felt as a wound, by comparison with what we saw as the omnipotence and complete freedom of action of the grown-ups in our lives. How we longed to grow up, so that we might be like them, free to do as we liked and give orders to others, as they gave orders to us! We never suspected that adulthood would bring its own frustrations, responsibilities, and restrictions: we looked forward to the time when our own whim would be law, when our egos would be free to soar wherever they chose. Until then, the best we could do was to rebel against a symbol of our subjection to others. If we could not be as adults were, we could at least destroy a little of the adults' world.

I saw the revolt against civilization and the restraints and frustrations it entails in many countries, but nowhere more starkly than in Liberia in the midst of the civil war there. I arrived in Monrovia when there was no longer any electricity or running water; no shops, no banks, no telephones, no post office; no schools, no transport, no clinics, no hospitals. Almost every building had been destroyed in whole or in part: and what had not been destroyed had been looted.

I inspected the remains of the public institutions. They had been destroyed with a thoroughness that could not have been the result of mere military conflict. Every last piece of equipment in the hospitals (which had long since been emptied of staff and patients) had been laboriously disassembled beyond hope of repair or use. Every wheel had been severed by metal cutters from every trolley, cut at the cost of what must have been a very considerable effort. It was as if a horde of people with terrible experiences of hospitals, doctors, and medicine had passed through to exact their revenge.

But this was not the explanation, because every other institution had undergone similar destruction. The books in the university library had been one and all—without exception—pulled from the shelves and piled into contemptuous heaps, many with pages torn from them or their spines deliberately broken. It was the revenge of barbarians upon civilization, and of the powerless upon the powerful, or at least upon what they perceived as the source of their power. Ignorance revolted against knowledge, for the same reasons that my brother and I smashed the radio all those years before. Could there have been a clearer indication of hatred of the lower for the higher?

In fact there was—and not very far away, in a building called the Centennial Hall, where the inauguration ceremonies of the presidents of Liberia took place. The hall was empty now, except for the busts of former presidents, some of them overturned, around the walls—and a Steinway grand piano, probably the only instrument of its kind in the entire country, two-thirds of the way into the hall. The piano, however, was not intact: its legs had been sawed off (though they were by design removable) and the body of the piano laid on the ground, like a stranded whale. Around it were disposed not only the sawed-off legs but little piles of human feces.

I had never seen a more graphic rejection of human refinement. I tried to imagine other possible meanings of the scene but could not. Of course, the piano represented a culture that was not fully Liberia's own and had not been assimilated fully by everyone in the country: but that the piano represented not just a particular culture but the very idea of civilization itself was obvious in the very coarseness of the gesture of contempt.

Appalled as I was by the scene in the Centennial Hall, I was yet more appalled by the reaction of two young British journalists, also visiting Monrovia, to whom I described it, assuming that they would want to see for themselves. But they could see nothing significant in the vandalizing of the piano—only an inanimate object, when all is said and done—in the context of a civil war in which scores of thousands of people had been killed and many more had been displaced from their homes. They saw no connection whatever between the impulse to destroy the piano and the impulse to kill, no connection between respect for human life and for the finer productions of human labor, no connection between civilization and the inhibition against the random killing of fellow beings, no connection between the book burnings in Nazi Germany and all the subsequent barbarities of that regime. Likewise, the fact that the Red Guards during the Cultural Revolution in China had destroyed thousands of pianos while also killing one million people conveyed no meaning or message to them.

If anything, they "understood" the destruction of the piano in the Centennial Hall and even sympathized with it. The "root cause" of Liberia's civil war, they said, had been the long dominance of an elite—in the same way, presumably, that poverty is often said to be the "root cause" of crime. The piano was an instrument, both musical and political, of that elite, and therefore its destruction was itself a step in the direction of democracy, an expression of the general will.

This way of thinking about culture and civilization—possible only for people who believe that the comforts and benefits they enjoy are immortal and indestructible—has become almost standard among the intelligentsia of Western societies. The word *civilization* itself now rarely appears in academic texts or in journalism without the use of ironical quotation marks, as if civilization were a mythical creature, like the Loch Ness monster or the Abominable Snowman, and to believe in it were a sign of philosophical naiveté. Brutal episodes, such as are all too frequent in history, are treated as demonstrations that civilization and culture are a sham, a mere mask for crassly material interests—as if there were any protection from man's permanent temptation to brutality except his striving after civilization and culture. At the same time, achievements are taken for granted, as always having been there, as if man's natural state were knowledge rather than ignorance, wealth rather than poverty, tranquility rather than anarchy. It follows that nothing is worthy of, or requires, protection and preservation, because all that is good comes about as a free gift of Nature.

To paraphrase Burke, all that is necessary for barbarism to triumph is for civilized men to do nothing: but in fact for the past few decades, civilized men have done worse than nothing—they have actively thrown in their lot with the barbarians. They have denied the distinction between higher and lower, to the invariable advantage of the latter. They have denied the superiority of man's greatest cultural achievements over the most ephemeral and vulgar of entertainments; they have denied that the scientific labors of brilliant men have resulted in an objective understanding of nature, and, like Pilate, they have treated the question of truth as a jest; above all, they have denied that it matters how people conduct themselves in their personal lives, provided only that they consent to their own depravity. The ultimate object of the deconstructionism that has swept the academy like an epidemic has been civilization itself, as the narcissists within the academy try to find a theoretical justification for their own revolt against civilized restraint. And thus the obvious truth—that it is necessary to repress, either by law or by custom, the permanent possibility in human nature of brutality and barbarism—never finds its way into the press or other media of mass communication.

For the last decade I have been observing close-up, from the vantage point of medical practice, the effects upon a large and susceptible population of the erosion of civilized standards of conduct brought about by the assault upon them by intellectuals. If Joseph Conrad were to search nowadays for the heart of darkness—the evil of human conduct untrammeled by the fear of legal sanction from without or of moral censure from within—he would have to look no further than an English city such as mine.

And how can I not be preoccupied with the search for the origins and ramifications of this evil when every working day I come upon stories like the one I heard today—the very day I write these words?

It concerns a young man aged twenty who still lived with his mother and who had tried to kill himself. Not long before, his mother's current boyfriend, a habitual drunkard ten years her junior, had, in a fit of jealousy, attacked the mother in the young man's presence, grabbing her round the throat and strangling her.

The young man tried to intervene, but the older man was not only six inches taller but much stronger. He knocked the young man to the ground and kicked him several times in the head. Then he dragged him outside and smashed his head on the ground until he was unconscious and blood ran from a deep wound.

The young man regained consciousness in the ambulance, but his mother insisted that he give no evidence to the police because, had he done so, her lover would have gone to jail: and she was most reluctant to give up a man who was, in her own words to the young man's eleven-year-old sister, "a better f—k than your father." A little animal pleasure meant more to the mother than her son's life; and so he was confronted by the terrifying realization that, in the words of Joseph Conrad, he was born alone, he lived alone, and would die alone.

Who, in listening to such cases day after day and year after year, as I have, could fail to wonder what ideas and what social arrangements have favored the spread of conduct so vile that its contemplation produces almost physical nausea? How can one avoid driving oneself to distraction by considering who is more to blame, the man who behaves as I have described, or the woman who accepts such behavior for the sake of a moment's pleasure?

This brutality is now a mass phenomenon rather than a sign of individual psychopathology. Recently I went to a soccer game in my city on behalf of a newspaper; the fans of the opposing teams had to be separated by hundreds of policemen, disposed in military fashion. The police allowed no contact whatever between the opposing factions, shepherding or corralling the visiting fans into their own area of the stadium with more security precautions than the most dangerous of criminals ever faces.

In the stadium I sat next to a man who appeared perfectly normal and decent, and his eleven-year-old son who seemed a well-behaved little boy. Suddenly, in the middle of the match, the father leaped up and, in unison with thousands of others, began to chant: "Who the f—k do you think you are? Who the f—k do you think you are?" while making, also in common with thousands of others, a threatening gesture in the direction of the opposing supporters that looked uncommonly like a fascist salute. Was this the example he wanted to set for his son? Apparently so. The frustrations of poverty could hardly explain his conduct: the cost of the tickets to the game could have fed a family more than adequately for a week.

After the game was over, I saw more clearly than ever that the thin blue line is no metaphor. Had it not been for the presence of the police (whose failures I have never hesitated to criticize), there would have been real violence and bloodshed, perhaps even death. The difference between an event that passed off peacefully and one that would end in mayhem, destruction, injury, and death was the presence of a relative handful of resolute men prepared to do their duty.

Despite the evidence of rising barbarism all around us, no betrayal is too trivial for the Quislings of civilization to consider worthwhile. Recently, at the airport, I noticed an advertisement for a firm of elegant and costly shirt- and tie-makers, headquartered in London's most expensive area. The model they chose to advertise their products was a shaven-headed, tattooed monster, with scars on his scalp from bar brawls—the human type that beats women, carries a knife, and throws punches at soccer games. The advertisement is not ironical, as academic cultural critics would pretend, but an abject capitulation to and flattery of the utmost coarseness and brutality. Savagery is all the rage.

If any good comes of the terrible events in New York, let it be this: that our intellectuals should realize that civilization is worth defending, and that the adversarial stance to tradition is not the beginning and end of wisdom and virtue. We have more to lose than they know.

2001

How to Read a Society

◆ IN THE DAYS—simultaneously not so very long ago and in the ancient past—when communism seemed a permanent feature of the political landscape, I traveled extensively on the other side of the looking glass that divided the world into two opposed camps. I did not take with me as literary guide and compass to my travels one of the Marxist-Leninist "classics": not because the works of Marx and Lenin failed to explain anything I found through that looking glass, but because the explanation they offered was all too obvious and self-evident. If it was difficult for a visitor to find anything to eat impromptu in Moscow, Havana, Tirana, Bucharest, or Pyongyang, it took little effort to understand the connection of this difficulty with the vulgar anti-commercialism of St. Karl and St. Vladimir. Indeed, it would have taken all the ingenuity of the cleverest academics *not* to have understood it.

I took with me instead a work by a nineteenth-century French aristocrat, the Marquis de Custine. First published as a series of letters in 1843 under the title *La Russie en 1839*, the book has since appeared in a multiplicity of formats and abbreviated versions, with various titles in English, suggesting that even its translators and most fervent admirers do not consider it a flawless work of literary art. And yet this travel book is undoubtedly a masterpiece, a work of such penetration and prescience that it is worth reading more than a century and a half after its composition, not only for its antiquarian or historical interest but because of the incomparably brilliant light it sheds on one of the most important phenomena of the last hundred years: the spread of com-

munism throughout the world. Writing before the development of
modern "scientific" sociology, whose achievement has been to obscure by means of statistical legerdemain the importance of human
consciousness, Custine analyzed Russian society by reference to
the psychology of the individuals who made it up. His work is a
supreme example of the subtle interplay between the abstract information about a political system and the imaginative entry into
the worldview of the people who live in it that is necessary for the
understanding of any society.

Custine's book is a prolonged meditation upon the effect of a
particular political regime and its institutions upon human character, thought, and action—and, by implication, a meditation upon
the dialectical interplay of political conditions and human character everywhere. As Custine well understood, the effect of tsarism
upon the Russian psyche was pregnant with significance for the
future, not just for the Russians themselves but for the whole
world, because Russia was destined to play so large a part in the
world's history.

For when you read Custine, you realize that the spread of communism was not of an ideology alone but of an entire political
culture: the culture of Russian despotism, which paved the way intellectually, and served as a practical exemplar, for Marxism's mil-
lenarian totalitarianism. Without the prologue of tsarist
despotism, Marxism would not have triumphed in Russia. And
without the Russian Revolution, whose "success" so many foreigners strove to imitate, far fewer Marxist regimes would have
been set up throughout the world, and none in Eastern Europe. As
Stalin's literary commissar, Zhdanov, might have put it, the Communist regimes that proliferated in the twentieth century were
Russian in form but Marxist in content—just as approved literature by non-Russian-language authors in the Soviet Union was
supposed to be national in form but socialist in content.

Custine visited Russia for only three months; he spoke no
Russian (though the Russian upper class of the time spoke French
fluently and even preferred to converse and think in that language). While he had read books about Russia, he was in no sense
a scholar of Russian affairs. Yet the book he wrote after so short a

sojourn in the country was infinitely more valuable than those written by men with a vastly more detailed knowledge of Russia than his. On reading *La Russie en 1839*, the exiled Alexander Herzen declared it the best book ever written on the subject and lamented that only a foreigner could have written it.

A third of Custine's long book concerned only his first few days in Russia, when his impressions were no doubt at their most intense, as travelers' impressions always are on their first arrival: but even had Custine returned to France after those few days and written nothing more than the first third of his book, he would have provided more insights into Russia, and hence into the subsequent fate of an all too considerable proportion of humanity, than any other writer of the nineteenth century.

How was this feat possible? What distinguished Custine from so many other observers? What were the methods and underlying assumptions that enabled him to penetrate so deeply in so short a time?

Custine displayed a remarkable talent for extracting the social and psychological meaning of small events that to others might have seemed insignificant. For example, on his arrival in St. Petersburg, border guards and customs staff subjected him to a minute and pointless examination the like of which he had not remotely experienced anywhere else, though he was a well-traveled man. "Each of these men discharges his duty with a pedantry, a rigour, an air of importance uniquely designed to give prominence to the most obscure employment," he noted. "He does not permit himself to say so, but you can see him thinking approximately this: 'Make way for me, I am one of the members of the great machine of the State.'" Unlike less reflective observers, Custine asked why the Russian officials should have behaved with such a manner, keenly aware that men inhabit a mental and not just a physical world and that their conduct is determined by their thoughts about the world as they have experienced it. He surmised that these border officials had been deprived of all true discretion and were deeply fearful themselves of the power to which they were subordinate. Custine described them as "automata inconvenienced with a soul": a description true, perhaps, of all bureaucrats fearful for their jobs but truest of all where power is both arbitrary and completely centralized, as it was in Russia. Their conduct was the revenge of men constrained to behave like machines: a revenge not upon the author of their servitude, of course, for that was impossible at the time, but upon those who fell within their extremely limited power.

No doubt Custine's family history and upbringing had heightened his acuity. His grandfather was a liberal aristocrat who became a general in the revolutionary army but whom the Jacobins guillotined as not sufficiently devoted to the cause. Custine's father went to the guillotine for having tried to defend him. Custine's mother, imprisoned as an enemy of the people for having tried to defend her husband, narrowly escaped execution herself, largely because one of the revolutionary fanatics who arrested her fell in love with her. Astolphe de Custine was brought up for a time by a faithful servant, living in penury with her in the only room of the Custine home that had not been looted and sealed off by Jacobin zealots and thieves. Such a background was likely to produce a man aware of the deep subterranean currents in life and not easily deceived by appearances. The evils of envy and hatred masquerading as humanitarian idealism had darkened his life from its outset, stamping him as a man quick to search for the reality behind the expression of fine sentiments.

He needed all his shrewdness to penetrate behind the veneer of Russia. He frequented mainly upper-class circles, traveled comparatively little, and studied no statistics. Accused of having visited Russia for too short a time to have drawn conclusions, he replied, *"Il est vrai, j'ai mal vu, mais j'ai bien déviné"*: which might be translated as, "Yes, I have seen little, but I have understood much."

Custine grasped that the propensity to deceive and to be (or to pretend to be) deceived lay at the heart of Russia's evident malaise. The maintenance of despotism depended upon this universal vocation for untruth, because without the fiction that the despotism was necessary, that it conduced to the happiness and well-being of all, and that any alternative would be disastrous, the subject population would cease to be controllable. The inability to speak even the most evident truth perverted all human relationships and institutions. And of course the lie came to be the foundation of all twentieth-century totalitarian regimes, without which they could not survive. "The political system of Russia," wrote Custine, "could not withstand twenty years of free communication with Western Europe."

Unlike so many gullible intellectuals of the twentieth century who visited Communist countries in the spirit of religious pilgrims, Custine understood only too well both the techniques and the meaning of the attempts to deceive him. "Russian hospitality, bristling with formalities . . . is a polite pretext for hampering the movements of the traveller and limiting his license to observe," he concluded. "Thanks to this fastidious politeness, the observer cannot visit a place or look at anything without a guide; never being alone he has trouble judging for himself, which is what they want. To enter Russia, you must deposit your free will as well as your passport at the frontier. . . . Would you like to see . . . a hospital? The doctor in charge will escort you. A fortress? The governor will show it to you, or rather, politely conceal it from you. A school, any kind of public establishment? The director, the inspector, will be forewarned of your visit. . . . A building? The architect will take you over all its parts and will, himself, explain everything you have not asked in order to avoid instructing you on the things you are interested in learning." No wonder, he added, that "the most highly esteemed travellers are those who, the most meekly and for the longest time, allow themselves to be taken in." No visitor to a Communist country could fail to recognize the description.

For the whole elaborate charade of despotism to work, for the pretense that the despotism is both indispensable and conducive to the welfare of all, everyone must appear to believe in it—including the despot himself. The tsar, as a consequence, remains trapped in a permanent state of fear and irritation, because he knows that he is not in fact omnipotent, but he cannot acknowledge openly this obvious fact and he cannot permit anyone or anything else to question the pretense on which his authority depends. "Subjecting the world to his supreme commands," Custine says of him, "he sees in the most insignificant events a shadow of revolt. . . . A fly that buzzes unseasonably . . . humiliates the Czar. The independence of Nature seems to him a bad example." Any rebellious behavior on the part of the meanest of his subjects assumes a disproportionate importance and must be ferreted out and put down. So the tsar, through an army of spies, must keep an eye on everyone. He is "both eagle and insect, soaring above the rest of humanity and at the same time insinuating himself into the fabric of their lives like a termite into wood." His position compels him to be paranoid: "an Emperor of Russia," wrote Custine, "would have to be a genius . . . to keep his sanity after twenty years of ruling." Such, of course, was precisely the problem all Communist dictators faced.

If the tsar is all-powerful, he is of course responsible for everything: therefore nothing untoward can happen in the country without the imputation of the tsar's ill will. But in that case, how is the imputation of omnipotence to be reconciled with that of perfect benevolence? If something terrible happens to innocent people, either the tsar must not be omnipotent or must not be benevolent. The only way to square the circle is to lie oneself and be deceived when others lie in similar fashion: to see no evil, hear no evil, and speak no evil, even when evil abounds.

For example, shortly after his arrival in Russia, Custine went to the annual festival at the palace of Peterhof, a festival of such magnificence that it took 1,800 servants to light 250,000 lamps for it. Visitors reached the palace by boat from St. Petersburg, and one boat had sunk in a storm on the way to the festival with the loss of all its passengers and crew. But because "any mishap [in Russia] is treated as an affair of State" in Russia, and because "to lie is to protect the social order, to speak the truth is to destroy the State," there followed "a silence more terrifying than the disaster itself." In Russia, people of the highest social class—as were the boat's passengers—could disappear not only without a trace but without comment. Who in such a country could ever feel safe?

The silence encompassed not only current events but extended back into history. A Russian nobleman, Prince Peter Koslovsky, had warned Custine before his arrival in Russia that in his country "despotism not only counts ideas and sentiments for nothing, but remakes facts. It wages war on evidence and triumphs in the bat-tle. . . . [The emperor's] power is more far-reaching than God's, for God makes only the future, while the Czar remakes the past." Custine's experience repeatedly proved this insight true. No previ-ous tsar was ever mentioned in conversation, he learned, to avoid the suggestion that the present tsar was not immortal. For this same reason, Custine noted that Russians did not dare look at the palace in which the tsar's father, the emperor Paul, was murdered: for "it is forbidden to recount, in the schools or elsewhere, the story of the death of the Emperor Paul."

When a man fell from grace, he not only ceased to exist, he ceased ever to have existed. "M. de Repnin governed the Empire and the Emperor. M. de Repnin has been in disfavour for two years and for two years Russia has not heard this name spoken—this name which two years ago was on every tongue. No one dares to remember him or even to believe in his existence—either his present existence or his past existence. In Russia, the day a minis-ter falls, his friends become deaf and blind. A man is buried as soon as he appears to be in disfavour."

Communist regimes went yet further in the creation of unper-sons, of course, striking them out of photographs and encyclope-dias (on the fall of a formerly prominent Soviet personage, the publishers of the *Great Soviet Encyclopaedia* would send out sub-stitute entries to paste over that unpersonage's entry). But the precedent had been set many years before.

Custine appreciated only too well the violence that this remak-ing of history did to the minds of men, and the consequences it had for their character and behavior. In order not to look at the palace in which the emperor Paul was murdered, a person had to know that he was killed there; but his whole purpose in not looking at the palace was to demonstrate in public his ignorance of the murder. He thus had not only to assert a lie but also to deny that he knew it was a lie. And all officials—the emperor included—had likewise to pretend that they did not know they were being lied to, or else the whole edifice of falsehood would have come tumbling down.

The need always to lie and always to avoid the truth stripped everyone of what Custine called "the two greatest gifts of God—

the soul and the speech which communicates it." People became hypocritical, cunning, mistrustful, cynical, silent, cruel, and indifferent to the fate of others as a result of the destruction of their own souls. Moreover the upkeep of systematic untruth requires a network of spies: indeed, it requires that everyone become a spy and potential informer. And "the spy," wrote Custine, "believes only in espionage, and if you escape his snares he believes that he is about to fall into yours." The damage to personal relations was incalculable.

If Custine were among us now, he would recognize the evil of political correctness at once, because of the violence that it does to people's souls by forcing them to say or imply what they do not believe but must not question. Custine would demonstrate to us that, without an external despot to explain our pusillanimity, we have willingly adopted the mental habits of people who live under a totalitarian dictatorship.

Custine could wring meaning even from stones: a great interpreter of the meaning of architecture, he caught from the buildings and streets of St. Petersburg another deep glimpse into the Russian soul. The city, to which he did not deny a certain beauty, was to him the physical embodiment of despotism. It was founded as the imperial capital not for the benefit of the Russians, as the natural expression of their economic or social activity, but as a permanent bulwark of the tsarist regime in the Baltic against the Swedes. The very selection of the terrain—a freezing swamp—for the construction of a city by the fiat of the tsar was an expression of contempt for humanity, for in such a place construction necessarily entailed the deaths of hundreds of thousands of men. Custine noted that the stucco that veneered St. Petersburg's grandiose government office buildings—"temples erected to clerks," he called them—was a material peculiarly unsuited to the Russian climate, such that it took thousands of workmen to restore the crumbling stucco in the three-month plastering season every year, large numbers of them meeting death in the process because of the flimsy scaffolding on which they worked. Only where human labor—and life itself— ostentatiously counted for nothing could such a system of building maintenance have been envisaged, let alone tolerated.

Custine noted that the streets of St. Petersburg were much too wide for the city's population and that the vast public spaces were bound to make a man feel overwhelmed and insignificant. In such vastnesses, no assembly would constitute a crowd unless it were scores of thousands strong. And this was the political purpose of such spaces: for in St. Petersburg, as Custine wrote, "a crowd would be a revolution." Intimidating gigantism of this kind— a constant feature of Communist town planning, from Bishkek in Kirghizia to Bucharest in Romania, from Pyongyang in North Korea to Minsk in Byelorussia—discouraged spontaneity, the enemy of all despotism.

But if no crowds could spontaneously gather, organized parades often filled the vast public spaces. "The taste for [military] reviews is pushed in Russia to the point of madness," Custine wrote. "I am not moved to laughter; puerility on a vast scale is to me an appalling thing. . . . [I]t is only with blindly submissive peoples that a ruler can demand immense sacrifices to produce trifles."

So I witnessed in North Korea, when a parade of hundreds of thousands of people—men, women, and children—marched past the despot, for no better reason than that there were delegations of foreigners in the city. They had been rehearsing the parade, so a diplomat told me, for six months beforehand, often until two or three in the morning. The military order of these ranks of civilians was terrifyingly impeccable: they performed maneuvers with the precision of a machine. But their faces were blank with exhaustion and permanent terror. Their immense sacrifices had been made toward their own complete subjugation as human beings, while the despot smiled at and waved to them, as if he imagined the whole event were a spontaneous demonstration of their affection for him.

Custine would have understood. "This member of the machine," he wrote of a Russian official, "functioning according to a will which is not his own, lives as much as the movement of a clock. . . . One asks oneself what [such men] can do with their excess of thought and you feel uncomfortable at the idea of the force that had to be exerted against intelligent beings to succeed in making them only things."

Whether describing a building or a social institution, Custine never lost sight of, for him, the key question: what was its effect upon the minds of men? For Custine, man was above all a thinking, conscious being: not even despotism could negate that. Without understanding the thoughts of the population, you could understand nothing about Russia, and its future would remain inexplicable to you. But, on the basis of his understanding of the Russian character, Custine could prophesy that within two or three generations a violent cataclysm would occur that would spell not liberation but a renewed and more terrible form of despotism, for men with souls molded by tsarism would have no vocation for freedom. The turmoil that Russia has experienced in escaping the legacy of communism would not have surprised Custine in the least, nor would he have expected a happy outcome at any time in the foreseeable future.

Another traveler, Custine's younger but more eminent and scholarly contemporary, Alexis de Tocqueville, took with him the same methods and the same assumption that no society can be understood without reference to the psychology of its members, and he famously produced classic accounts both of America and Britain. He too analyzed societies by reference to the interplay between political arrangements and the minds of men. These two men shared not just similar assumptions but a similar background. Both were scions of the French aristocracy, with reason to dislike the excesses of the French Revolution and its rhetoric. Both had a visceral mistrust of democratic government, but both came—with qualifications—to admire it, Tocqueville because of the positive example of the United States, Custine because of the negative example of Russia. (It is even possible that Custine chose Russia as a destination because the first volume of Tocqueville's *Democracy in America*, published in 1835 to immediate acclaim, stated that Russia seemed destined, along with the United States, to hold sway over half the world.) Before visiting America, Tocqueville, trained as a lawyer, had served as a judge; after his return, he served in France's Chamber of Deputies and became, briefly, foreign minister in 1849.

Where Custine had studied the effect of despotism upon the human psyche and character, Tocqueville studied the effect of political liberty and legal equality upon them. Liberty had certain disadvantages, he thought, but the price was worth paying (the mirror image of Custine's conclusion that any good the tsarist regime did was bought at far too high a cost). In many respects, freedom's consequences were the opposite of despotism's. Men became honest when they had to deal with one another on the basis of legal equality, rather than sly, underhanded, and dissimulating, as they were under despotism. When a man's reputation depended more upon his activity than upon his position in a social hierarchy, conferred at birth, as in Russia, he was inclined to virtue without any obvious external compulsion. In addition, the comparative absence of governmental interference in his life rendered him energetic, enterprising, and thoughtful in pursuit of his own economic interests.

For that reason, a society of free men could organize itself to produce impressive public works without the coercion applied by Peter the Great and his successors—provided only that the public works were of genuine public utility and not merely the whim of one man. The interests of the individual and those of the political power—which is to say, the chosen representatives of the community at large—were united by a thousand small bonds.

But it was from this initial identity of interest that a potential danger arose. By small degrees—though this was only a possibility, not an inevitability—men might cede their independence to a government that represented them, that was believed to have their interests at heart, and that was (after all) composed of men very like themselves. In a passage that united prophetic with psychological insight, Tocqueville (who rightly foresaw that democratic government was destined to spread widely, if not throughout the entire world) described the future soul of man under a seemingly benevolent and democratic government that willingly labored for the happiness of the people "but chose to be the sole agent and only arbiter of that happiness." Such a government would "supply [the people] with their necessities, facilitate their pleasures, manage their principal concerns." What would remain but to "spare them all the care of thinking and all the trouble of living"? When this came to pass, "the will of man will not be shattered, but softened, bent and guided." Men would not be forced to act but prevented from acting; the government would not destroy but prevent a full human existence. It would not tyrannize but "enervate, extinguish and stupefy a people."

And this is exactly the condition to which a part of the population had been reduced under irreproachably democratic governments. Living in subsidized housing, its children educated free of charge and its medical bills paid (all for its own good, of course), with an income sufficient to guarantee both enough food and perpetual entertainment in the form of television, all its "principal concerns" are "managed," just as Tocqueville said they would be, and it is thus spared "the care of thinking and all the trouble of living." This is the welfare-dependent population among which I work: so enervated and stupefied that it cannot cook for itself even when it has nothing else to do but eats only pre-cooked food, and so enervated and stupefied that when trash appears in its own front yard, it cannot summon the initiative to clear it away by itself but—if it notices the mess at all—summons officialdom to do so on its behalf.

If I took Custine with me as a guide each time I traveled in the Communist world, I could, with equal reason, take a short essay by Tocqueville on the subject of pauperism with me each time I go to work in my hospital in the slums—which is, in a certain sense, to travel abroad. For I work among people who are in effect paupers: and Tocqueville understood, as few modern writers do, that pauperism is above all a psychological, not an economic, condition. And he saw in the English system of social assistance to the poor the same insidious threat to men's independence of character that he saw, only as a potentiality, in American democracy.

Tocqueville's *Memoir on Pauperism* was published in 1835, shortly after the first volume of *Democracy in America*. He had visited England, then by far the most prosperous country in Europe, if not the world. But there was a seeming paradox: a sixth of the population of England were—or had made themselves—paupers, completely reliant upon handouts from public charity. This was a proportion greater than in any other country in Europe, even in such incomparably poorer ones as Spain and Portugal. In the midst of what was then the utmost prosperity, Tocqueville found not only physical squalor but moral and emotional degradation.

Tocqueville surmised that the reason lay in the fact that England was then the one country in Europe that provided public assistance, as of right, to people who lacked the means to support themselves. The reign of Elizabeth I had conferred this right, as a way of dealing with the epidemic of begging that followed the dissolution of the monasteries. In the past they had provided essentially private and voluntary charity to the poor, on a discretionary basis.

At first sight, remarked Tocqueville, the replacement of discretionary charity by public assistance granted as of right appeared deeply humane. What, he asked, could be nobler than the determination to ensure that no one went hungry? What could be more fair and reasonable than that the prosperous should give up a little for the welfare of those with nothing?

If men were not thinking beings who react to their circumstances by taking what they conceive to be advantage of them, this system doubtless would have had the desired effect. But instead, Tocqueville observed the voluntary idleness to which the seemingly humane system of entitlement gave rise—how it destroyed both kindness and gratitude (for what is given bureaucratically is received with resentment), how it encouraged fraud and dissimulation of various kinds, and above all how it dissolved the social bonds that protected people from the worst effects of poverty. The provision of relief by entitlement atomized society: Tocqueville cited the case of a man who, though financially able to do so, refused to support his daughter-in-law and grandchild after his son's death, precisely because public support was available to them as of right. Having paid his taxes, why should he do more? The provision of charity as of right destroyed the motive for human solidarity in the face of hardship, and undermined both ties of personal affection and the sense of duty toward close relations. Intended as an expression of social responsibility, it liberated selfishness. As Tocqueville grasped, the shift of responsibility from individual to collectivity had an enormous and deleterious effect on how people thought and felt, and therefore upon society as a whole. Where this shift had taken place, economic progress was perfectly compatible with squalor of every kind, and general wealth with degradation.

It wasn't until the end of the twentieth century, with its unprecedented prosperity and its militant moral relativism, that Tocqueville's prescience became clear. Until very recently in human history, sheer physical poverty has seemed much more a menace than any attempt to relieve it could ever be. But none of the social pathology of a modern British or American slum would have surprised Tocqueville, who foresaw it all 165 years ago.

Custine and Tocqueville analyzed the subtle interplay of culture, political regime, and human character in two very different—one might almost say, opposite—societies and came to similar political conclusions. Underlying their analysis was a shared understanding: that societies alien to them were comprehensible because there existed a fundamental human nature, in which they themselves shared, and that some political and social arrangements nurture all the excellences of which human nature is capable, while others might stunt and deform it. They did not aspire to the pseudo-scientific detachment that is the hallmark of so much modern social commentary: and they will therefore continue to be read long after the tabulators and statistical correlators are forgotten.

2000

Why Havana Had to Die

DECAY, when not carried to excess, has its architectural charms, and ruins are romantic: so romantic, indeed, that eighteenth-century English gentlemen built them in their gardens, as pleasantly melancholic reminders of the transience of earthly existence. But Fidel Castro is no eighteenth-century English gentleman, and Havana is not his private estate, for use as a personal *memento mori*. The ruins of Havana that he has brought into being are, in fact, the habitation of more than a million people, whose collective will, these ruins attest, is not equal in power to the will of one man. "*Comandante en jefe*," says one of the political billboards that have replaced all commercial advertisements, "you give the orders." The place of everyone else, needless to say, is to obey.

Havana has changed a little since I was last there, a dozen years ago. The vast Soviet subsidy has vanished; the economy now depends on European tourism. The influx of tourists, most of them in search of a cheap holiday in the tropics and cheerfully oblivious to Cuba's politics, has necessitated a slight degree of flexibility. Small private family restaurants, called *paladares* (*paladar* is Spanish for palate), with no more than twelve seats, are now tolerated, though the hiring of nonfamily labor, deemed exploitative by definition, is still not permitted. Only certain dishes are allowed—not fish and lobster, reserved to the state restaurants—and those *paladares* that break the rules operate like speakeasies in the time of Prohibition, the fish-bootlegging owners keeping a nervous eye out for informers. (Committees for the Defense of the Revolution still operate everywhere.) The owner of one such that I visited—with no sign outside to mark its existence—anxiously looked through the peephole of the door before letting anyone in. The taking of a simple meal at one of the three tables turned into a scene from a spy novel.

Flea markets are also now legal in Cuba, and a petty trade in cast-off clothing and household goods takes place. Twelve years ago it was unthinkable for anyone to buy or sell anything in the open, for buying and selling were symptoms of bourgeois individualism and contrary to Fidel's socialist vision, in which everything is to be rationed—rationally, as it were—according to need. (In practice, of course, this meant rationing according to what there was, which was not much.)

Openings to small-scale commerce have occurred earlier during Castro's forty-three-year rule, but they have always soon succumbed to periods of "rectification," after it became all too apparent that people were responding more vigorously to economic incentives than they ever had to the "moral" ones praised in the adolescent theories of Che Guevara. But this time the commercial activity is more secure, because it is essential to the regime's economic survival. When last I was in Havana, even the dollar-laden foreigner couldn't find food to eat outside his hotel— a situation that hardly encouraged mass tourism. Now, of necessity, cafés and bars aplenty cater to the visitor.

The economy is now extensively dollarized, a curious and ironic denouement to decades of impassioned nationalism. When I asked in my hotel to change money into pesos, I was told—quite rightly, it turned out—that I would not need them. The few dusty shops that were prepared to exchange goods for pesos—for *moneda nacional*—advertised this extraordinary fact in their windows, as if performing a miracle, though the goods for sale were few and of the lowest quality. Last time I was in Cuba, the possession of a dollar by an ordinary Cuban was a crime, virtually proof of disloyalty and disaffection, if not of outright economic sabotage of the revolution. Dollars were handled as if they were nitroglycerine, liable to blow up in your face at the slightest jolt; but now they are merely units of currency, which anyone may safely handle.

The sheer number of foreign visitors to Cuba means that, though the hotel lobbies are still patrolled by security men with walkie-talkies to ensure that no unauthorized Cubans enter, relations between Cubans and foreigners are more relaxed than they once were. To talk to a foreigner is no longer a sign of political unreliability, and conversations do not have to be carried out in a hole-and-corner fashion, behind walls, with one nervous eye open for spies and eavesdroppers. I even received a few requests that I send medicine, since none was available in the local pharmacies—an admission, unthinkable a few years ago, that all is not well in the much-vaunted health-care system.

People will even speak of *lo bueno* and *lo malo*, the good and the bad, of the revolution—usually adding that *lo malo* was very, very bad. One man, brought up in the 1970s, told me that he had been fired by revolutionary romanticism, with Che Guevara and John Lennon as his heroes (he told me proudly that Havana was one of three cities with memorials to Lennon, the others being Liverpool and New York). He thought then that a new world had been in construction: but he knew now that it had been a dead end. And old people in particular are inclined to murmur *jabón* (soap) as you pass, in the hope that you might have some of this rare and precious commodity to give away. When the first old lady came up to me and said *jabón*, I thought she was mad; but she was only the first of many.

There are now signs of a slight intellectual opening. In *La Moderna Poesía*, a bookshop in an art deco building on the Calle Obispo, I found a Spanish translation of Karl Popper's *The Open Society and Its Enemies*. The price in dollars was unlikely to attract many Cuban buyers. Perhaps it was there only to convince foreigners of the regime's intellectual tolerance; perhaps any Cuban who tried to buy it would be reported at once to the authorities: but even so, the mere public presence of a work so antithetical to the regime's philosophy would have been unthinkable a dozen years ago.

By contrast, the newspapers, *Granma* and *Rebelde*, have not changed at all: to have read them forty years ago is to have read them today and tomorrow and in ten years' time, if the regime lasts that long. The incessant recital of social progress in Cuba in the face of adversity, and horrible social breakdown everywhere else (especially, of course, in the United States), would bore even the truest of believers. No doubt that is why I saw not a single Cuban reading a newspaper or taking any notice of the aged itinerant salesmen, each with about five copies to dispose of. When I expressed an interest in buying one, the old men took the opportunity openly to ask me for money: selling the newspaper was only a pretext to approach and beg. The question "How much is the newspaper?" always drew the answer "Whatever you would like to give."

Forty-three years of totalitarian dictatorship have left the city of Havana—one of the most beautiful in the world—suspended in a peculiar state halfway between preservation and destruction. For myself, I found the absence of the most grating aspects of commercialism aesthetically pleasing: McDonald's restaurants (and their like) would ruin Havana as a townscape as comprehensively as time and neglect. And the comparative lack of traffic in Havana demonstrates how mixed a blessing the inexorable spread of the automobile has been for the quality of city life. Had Havana developed "normally," its narrow grid-pattern streets would by now be choking with traffic and pollution, a suffocating inferno like Guatemala City or San José, Costa Rica, where to breathe is to grow breathless, where noise makes the ears sing, and where thoughts turn to escape as soon as possible.

The streets of Havana, not like that at all, are pleasant to walk in. The air is clean, and there is no honking of horns. You can hear yourself think and talk. Most of the few cars that pass are American relics of the Batista era, battered but much restored; they rattle and wheeze like beasts of burden driven forward under duress. Some seem to progress crabwise, not straight ahead but sideways; and with the patina of time, these vehicles, which once would have seemed the commonplace, throwaway mass products of an industrialized society, have taken on an aura of romance, almost of personality. They are loved and treasured as irreplaceable old friends, and when you look at them you wonder how many of the objects that you take so much for granted might one day be regarded in like fashion. It helps you to see the world anew.

Few new buildings have been added to Havana, which is just as well, of course, since those few are in the style of totalitarian modernism, and ruin the neighborhood. In the very center of the city, moreover, which UNESCO has declared to be part of humanity's patrimony, tasteful restoration work is under way. In the Plaza Vieja, a grand colonial building has been transformed into luxury apartments for tourists to rent, with an excellent restaurant downstairs (the very idea of an excellent restaurant in Cuba was unthinkable twelve years ago). The bourgeoisie is thus a little like nature: though you pitch it out with a revolution, yet it will in the end return.

But the scale of the restoration of Havana is as nothing compared with the scale of its ruination. It is quite literally crumbling away. One of the most magnificent of its many magnificent streets is known as the Prado, a wide avenue that leads to the sea, with a central tree-lined marble walkway down which people stroll at night in the balmy air. Some of the beautifully proportioned mansions along the Prado have collapsed into rubble since the last time I was there; others have their façades—all that remains of them—propped up by wooden struts. The palace along the Prado that houses the national school of ballet is a mere shell, the ground floor containing nothing but rubble: it is extraordinary to hear the sound of *répétiteurs* emerging from the upper floor of this shell. Havana is like Beirut, without having gone through the civil war to achieve the destruction.

No words can do justice to the architectural genius of Havana, a genius that extended from the Renaissance classicism of the sixteenth century, with severe but perfectly proportioned houses containing colonnaded courtyards cooled and softened by tropical trees and shrubs, to the flamboyant art deco of the 1930s and '40s. The Cubans of successive centuries created a harmonious architectural whole almost without equal in the world. There is hardly a building that is wrong, a detail that is superfluous or tasteless. The tiled multi-coloration of the Bacardi building, for example, which might be garish elsewhere, is perfectly adapted—natural, one might say—to the Cuban light, climate, and temper. Cuban architects understood the need for air and shade in a climate such as Cuba's, and they proportioned buildings and rooms accordingly. They created an urban environment that, with its arcades, columns, verandas, and balconies, was elegant, sophisticated, convenient, and joyful.

Of course, not every Cuban shared it: there were large shantytowns outside the city, and in the countryside much of the peasantry lived in grinding poverty. In 1958, Cuba might have had Italy's overall levels of consumption per capita, more or less, but the consumption was unevenly distributed. Yet what is so striking about Havana's grandeur and beauty is how extensive it is, and how wealthy (as well as sophisticated) the society that produced it must have been. The splendor of Havana, rather than being confined to a small quarter of the city, extends for miles.

The splendor is very faded now, of course. The city is like a great set of Bach variations on the theme of urban decay. The stucco has given way to mold; roofs have gone, replaced by corrugated iron; shutters have crumbled into sawdust; paint is a phenomenon of the past; staircases end in precipices; windows lack glass; doors are off their hinges; interior walls have collapsed; wooden props support, though not with any degree of assurance, all kinds of structures; ancient electrical wiring emerges from walls like worms from cheese; wrought ironwork balconies crumble into rust; plaster peels as in a malignant skin disease; flagstones are mined for other purposes. Every grand and beautifully proportioned room—visible through the windows or in some places through the walls that have crumbled away—has been subdivided by plywood partitions into smaller spaces, in which entire families now live. Washing hangs from the windows of what were once palaces. Every entranceway is dark, and at night the electric lights glimmer rather than shine. No ruination is too great to render a building unfit for habitation: Havana is like a city that has been struck by an earthquake and its population forced to survive among the wreckage until relief arrives.

It cannot be said, however, that the inhabitants of Havana appear notably unhappy—far from it. The children play baseball cheerfully in the street with balls of compressed rags and bats of metal piping. (Curiously, the Latin American countries with the strongest anti-Yanqui political tradition are those where baseball is most enthusiastically played, as if the politics aimed to assuage the guilt at having taken up the pastime of the enemy.) There is plenty of social life in the streets, much smiling and laughter, and it isn't hard to find a small fiesta with music and dancing. When you look into the homes that the people have made among the ruins, there are the small, heartbreaking signs of pride and self-respect that one also sees in the huts of Africa: the carefully tended plastic flowers and other cheap ornaments, for example. A taste for kitsch among the well-to-do is a sign of spiritual impoverishment; but among the poor it represents a striving for beauty, an aspiration without the likelihood of fulfillment. Only the old look downcast or crushed: old people's thoughts turn naturally to the past, and the contrast between the Havana of their youth and the Havana of their dotage must be painful to contemplate.

The evident contentment of the population among the ruins, though, does not lessen my profound sorrow (and worse than sorrow, it is something indefinable that weighs on the heart) to see the destruction of a masterpiece of collective human endeavor down the ages, Havana. On the contrary, I find the very unconcern profoundly disturbing. What can it mean that people should live contentedly in the ruins of their own capital city, the ruination having been wrought not by war or natural disaster but by prolonged (and in my view deliberate) neglect? They are not barbarians who actively smash or destroy what they do not understand and value; nor do they fail to notice—how could they?—that the buildings in which they live are on the verge of collapse. It is not difficult to get people to show you the ramshackle ruins they inhabit, a service they perform with a laugh and a smile; it is simply that to live thus has become natural for them, and the collapse of walls and staircases seems no more avoidable than the weather.

An artist to whom I spoke, who was tentatively trying to use his photographs to draw the attention of his countrymen to the decay and destruction of their architectural inheritance occurring all around them, explained the neglect of the city as a manifestation of the government's priorities. It had always been more concerned about education and the health service, he said, than with preservation of the fabric of Havana. Though he understood why the government should have considered the reduction of the infant-mortality rate to be more important than the care of mere material objects such as buildings, he himself had gradually come to see the importance of preserving that inheritance: once gone, it was irrecoverable. But in his opinion, most people were unconcerned by it.

Alas, I suspect that the neglect of Havana has a deeper and more sinister rationale than the one the artist proposed. It is not difficult to imagine Castro's angry response to the accusation that he has let Havana fall into ruins. He would argue that, largely because of the American embargo, he had always had to establish clear spending priorities, and that schools, hospitals, and medicines mattered more for the life of a people than the upkeep of a capital city in which only a minority of the population lived. Life itself was more important than objects: and Cuba's low infant-mortality rate and high life expectancy were justification of his policies.

But this answer would not, in my view, be entirely honest—even beyond the question of whether Cuba's progress in literacy and public health necessitated Castro's policies or justified the evident lack of freedoms enjoyed by Cubans. I suspect that the neglectful ruination of Havana has served a profoundly ideological purpose. After all, the neglect has been continuous for nearly half a century, while massive subsidies from the Soviet Union were pouring in. A dictator as absolute as Castro could have preserved Havana if he had so wished, and could easily have found an economic pretext for doing so.

Havana, however, was a material refutation of his entire historiography—of the historiography that has underpinned his policies and justified his dictatorship for forty-three years. According to this account, Cuba was a poor agrarian society, impoverished by its dependent relationship with the United States, incapable without a socialist revolution of solving its problems. A small exploitative class of intermediaries benefited enormously from the neocolonial relationship, but the masses were sunk in abject poverty and misery.

But Havana was a large city of astonishing grandeur and wealth, which was clearly not confined to a tiny minority, despite the coexistence with that wealth of deep poverty. Hundreds of thousands of people obviously had lived well in Havana, and it is not plausible that so many had done so merely by the exploitation of a relatively small rural population. They must themselves have been energetic, productive, and creative people. Their society must have been considerably more complex and sophisticated than Castro can admit without destroying the rationale of his own rule.

In the circumstances, therefore, it became ideologically essential that the material traces and even the very memory of that society should be destroyed. In official publications (and all publications in Cuba are official) the only positive personages from the past are rebels and revolutionaries, representing a continuing nationalist tradition of which Castro is the apotheosis: there is no god but revolution, and Castro is its prophet. The period between Cuban independence and the advent of Castro is known as "the Pseudorepublic," and the corrupt thuggery of Batista, as well as the existence of poverty, is all that needs (or is allowed) to be known of life immediately before Castro.

But who created Havana, and where did the magnificence come from, if before Castro there were only poverty, corruption, and thuggery? Best to destroy the evidence, though not by the crude Taliban method of blowing up the statues of Buddha, which is inclined to arouse the opprobrium of the world: better to let huge numbers of people camp out permanently in stolen property and then let time and neglect do the rest. In a young population such as Cuba's, with little access to information not filtered through official channels, life among the ruins will come to seem normal and natural. The people will soon be radically disconnected from the past of the very walls they live among. And so the present ruins of Havana are the material consequence of a monomaniacal historiography put into practice.

Yet foreshortened memory can be made to serve an ideological turn, as has happened with the restoration of a small area of the city—a much-needed restoration, for inhabited ruins will not long attract mass tourism. And so a large and glossy book has appeared, recording by means of before-and-after photographs the Herculean efforts of the regime to restore some of the buildings of old Havana that had fallen practically into ruins. Entitled *Lest We Forget*, the book omits to mention how the ruination came about in the first place. The restoration is thus one triumph more for the revolution.

The terrible damage that Castro has done will long outlive him and his regime. Untold billions of capital will be needed to restore Havana; legal problems about ownership and rights of residence will be costly, bitter, and interminable; and the need to balance commercial, social, and aesthetic considerations in the reconstruction of Cuba will require the highest regulatory wisdom. In the meantime, Havana stands as a dreadful warning to the world—if one were any longer needed—against the dangers of monomaniacs who believe themselves to be in possession of a theory that explains everything, including the future.

2002

The Uses of Corruption

◈ I FIRST WENT to Italy as a boy in 1960, the year of the Rome Olympics, and it was still recognizably a poor country. The standard of living was not very different from that of Cuba before the overthrow of Batista. In one town in Sicily, the country's poorest region, 3,404 humans shared 700 rooms with 5,085 animals, among them pigs, goats, and donkeys. Animal dung, still used as fertilizer, was piled up in the Sicilian streets awaiting use. Visitors from Britain to the Italian peninsula had to treat the water supply with suspicion. My first Italian sojourn ended abruptly when, aged ten, I became delirious from fever and had to be moved to Switzerland to recover; despite the many and dire warnings, I had drunk the Italian tap water. I had not liked to ask my parents all the time for *acqua minerale*.

The infant mortality rate in the year in which I was born was at least three times higher in Italy than in Britain. Now, half a century later, it is lower than in Britain, and Italians in general live longer and healthier lives than Britons. Not only is Italy noticeably richer than Britain, but it is also considerably cleaner. Recently the newspaper *La Repubblica* carried an article wondering why the British food supply was so unclean and unsafe.

This is an astonishing reversal: for two and a half centuries at least, Britain was much richer than Italy in almost everything except its past. Britons pitied and condescended to their Italian contemporaries. Italy was a country of inexhaustible charm, sybaritic pleasure, and cultural wealth, of course, but it was not to be taken quite seriously in an economic or political sense. Even Mussolini concluded toward the end of his life that Italy was not really a serious country.

According to most published figures, Britain and Italy are now about equal in gross national product per head. No two sources agree on the precise numbers, and of course fluctuations in the value of currencies can alter the relative wealth of two countries without anything else having changed. No source suggests that the difference between the two countries is very great, though. In 1950 the same sources put Italy's per capita GNP at about 40 percent of Britain's.

I have learned, however, not to trust such measurements entirely. It is all too easy to suppose that a precise figure represents an indubitable fact, like a bank account balance. But the very precision of these figures is suspect. I have been to countries (such as Romania) whose economies were said by professional GNP measurers to have been growing at a phenomenal rate for many years, where people nevertheless had to line up for several hours to buy a few rotten potatoes on the rare occasions when they were available. How many years of breakneck growth would it have taken for potatoes to become generally available in Romania? Commonsense observation as well as statistics are necessary for assessing the success of an economy.

And by commonsense comparison with Britain's, Italy's economy clearly is very successful. Merely to have caught up with Britain would represent its greater success, but *il sorpasso*, the overtaking of Britain, is evident almost everywhere you look. For example, you do not see in Italy the miles of urban desolation and squalor that characterize so much of Britain. Squalor, upon which British visitors to Italy used to remark with effortless and eloquent superiority, is now far more prevalent at home. The Italian population does not look nearly so grey or crushed by circumstance as the British. The shops in every small provincial town in Italy, even in Sicily, offer luxury goods of a range and quality not to be found even in the largest British cities outside London. Bari is incomparably richer and less dilapidated than Dover.

In 1950 the British owned 12 times as many cars as did Italians: now the Italians own more cars than the British. In that year the British car industry was the second largest in the world, but now the only British-owned car manufacturer, Rover, makes a mere 200,000 vehicles a year, and Italy has three car manufacturers, one of them, Fiat, among the largest in the world.

How has this reversal of fortunes come about, and what accounts for it? The two countries are almost identical as far as population density is concerned, and natural resources play a very small part in their economies. If anything, Britain is at an advantage in this respect: for more than twenty years it has extracted large quantities of oil from the North Sea, partly offsetting its other difficulties in paying its way in the world.

A comparison of the two countries' political stability clearly favors Britain. Silvio Berlusconi, recently elected Italy's prime minister, heads his country's fifty-ninth government since the end of the war. This is a rate of government formation and dissolution equaled only by Bolivia. British governments, by contrast, last at least six times as long. The stable alternation in power of two well-established political parties appears, even now, to be a permanent feature of Britain's political landscape.

Nor does economic policy explain the two countries' different growth rates. Italian economic management—or mismanagement—has not differed much from British. Italian inflation has, if anything, been worse; the lira has declined in value nearly twice as far as the pound in the last forty years. Income distribution in Britain and Italy is very similar, with the top and bottom centiles receiving the same proportion of the national income. Neither greater economic equality nor inequality explains the difference.

As for the Italian state, it has consumed for many years more of the Italian economic product than has the British state. With officially equivalent per capita GNPs in 1992, the Italian state spent about 25 percent more than the British.

At first sight you might think this fact vindicates economic *dirigisme*—but only if you had no idea what the Italian state is actually like. The Italian bureaucracy's sole product is seemingly insuperable obstacles to productive activity, even more of them (because the bureaucracy is larger and more convoluted) than its British equivalent. The simplest procedures that involve an Italian bureaucracy rapidly turn—for the uninitiated—into a maze of byzantine complexity, from which it is almost impossible ever to emerge. Foreigners who have lived in Italy invariably recount their epic struggles with public utilities, the legatees of state monopolies, to have a telephone connected, for example, or to pay the gas bill. How can a modern economy not only function but flourish in such circumstances?

The Italian public administration has traditionally had one saving grace by comparison with its British counterpart, however: its corruption.

Admittedly, corruption is a strange kind of virtue: but so is honesty in pursuit of useless or harmful ends. Corruption is generally held to be a vice, and viewed in the abstract it is. But bad behavior can sometimes have good effects, and good behavior bad effects.

Where administration is light and bureaucracy small, bureaucratic honesty is an incomparable virtue; but where these are heavy and large, as in all modern European states, Britain and Italy not least among them, they burden and obstruct the inventive and energetic. Where bureaucrats are honest, no one can cut through their Laocoönian coils: their procedures, no matter how onerous, antiquated, or bloody-minded, must be endured patiently. Such bureaucrats can neither be hurried in their deliberations nor made to see common sense. Indeed, the very absurdity or pedantry of these deliberations is for them the guarantee of their own fair-mindedness, impartiality, and disinterest. To treat all people with equal contempt and indifference is the bureaucrat's idea of equity.

In such circumstances the use of personal influence or bribery by a petitioner at the bar of bureaucracy may actually represent an increase in efficiency. It would be better that the bureaucracy did not exist at all, of course; but it does exist and is unlikely soon to disappear. (My experience in Britain suggests that all official attempts to reduce bureaucracy actually increase it.) The man who can bribe or call upon the illicit influence of his brother-in-law is not obliged passively to await a decree from the bureaucratic Olympus: he retains some control over the situation (and also, therefore, some self-respect).

Where the state looms large in everyone's life, a degree of corruption exerts a beneficial effect upon the character of the people. Only up to a point, of course: when the state is all-embracing and official corruption becomes total, both together stifle wealth creation, and general impoverishment results. In the end, the demonetarization of the economy ensues, as under communism. Italy never came near this stage, however, and Italian bureaucrats were astute enough not to kill the goose that laid the golden eggs. The richer the society around them, the more they could themselves extract from it. What was good for business was good for them. (Officials in China's relatively flourishing Guangdong province appear to have grasped this principle too.)

The thoroughly obvious corruption of Italian officials convinced the population that the state was their enemy, not their patron or protector, and they regarded it with profound mistrust. Accordingly, people of all classes evaded taxes, without moral opprobrium; everyone regarded the idea of revealing one's entire income to the authorities and paying the taxes upon it as laughable in its naiveté. As far as possible, people concealed their economic activity from the eyes of the state, giving rise to Italy's notorious "black" economy, a kind of parallel market, which is by common consent larger and more sophisticated than in any other European state. The size of this parallel market probably explains why the country, with an official per capita GNP the size of Britain's, looks very much more prosperous than Britain.

The need to evade the depredations of the state and to make alternative arrangements for functions (like social security) that the state claimed, but usually failed, to carry out meant that the Italian population had to fend for itself. With governments that fell like skittles—and quite long periods without any government at all—no Italian could possibly imagine that the politicians or the state they governed held the key to their prosperity. Necessity in Italy was not so much the mother of invention as of economic flexibility, opportunism (in the best sense), and family solidarity. Not coincidentally, the Italian divorce and illegitimacy rates are a sixth of the British—a product not only of Italy's Catholicism.

In Britain, by contrast, the financial probity of the public administration, a legacy of the Victorian era (in which the state hardly impinged on the lives of individuals at all), misled people into a fatal misapprehension. They supposed that, because no public official ever asked for or expected a bribe, or could be easily swayed by other forms of illicit influence, public officials actually worked both for the public good and the good of individuals. People therefore came to believe in the beneficence, or at least the benevolent neutrality, of the state. Its officials were honest and fair, and therefore it was good.

I see the deleterious consequences of this mistaken belief in many of my patients. They often devote their lives to trying to extract what they believe is their due from the authorities, whose failure to provide it is to them inexplicable, since no one appears personally to benefit from it. If only someone in the administration would say to them, "Give me £100 and I'll do it," all would make sense to them: but no one ever does. The illusion thus persists, sometimes for years, that the authorities are genuinely looking into it. The British national pastime is Waiting for Godot.

My patients who live in public housing, for example, inhabit a world of endless, inexplicable official delay and prevarication. The rhetoric of politicians and the financial integrity of the housing department have convinced them that public housing exists for the benefit of those who live in it, so they suffer from paralyzing cognitive dissonance when problems arise. I see this often. When a damp patch appeared on the living-room wall of one of my patients and then spread throughout his apartment to such an extent that the electricity blew out and he and his family had to live in the only room not yet affected, he found the authorities distinctly—and mysteriously—unhelpful. For eighteen months he sought their assistance, but they lost his letters, denied they had ever received them, sent an inspector who said there was no damp present despite the fact that black mold was attacking everything in the affected rooms, sent a contractor who simply covered the damp walls with cardboard that the mold soon ate away, and finally accused the tenant himself of being responsible for the damp because he had overheated the rooms with the windows shut. Therefore, they declared, they could do nothing further to help him. Because it had not occurred to him that there might be other forms of dishonesty than financial, my patient persisted in his search for satisfaction for a long time, believing himself to be the isolated victim of bad luck rather than of systematic neglect.

When finally he realized that bad luck alone could not explain his experience, his willing and patient dependence gave way to angry resentment: but neither dependence nor resentment is constructive. A large and honest, but indifferent or incompetent, state bureaucracy creates expectations that give rise to this dialectic of dependence and resentment, which does not exist in Italy, where no one would assume the honesty and therefore the benevolence of the public administration in the first place.

The vast and seemingly benevolent state has completely eroded the proud and sturdy independence of the British population, once remarked upon by visitors. Forty percent of Britons now depend on government subsidy, receiving direct payment from the public purse as part, or all, of their income. Even so, the government regularly mounts advertising campaigns to ensure that people claim all their entitlements. Moreover the British state has removed several important areas of human life from the responsibility of individuals to arrange for themselves or their families: health, education, social security, pensions, and (for at least a quarter of the population) housing. The income left to them after taxation—or received from the government dole—is thus a kind of pocket money, the more serious, if more vexatious and boring, aspects of a personal budget having been already taken care of by the government. This explains why, whenever the British government considers a tax cut, almost all newspapers, no matter of what political tendency, describe the measure as giving money away—indulging in a handout, like a parent doling out a weekly allowance to children.

The entrapment of people in the psychologically and economically debilitating dialectic I have described is not a marginal but a mass phenomenon. It addles the brain and paralyzes action. It helps to explain the degradation and lack of self-respect that is so obvious in the streets of Britain but so absent from those of Italy.

When I worked in East Africa, I saw an instructive contrast between an Italian and a British construction project within a few miles of each other. The British construction workers were drunken, violent, debauched, and dirty, without shame or dignity. Utterly egotistical, yet without much individuality, they wrecked hugely expensive machinery when drunk, without a moment's regret, and responded with outrage if reprimanded. They intimidated their managers, who made little attempt to control them. They were truly representative of a population that has lost any pride in itself or in what it does, and that somehow contrives to be frivolous without gaiety.

By contrast, the Italians were hardworking, disciplined, and clean, and could enjoy themselves in a civilized way even in the African bush, drinking without drunkenness or that complete loss of self-control characteristic of today's British. Unlike the British, they never became a nuisance to the local population, and everyone saw them as people who had come to do a job of work. At once more social and more self-reliant than their British counterparts, they were men whose dignity had not been destroyed by a culture of dependence.

Italy's public administration vastly surpasses Britain's in only one area: the preservation of the country's urban heritage. This single bureaucratic success is crucial, however, for it greatly elevates Italy's standard of living over Britain's. The destruction of Britain's urban patrimony and its replacement by hideous modernist multi-story parking garages and office buildings, while inflating the GNP, represent a lowering of every Briton's quality of life.

You would think that Britain, with a less rich architectural heritage to preserve than Italy, would preserve what it had all the more zealously. But no: Britain's townscape, once civilized and gracious, has fallen prey to an ideological pincer movement. At one end of the political spectrum, the rawest and shortest-sighted commercial interests demanded and won freedom to do whatever they wished with the inherited townscape, in the cheapest and most profitable way, so that harmonious assemblages of buildings centuries old suffered the most philistine and incongruous redevelopment that ruined them beyond hope of restoration. At the other end of the spectrum, radical reformers fanatically hated the architectural symbols of the past, merely because they were symbols of the past, whose despised elitist culture supposedly rested solely on exploitation, racism, slavery, and so forth.

The official architect and town planner of the city in which I live, for example, wanted—quite literally—to pull down every single local building that dated from before the second half of the twentieth century, including entire Georgian streets and many masterpieces of the Victorian gothic revival. Fortunately he retired when perhaps a tenth of the old buildings still remained: the rest having by then been replaced by Le Corbusian leviathans so horrible and inhuman that many of them are now scheduled for demolition in their turn, less than thirty years after their erection. The Georgian spa city of Bath offers an even more startling example: in the 1950s the city council wanted to raze it to the ground and replace it with something more in tune with the times.

Such barbarous thoughts would never have occurred to any Italian, however corrupt or politically extreme he might otherwise have been. As Giorgio Bassani observes of the street of palaces where his protagonists live in *The Garden of the Finzi-Continis*: "[The] Corso Ercole I d'Este is so fine, and such a tourist attraction, that the left-wing council that has been running Ferrara for nearly fifteen years has realized it must be left as it is and strictly protected against speculative builders and shopkeepers; in fact, that its aristocratic character must be preserved exactly as it was." Never in England.

Actually, Italian municipal policy has been even more enlightened than this passage suggests. Commercial enterprises in old towns and cities must conform to aesthetic standards, so as not to do violence to the appearance of buildings, with the result that the Italians are not, like the British, modern barbarians camped out in the relics of an older and superior civilization to whose beauties they are oblivious. Italian municipalities have also kept their cities vibrant by capping the local taxes of small businesses, thus nurturing a variety of shops that in turn nourish many crafts, from papermaking to glass-blowing, that might otherwise have died. Thus, an uneducated man in Italy can still be a proud craftsman, while in Britain he must take a low-paid, unskilled job—if he takes a job at all. Italian downtowns are not as British city centers are, the location of depressingly uniform chain stores without character or individuality, plateglassed emporia hacked into the ground floors of historic buildings without regard to the original architecture. The Italians have solved, as the British have not, the problem of living in a modern way in ancient surroundings that, looked at in economic terms, constitute inherited wealth.

The preservation of the aesthetic quality of Italian life, but its utter destruction in Britain, whose streets have been coarsened to a degree unequaled in Europe, has had profound social and economic consequences. Where all is ugliness and indifference to aesthetic considerations, it is easy for behavior to become ugly and crude and for collective municipal pride to evaporate. It seems not to matter how people conduct themselves: there is nothing to spoil. Attention to detail, important in both the manufacture of goods and the provision of services, attenuates in an environment of generalized ugliness. What is the point of wiping a table if the world around it is irredeemably hideous? To be sure, self-respect can encourage people to make the best of a bad job, but dependency on the state has destroyed the basis of self-respect.

In a world grown richer, aesthetic quality has obvious economic benefits. Given the gulf between the excellence of Italian design, educated by the beauties of the past, and the unremitting tastelessness of British modernity, it is not a coincidence that Italy has one of the largest trading surpluses of any nation, while Britain has one of the largest deficits.

Italy has long cherished a certain Anglophilia, or at least an admiration for the supposed uprightness of British life, which Italians considered a model worthy of imitation. This uprightness, Italians believed, characterized the conduct both of the government and of the population, which was too proud and self-reliant to stoop to dishonesty. Alas, this is a vision of the past, not of the present.

In any case, the Italians know themselves well enough not to believe wholeheartedly in the possibility of honest government in their country: which is why the allegations of dishonesty hurled against Prime Minister Berlusconi before his election were beside the point. Even if such accusations were true, the new prime minister would only have done on a grand scale what most Italians have done on a small one. The electorate probably appreciated that a leviathan state is harmful because it is leviathan, not because it is corrupt. An uncorrupt leviathan state is, in fact, more to be feared than a corrupt one. Indeed, if the Italian state were to turn honest without a simultaneous reduction in its size, the result would be an economic and cultural catastrophe for Italy.

The British, by contrast, are still attached to their state as calves to the udder. They have just voted massively for a party and a man who claim to be responsible for everything—whose government has recently issued, for example, an official booklet to every engaged couple outlining the advantages and disadvantages of marriage, as if the population were incapable of thinking for itself even about those things that most intimately concern it (which, under a regime like this, is increasingly the case).

What can be the future of a country whose government believes that the population needs to be told that marriage can sometimes result in marital disharmony?

2001

The Goddess of Domestic Tribulations

I FIRST LEARNED of the death of Princess Diana on Sunday morning at the prison. The flag was at half-mast, and I asked a prison officer why.

"Haven't you heard?" he replied. "Diana's dead—killed in a car crash in Paris while being chased by paparazzi."

I felt a moment of sorrow for a young life so needlessly and pointlessly ended, but duty called. A hunger-striking prisoner was close to death: he was protesting what he considered the injustice of the security precautions taken in his case, though the last time they were relaxed he had tried to escape by blowing up the Black Maria carrying him to court. Another prisoner had tried to hang himself. A new recruit to prison culture, as anthropologists would call it, he made the mistake of reporting the theft of his radio to the officers, who had recovered it for him. But he was thenceforth known as a *grass*, an informer, the only form of prison life lower than a *nonce*, or sex offender; and he thought he had better hang himself at once, before the other prisoners did it for him. And then there was a prisoner to attend to who had slashed his forearm some days before and had refused the operation necessary to stitch him up. He was now busily stuffing tissue paper and broken bits of plastic spoon deep into the wound.

In short, everything was proceeding much as normal in the prison, despite the death of Diana. It was only much later that I realized that a mass hysteria had been unleashed that makes the death of Little Nell look like a detached clinical report.

While Diana was being killed in the Paris tunnel, the presses of the *Observer* newspaper, the Sunday journal of Britain's liberal intelligentsia, were printing the following item in a satirical column entitled MRS. BLAIR'S DIARY: "It always amazes me that the press picks up on [what Diana says] as if it were compelling genius insight of Aristotelian wisdom and Shavian wit, as opposed to the twitterings of a woman who, if her IQ were five points lower, would have to be watered daily." So proud was the newspaper of this delicious shaft of satire that it headlined the entire column: IF HER IQ WERE ANY LOWER, SHE'D NEED DAILY WATERING. Elsewhere in the newspaper, a picture of Diana bore the caption: "Woodentop."

This crudely satirical tone could not survive the tragic events of the day, of course. But if civilized convention demands that one should not speak ill of the (recently) dead, it surely does not demand either that one eulogize them to excess. Nevertheless, the *Guardian*—owned, edited, written, and read by the same people as the *Observer*—soon began to write of the late princess in the most nauseatingly fulsome fashion. Among other miracles, the paper credited her with a beneficial revolution in our manners: on the Tuesday following her death, for example, two commentators in the *Guardian*, one of them a professor of politics at Oxford University, asserted that she both created and reflected a more compassionate Britain after the heartless years of Thatcherite selfishness. She also changed us from a nation of people who keep our feelings bottled up inside into one of frank and openhearted self-revelation—a change all for the better, of course.

"She preached a doctrine of hugs, warmth and confession," wrote one of the commentators approvingly, "a revolutionary doctrine whose enemy was the frigidity of our habitual reserve." That the loss of reserve might entail other losses—depth, for example—was a thought not to be entertained at such a moment.

What accounted for this sudden shift from cruel personal abuse to absurdly exaggerated respect? Princess Diana was useful both alive and dead to British liberals, who habitually measure their own moral standing and worth by their degree of theoretical hatred for and opposition to whatever exists. Diana was useful because she was both an insider and an outsider, who could be represented either as a symbol of the establishment or as an enemy of it. Spurned as she was by the royal family, she remained an aristocrat who led an extremely privileged life.

Alive, she was handy proof that people of no particular merit or intelligence had undue social prominence in this country, which necessitated radical reforms as demanded by the liberal intelligentsia; dead, she was equally useful to demonstrate that the rottenness of our institutions (such as the monarchy) had destroyed a splendid woman for whom the establishment could find no place. Solution: more radical reform, as demanded by the liberal intelligentsia.

What is more certain than that the sun will rise tomorrow is that once Diana, having undergone temporary secular canonization, has served her turn to inflict whatever damage can be inflicted upon our institutions, the *Observer* and the *Guardian* will debunk her, in order to establish their credentials as journals of fierce independent-mindedness. They will reveal her as a hysterical, self-serving, scheming, and manipulative minx. The wheel will have made its revolution.

As for the gutter press—the one field of production in which Britain undoubtedly still leads the world, and a faithful reflection of the cultural and educational level of the population as a whole—it momentarily lost its swagger at the suggestion that the photographers it routinely showered with money to snap the princess from every conceivable angle had been responsible for her untimely demise. It even shrank from publishing the photographs of Diana in the crash.

But when it was established that the driver of Diana's car was drunk, and that he had been going absurdly fast through the tunnel, the gutter press regained its confidence and immediately mounted a campaign to force the queen to express her grief in public and to fly the national flag at half-mast over the royal palace, though this was against the custom and usage of centuries. The combined circulation of these newspapers is twelve million, and perhaps half the population of the country reads one or the other of them; so the queen bowed to what must have seemed like popular pressure, though it was in fact the simulated rage of a handful of editors who were conducting a struggle to maintain circulation at a difficult time. No one stopped to think that the tradition of not flying the flag at half-mast over the palace was a symbolic representation of the idea that, while individuals come and go, the institution survives them and is more important than they; or that, by demanding that the queen express grief in public, the newspapers were demanding either that she express an emotion she did not feel, or that she should not be allowed to grieve in private. Either way was to trivialize and cheapen the emotion.

But the queen outwitted the editors. In her television address to the nation, which they had demanded, she managed to avoid what would have been patently dishonest avowals of affection for her ex-daughter-in-law while avowing admiration for such qualities as her energy—a distinctly double-edged quality in someone of whose activities one does not entirely approve.

The new prime minister, Tony Blair, exactly caught (indeed, in part created) the mood of the nation when he called Diana "the people's princess." The appellation instantly became universal, and made it doubly difficult to express reservations about the adulation being offered her memory or to cast doubt on the historical importance ascribed to her life and her unfortunate death. Because she was the people's princess, such reservations branded one an anti-democratic elitist, opposed to the people. A name once conferred and accepted can stand in the way of proper thought.

But did the people's princess have anything more in common with the people than the People's Democratic Republic of Korea has in common with either democracy or the Korean people? Yes and no: she was undoubtedly a popular figure, though her life was as remote from that of the people as that of an anchorite who lives in a desert cave.

Her popularity rested upon both her extreme difference from common people and her similarity to them. She was aristocratic, rich, and glamorous. Born to the purple, she married a prince: her life had a fairy-tale quality to it, acknowledged throughout the world. How well I remember watching her wedding on Peruvian television, which billed it as *La Boda del Siglo*, the Wedding of the Century. I little thought—no one then imagined—that it would end as *Los Funerales del Siglo*, the first truly global funeral.

In her, the mystique of royalty to which Bagehot referred in *The English Constitution* was replaced by the mystique of celebrity: and while the former mystique depended upon concealment, the latter depends upon revelation, usually of the most vulgar, prurient, trite, and debased variety. The cult of royalty, while the mystique lasted, suggested to those who followed it that there was a plane of existence that transcended the everyday world, and that there existed something greater and more important than themselves; whereas the cult of celebrity is but a disguised worship of our own, generally uncultivated, tastes and desires. Quiet reverence for the unseen has become noisy tittle-tattle about the ubiquitous, which has resulted in a vicious spiral of ever-coarsening public appetites, because tittle-tattle must be ever more salacious to satisfy us.

If Diana's life was inaccessible to the commonalty, and therefore the stuff of dreams, it was highly accessible also. Her prince turned out to be not so charming, at least to her. His heart was set on another, even as he walked down the aisle. She had been selected for marriage in much the same way as a horse breeder selects a horse, and for much the same reasons: the bloodline must go on. Her teeth were good, and she was fertile. Moreover, the family into which she married, interesting only by virtue of its position, was not at all normal. Difficulties ensued.

Diana therefore had a constituency of all those who have been unhappy in their marriages, whose husbands or wives have deserted or betrayed them, who have had contretemps with their mothers-in-law, who have suffered humiliation at the hands of others: that is to say, a very high percentage of the human race. Her problems were those that might afflict any ordinary person, especially any ordinary woman, and therefore ordinary people were able to identify with her easily. She was the goddess of domestic tribulations.

When she revealed that she suffered from bulimia, she sealed her universal popularity. In an age when strength of character consists of being able to flaunt one's weaknesses to the prurient gaze of millions of idle onlookers, nothing could establish her *bona fides* better than her confession that she induced herself to vomit after eating too much: just like a thousand or a million salesclerks anxious about their weight. She is one of us: an alcoholic, a drug addict, a sexual pervert, a kleptomaniac, an agoraphobic, an anorexic, or one of the thousand natural diagnoses of the *Diagnostic and Statistical Manual of the American Psychiatric Association* (Fourth Edition) that flesh is heir to.

So universally accepted has the pathologico-therapeutic approach to life become that the apostolic heir to St. Augustine—that is to say, the present Archbishop of Canterbury—offered up thanks to God at the funeral service for Princess Diana's vulnerability, as if an appointment with a psychiatrist were man's highest possible moral and cultural aspiration. Of course, prelates of the Church of England today have backbones of marshmallow; but still it seems to me absurd to offer up thanks to the Author of the Universe for a princess's shortcomings.

The other quality that made Diana the people's princess was, of course, the extreme banality of her tastes and pleasures. As she herself was the first to admit, she was not clever, at least in the intellectual sense, though she clearly had intuition. Apart from dress sense, she had the cheapest taste: in other words, she was not at all threatening to the man and woman in the street, who knew that she liked what they liked and that much of her life was lived as they would live, were they to win the lottery. Even her sympathy with the poor and wretched of the earth was such as the average man or woman feels from time to time. In this respect her similarity to Eva Perón, who embraced the conspicuously afflicted before the flashbulbs of photographers, is very striking, as is the similarity of the aura of sanctity that the public, quite incongruously, conferred upon "Evita" after her equally untimely death.

That her tastes were, despite her privileged upbringing, utterly banal and plebeian appeared very clearly at the funeral, where Elton John sang his bathetic dirge immediately after the prime minister read St. Paul's magnificent words in Corinthians. It was highly appropriate (and symbolic) that this lugubrious booby, with his implanted wig, should sing a recycled version of a song initially dedicated to the memory of Marilyn Monroe—a celebrity who at least had had to make her own way in the world, and who also made a few films worthy of commemoration. "Goodbye, England's rose," he intoned in a mid-Atlantic accent that spoke volumes for the loss of Britain's cultural confidence, "from a country lost without your soul."

You can say that again. In the orgy of sentimentality into which much of the country sank after Diana's death, and which reminds me of the hot bath into which I gratefully sink after a hard day at the hospital, one thing has become evident: that the British, under the influence of the media of mass communication, which demand that everyone wear his emotion or pseudo-emotion on his sleeve, have lost their only admirable qualities—stoicism, self-deprecation, and a sense of irony—and have gained only those worthy of contempt. They have exchanged depth for shallowness, and have thought they got the better of the bargain. They are like people who imagine that the answer to constipation is diarrhea.

TO SPEAK OF EMOTION CONVEYS SINCERITY, the headline in the *Guardian* graphically put it; and that is why the vast crowds outside Westminster Abbey widely applauded the Earl Spencer's address at the funeral, despite its obvious and grotesque dishonesty. That a speech can be heartfelt and mendacious at the same time is a thought too subtle for people reared on mass media culture. Not only had the great defender of Diana's children provided a less than stable home environment for his own four children and implied (more or less) that the Princes William and Harry were born by parthenogenesis, without any contribution by Prince Charles, but in castigating the odious tabloid newspapers he omitted to mention that they were pandering to the degraded tastes of the general public, two million of whom were gathered outside the abbey, mourning the fact that there would be no more photographs of Diana in bikinis, kissing the latest of her celebrity lovers. Indeed, the Earl Spencer (all too predictably dubbed "the people's earl") omitted to mention that Diana's fame was largely the creation of that odious press that he had excluded from the funeral, that the millions of mourners were in effect mourning the loss of a character from a soap opera, and that her own symbiotic relations with the reptile press were very far from straightforwardly adversarial. The good earl was like the anti-Semite of old, who blamed the Jews for the existence of usury.

He was hardly the only person who missed the connection between the demand for intrusions on privacy and the supply thereof in an age of celebrity. A patient of mine attempted suicide with tablets on the day of the funeral, feeling it incumbent upon him to express his loyalty to Princess Diana. He was a lonely man in his fifties, living on his own, who had made something of a cult of the princess. He told me he cut out and collected pictures of her. I asked him where he found the pictures that he collected.

"The *Sun*," he replied.

The *Sun*, needless to say, is one of those tabloids that have been most ruthless in procuring pictures of Diana, one of those tabloids that the earl held responsible for the death of his sister. But the irony was as entirely lost on my poor patient as it was on the earl.

Diana has already wrought the first of her miracles. A multimillionaire alcoholic patient has for many years insisted upon driving while drunk, but the accident in the Paris tunnel has caused him to forswear his drunken driving, where doctors, courts, friends, and relatives had previously produced no effect at all. Only two more miracles to go!

Conspiracy theories abound, of course, and they are already affecting patients. A French television channel, for example, has put it about that the royal family had Diana killed to save the embarrassment of having her marry a Muslim, a theory that will no doubt gain credence, especially as many suspect that her selection as a lover of the son of a man with whom the British government has been in acrimonious dispute for many years was not entirely coincidental. Many already believe she was assassinated, even without the publication of spurious "investigative" books, and when a patient of mine told me that her husband had better return to the paths of marital fidelity "or else," and I asked what the "or else" signified, she said darkly, "A road tunnel in Paris."

So not quite everyone has grown sentimental about the death of Diana, and even the funeral itself afforded one or two light moments. The commentator on one of the television channels, for example, made the Freudian slip of all time when, as Princess Diana's cortege was passing the Banqueting House, he noted that the magnificent building was the last surviving part of Westminster Palace, "on the steps of which," he added, "Prince Charles was executed." The declining remnant of the population that knows that England once had a King Charles who was beheaded fell about laughing at this conclusive proof that, after all, Freud knew what he was talking about.

But there were genuinely moving moments too, as when the ninety-seven-year-old queen mother climbed the steps of the Abbey and walked down the aisle unaided, thanks to a hip-replacement operation performed when she was ninety-five. I couldn't help recalling, however, that one of the surgeons who performed this astonishing technical feat had taken a month's leave from his hospital and returned as a woman, having previously been a man. What else can one expect in an age when it has been suggested (by the serious newspapers) that the royal family's insistence on the children of Charles and Diana behaving with dignity in public is a form of child abuse perpetrated by pre-Freudian dinosaurs?

I was reminded that restraint and reserve were once not confined to the upper reaches of the British aristocracy by another patient of mine, who consulted me a few days after Diana's death. She was a seventy-five-year-old working-class woman of dignified mien, who had lived through more than one tragedy in her life. Her brother died in a submarine sunk during the war, and her sister-in-law was killed in an air raid, leaving her the task of bringing up their orphaned child. Her own husband had died comparatively young, and her first son had died of a heart attack at the age of forty-two. ("He had just finished a game of football, doctor, and was in the changing rooms. He fell on the floor, and his mates thought he had slipped, and they told him to stop messing about. He just looked up at them—smiled—and he was gone.")

The bitterest blow of all was the death of another son, recently killed in an accident in which a heavy truck, carelessly driven, crushed his car. He was fifty. She brought me his photo, her hand trembling slightly as she gave it to me. He was a successful businessman who had devoted his spare time to raising money for the Children's Hospital and to producing programs for its own radio station.

"It doesn't seem right, somehow," she said, "that he should have gone before me."

Did she still cry?

"Yes, doctor, but only when I'm on my own. It's not right, is it, to let anyone see you. After all, life has to go on."

Could anyone have doubted either the depth of her feeling or of her character? Could any decent person fail to have been moved by the self-mastery she had achieved, the foundation of her dignity and her strength? Yet her fortitude is precisely the virtue that the acolytes of the hug-and-confess culture wish to extirpate from the British national character as obsolete, in favor of a banal, self-pitying, witless, and shallow emotional incontinence, of which the hysteria at the princess's death was so florid an example.

1997

The Starving Criminal

◆ RARELY DOES the *British Journal of Psychiatry* produce in the reader anything other than déjà vu at best and ennui at worst; but an article in the July issue was startling in its implications and accordingly won wide publicity.

Researchers carried out a double-blind trial of the effect of vitamin and mineral supplements on the behavior of prisoners aged eighteen to twenty-one. Two hundred and thirty-one such prisoners were divided randomly into two groups: one that received real vitamins, one that got only a placebo. Those who received the real vitamins committed about a third fewer disciplinary offenses and acts of violence during the follow-up period than those who took the placebo.

The researchers demonstrated that the two groups of prisoners did not differ in any respect before the trial (though, importantly, they did not control for previous or current usage of illicit drugs). Thus the reduction in anti-social behavior was in all probability attributable to the vitamins. True, the results have yet to be reproduced elsewhere, and reproducibility is the hallmark of genuine scientific discovery. True, too, the researchers offered no explanation of why the vitamins produced their alleged effects—and the supplements contained so many vitamins, minerals, and fatty acids that it would take several lifetimes to establish exactly which ones produced the alleged effect.

Still, the trial raised hopes of a breakthrough for Britain's crime-ridden, even crime-dominated, society. Could it be that simply handing out vitamin pills to our potential burglars and muggers could make our homes and streets more secure?

Those who have long been on the lookout for reasons to exempt criminals from responsibility for their acts—as a sign of their own generosity of spirit—will conclude from these results either that crime is a manifestation of physical illness of the brain or that it is the result of poverty that itself gives rise to that illness.

But we should exercise caution: other interpretations are, as always, possible. That many young inmates are grossly malnourished when they enter prison I have absolutely no doubt, because each day I see cases of severe malnutrition among those who have recently entered the adult prison in which I work. Of an average daily intake of 20 prisoners, perhaps 6, of whom 4 are drug addicts, show obvious outward signs of malnutrition. A rough estimate (allowing for recidivism) would suggest that perhaps 1,000 malnourished men arrive in my prison annually: that means (if my prison is typical, and there is no reason to suppose otherwise) that each year at least 25,000 malnourished men enter the British prison system. What is more, the malnutrition that I see in the prison is also to be found in the hospital in which I work, among men (and, to a lesser extent, among women) of the same social class as the prisoners.

Were a film director to need extras to play the part of starving Bosnians in a movie about the Serbian atrocities, he would need to look no further than my prison's daily intake. The prisoners' sunken eyes, which appear disproportionately large in the setting of their sunken cheeks and prominent cheekbones, their spindly limbs, and their hollow chests with paper-bag skin, punctuated with unhealing sores, over their bony rib cages, would fit the director's bill perfectly. The prisoners' teeth are falling out; their tongues are glisteningly smooth, angrily magenta red, and the corners of their mouths are cracked, as in vitamin B deficiency. They are in their early twenties to their early thirties.

From the dietary point of view, freedom has the same effect upon them as a concentration camp; incarceration restores them to nutritional health. This is a new phenomenon, at least on the scale on which I now see it. Last week, for example, I treated in my hospital a skeletal man who had been released from prison only two months before and had in that short time lost forty-four pounds. A recidivist, he had served many short sentences for theft, and his weight went up and down according to whether he was in prison or at liberty. This is a common enough pattern of weight gain and weight loss among the males of my city's underclass. It has a meaning quite alien to those who believe that modern malnutrition is merely a symptom of poverty and inequality.

About two-thirds of these malnourished young men take drugs, upon which they spend sums of money that, however obtained, would secure them nightly banquets. The drugs they take suppress their appetite: the nausea induced by heroin inhibits the desire to eat, while cocaine and its derivatives suppress it altogether. The prostitutes who stand on the street corners not far from where I live—they work a shift system and commute in from a nearby town in buses chartered by their pimps—are likewise grossly malnourished (they often end up in my hospital), and for the same reason. You'd think famine were stalking the land.

Not all the malnourished are drug-takers, however. It is when you inquire into eating habits, not just recent but throughout entire lifetimes, that all this malnutrition begins to make sense. The trail is a short one between modern malnutrition and modern family and sexual relations.

Take the young burglar whom I saw in the prison last week. There was nothing remarkable about his case: on the contrary, he was, if I may put it thus, an average British burglar. And his story was one that I have heard a thousand times at least. Here, if anywhere, is the true banality of evil.

He smoked heroin, but the connection between his habit and his criminality was not what is conventionally assumed: that his addiction produced a craving so strong, and a need to avoid withdrawal symptoms so imperative, that resort to crime was his only choice. On the contrary—and as is usually the case—his criminal record started well before he took to heroin. Indeed, his decision to take heroin was itself a continuation, an almost logical development, of his choice of the criminal life.

He was thin and malnourished in the manner I have described. Five feet ten, he weighed just over a hundred pounds. He told me what many young men in his situation have told me, that he asked the court not to grant him bail, so that he could recover his health in prison—something he knew he would never do outside. A few months of incarceration would set him up nicely to indulge in heroin on his release. Prison is the health farm of the slums.

I examined him and said to him, "You don't eat."

"Not much," he said. "I don't feel like it."

"And when you do eat, what do you eat?"

"Crisps [potato chips] and chocolate."

This pattern, however, was not the heroin talking, as addicts sometimes put it. Rather, it was the story of his life.

He had never known his father, who had not even achieved the status of myth in his mind. His father's existence was more of a logical deduction, the product of the syllogism that runs: all humans have fathers, I am a human, therefore I have a father. To make up for it, he had known stepfathers aplenty, the last of whom was in a steady, though violent, relationship with his mother, a relationship that required the frequent intervention of the police to prevent its premature end through murder. He had left home when he was sixteen because his stepfather had made it clear that he was *de trop*.

I asked the young man whether his mother had ever cooked for him.

"Not since my stepfather arrived. She would cook for him, like, but not for us children."

I asked him what they—he and his brothers and sisters—had eaten and how they had eaten it.

"We'd just eat whatever there was," he said. "We'd look for something whenever we was hungry."

"And what was there?"

"Bread, cereals, chocolate—that kind of thing."

"So you never sat round a table and ate a meal together?"

"No."

In fact, he told me that he had never once eaten at a table with others in the last fifteen years. Eating was for him a solitary vice, something done almost furtively, with no pleasure attached to it and certainly not as a social event. The street was his principal dining room, as well as his trash can: and as far as food was concerned, he was more a hunter-gatherer than a man living in a highly evolved society.

Far from being unique, his story was typical of those I have heard hundreds—no, thousands—of times. Another young man, also expelled from home at an early age because his new stepfather, only a few years older than he, found him surplus to requirements, had been obliged to drift from friend's house to friend's house for six years. Unfitted by training or education for any particular job, he had worked only casually, for a few weeks at a time, and so never had the financial stability to pay rent on a place of his own (in conditions of shortage, public housing goes preferentially to young single women with children, and he had made the situation worse by having two children of his own by two young women). Needless to say, he had no domestic skills either, never having been taught any; and his friends, coming from the same social milieu, were just as undomesticated. They too ate in an unsocial fashion and expected him to fend nutritionally for himself, which he did by eating chocolate, the only food he could remember having eaten with any consistency over the last few years. Apart from his time in prison (for stealing from cars), he hadn't eaten a meal in a decade. It can't be long before someone suggests that the solution to a problem like this is to fortify chocolate with minerals and vitamins.

I meet at least one young man every week in the hospital with a similar story to relate. It is a story that angers and frustrates me. These young men's malnutrition is the sign of an entire way of life, and not the result of raw, inescapable poverty. Another patient whom I saw soon after, similarly malnourished, told me that he ate practically nothing, subsisting on sugary soft drinks.

It never takes many links in a chain of reasoning to get from their smooth and raw magenta tongues to the kind of family breakdown favored by a certain ideology of human relations, encouraged by our laws and fiscal system, and made viable by welfare payments. It is the breakdown of the family structure—a breakdown so complete that mothers do not consider it part of their duty to feed their own children once they have reached the age at which they can forage for themselves in a refrigerator—that promotes modern malnutrition in Britain. Such malnutrition, according to the public health establishment, now affects millions of British households. And it is hardly surprising if young people who have not learned to socialize within the walls of their own homes, who have not learned even the minimal social disciplines required by people who eat together, should be completely antisocial in other respects.

One of the things British prisons could usefully do, therefore, but do not even attempt, is to teach young men how to eat in a social fashion. Instead they reinforce the pattern of solipsistic consumption by making prisoners take their food back to their cells, where they eat it in the same solitary and furtive fashion as they masturbate.

As to whether the malnutrition consequent upon a profoundly asocial way of life itself contributes to anti-social behavior, by affecting the brain and hence the capacity of the malnourished person to make reasonable choices, only future research will prove. I personally do not find the idea inherently improbable.

The existence of malnutrition in the midst of plenty has not entirely escaped either the intelligentsia or the government, which of course is proposing measures to combat it: but, as usual, neither pols nor pundits wish to look the problem in the face or make the obvious connections. For them, the real and most pressing question raised by any social problem is: "How do I appear concerned and compassionate to all my friends, colleagues, and peers?" Needless to say, the first imperative is to avoid any hint of blaming the victim by examining the bad choices that he makes. It is not even permissible to look at the reasons for those choices, since by definition victims are victims and therefore not responsible for their acts, unlike the relatively small class of human beings who are not victims. One might extend La Rochefoucauld's famous maxim that neither the sun nor death can be stared at for long, by saying that no member of the modern liberal intelligentsia can stare at a social problem for very long. He feels the need to retreat into impersonal abstractions, into structures or alleged structures over which the victim has no control. And out of this need to avoid the rawness of reality he spins utopian schemes of social engineering.

The British intelligentsia has thus come up with an abstraction that fits this particular bill perfectly—that is to say, the need to explain widespread malnutrition in the midst of plenty without resort to the conduct of the malnourished themselves: *food deserts*.

A food desert is a poor area of a town or city, in which there are few shops selling food, and in which those few offer a restricted range of unhealthy and unnourishing produce at relatively high prices. The huge supermarket chains, unwilling to carry out their social duty, have retreated to prosperous areas, where they can sell profitably to people who do not have to worry about what they spend on what they eat. Particularly lacking in a food desert are fresh comestibles: all food available is processed or precooked, full of salt and the worst kind of fat, and lacking in vital ingredients. The people who live in a food desert, therefore, have no choice but to eat unhealthily. Of course, the real—that is to say, ultimate—cause of food deserts is modern capitalism, the system that created and perpetuates the food deserts.

It has become a truth universally acknowledged that food deserts actually exist and must be the fault of the supermarket chains (and, by extension, the System). Indeed, the government, ever on the lookout for new areas of life to control with its dictatorial benevolence, has proposed a new law to eradicate what is now known as "food poverty" by irrigating these deserts with subsidies to food suppliers. As yet the additional provisions of the bill are not at all firm, except for the establishment of a Food Poverty Authority in every district, manned by bureaucrats, who will measure food poverty and count the miles people have to go to get fresh vegetables. One man's poverty is another man's employment opportunity: as long ago as the sixteenth century, a German bishop remarked that the poor are a gold mine.

Recently, at a lunch I attended, given by a left-wing magazine to which I sometimes contribute, the matter of food poverty and food deserts came up, and it was with some pride that I heard an area, not more than a mile from where I live, described as the very worst of these deserts, positively the Atacama of food.

As the only person present with personal knowledge—what Bertrand Russell used to call "knowledge by acquaintance"—of the area in question, I felt constrained to point out that I frequently shopped there, at a small Indian store in which one could buy, for example, twenty-two-pound sacks of onions for about $3.40, and in which a huge variety of extremely fresh vegetables could be bought at prices less than half of those in the supermarket chains. Yet the only poor people who shopped there were Indian immigrants or their descendants—housewives who sifted through the produce looking carefully for the best. Practically no poor whites (or blacks) ever went there, though plenty of both live in the area. Only a few members of the white middle class from outside the area took advantage of the wide range and exceptionally low prices.

Moreover, unlike the people who spoke so fluently of the food deserts, I had, in the course of my medical duties, visited many homes in the area. The only homes in which there were ever any signs of genuine cookery and of eating as a social activity, where families discussed the topics of daily life and affirmed their bonds to one another, were those of the Indian immigrants. In white and black homes, cookery meant (at its best) reheating in a microwave oven, and there was no table round which people could sit together to eat the reheated food. Meals here were solitary, poor, nasty, British, and short.

The Indian immigrants and their descendants inherited a far better and more elaborate cuisine than the native British, of course, but this is not a sufficient explanation of their willingness still to buy fresh food and to cook it: they continue to cook because they still live in families, and cookery is a socially motivated art. Even among Indian heroin addicts (principally Muslim), the kind of malnutrition I have described is rare, because they do not yet live in the solipsistic isolation of their white counterparts, who live alone, even when there are other people inhabiting the house or apartment in which they themselves live. Drug addiction is thus a necessary condition for much of the malnutrition that I see, but not sufficient.

The owners of the shop only a mile from my door, serving poor Indian immigrants, are almost certainly millionaires: and the fact that their customers are poor has not prevented them from establishing a conspicuously flourishing business. If, however, you examined the convenience stores in predominantly white working-class areas (where the per capita income is not lower), you would find a much reduced range of produce, very little of it fresh, and the great majority of it processed for ease of preparation. While the Indian store gives the impression of intense activity and hope, the convenience store in a white working-class area gives the impression of passivity and despair. If food deserts truly exist—and they cannot in these times of easy transport be very extensive—the explanation lies in demand, not in supply. And demand is a cultural phenomenon.

The connections I have drawn are obvious, yet denied—or rather avoided altogether—in the typical modern British approach to social problems. The article in the *British Journal of Psychiatry* at least refrains from trying to explain away the malnutrition of the young prisoners without reference to their choices, ideas, habits, way of life, and pattern of social and family relations. It is completely agnostic as to the source of, or reasons for, their dietary deficiencies. Nor does it attempt to disaggregate the results according to ethnic group: the numbers involved in the trial were probably too small for this to be feasible, even had the authors desired to do so.

The liberal intelligentsia has several reasons for failing to see or admit the cultural dimension of malnutrition in the midst of plenty—in failing to see its connection with an entire way of life—and in throwing the blame instead onto the supermarket chains. One reason is to avoid confronting the human consequences of the changes in morals, manners, and social policy that it has consistently advocated. The second is to avoid all appearance of blaming people whose lives are poor and unenviable. That this approach leads it to view those same people as helpless automata, in the grip of forces that they cannot influence, let alone control—and therefore as not full members of the human race—does not worry the intelligentsia in the least. On the contrary, it increases the importance of the elite's own providential role in society. To blame the supermarket chains is implicitly to demand that the liberal and bureaucratic elite should have yet more control over society.

This is how the British government's current Food Poverty Eradication Bill should be interpreted. By attempting to tackle the sources of supply rather than those of demand, it will sidestep the question of an entire way of life—a problem that it would take genuine moral courage to tackle—and aim at an easy target instead. The government will increase bureaucracy and regulation without reducing malnutrition.

This, in miniature, is the story of modern Britain.

2002

Don't Legalize Drugs

THERE IS a progression in the minds of men: first the un-thinkable becomes thinkable, and then it becomes an orthodoxy whose truth seems so obvious that no one remembers that anyone ever thought differently. This is just what is happening with the idea of legalizing drugs: it has reached the stage when millions of thinking men are agreed that allowing people to take whatever they like is the obvious, indeed only, solution to the social problems that arise from the consumption of drugs.

Man's desire to take mind-altering substances is as old as society itself—as are attempts to regulate their consumption. If intoxication in one form or another is inevitable, then so is customary or legal restraint upon that intoxication. But no society until our own has had to contend with the ready availability of so many different mind-altering drugs, combined with a citizenry jealous of its right to pursue its own pleasures in its own way.

The arguments in favor of legalizing the use of all narcotic and stimulant drugs are twofold: philosophical and pragmatic. Neither argument is negligible, but both are mistaken, I believe, and both miss the point.

The philosophic argument is that, in a free society, adults should be permitted to do whatever they please, always provided that they are prepared to take the consequences of their own choices and that they cause no direct harm to others. The *locus classicus* for this point of view is John Stuart Mill's famous essay *On Liberty*: "The only purpose for which power can be rightfully exercised over any member of the community, against his will, is to prevent harm to others," Mill wrote. "His own good, either physical or moral, is not a sufficient warrant." This radical individualism allows society no part whatever in shaping, determining, or enforcing a moral code: in short, we have nothing in common but our contractual agreement not to interfere with one another as we go about seeking our private pleasures.

In practice, of course, it is exceedingly difficult to make people take *all* the consequences of their own actions—as they must, if Mill's great principle is to serve as a philosophical guide to policy. Addiction to, or regular use of, most currently prohibited drugs cannot affect only the person who takes them—and not his spouse, children, neighbors, or employers. No man, except possibly a hermit, is an island; and so it is virtually impossible for Mill's principle to apply to any human action whatever, let alone shooting up heroin or smoking crack. Such a principle is virtually useless in determining what should or should not be permitted.

Perhaps we ought not be too harsh on Mill's principle: it's not clear that anyone has ever thought of a better one. But that is precisely the point. Human affairs cannot be decided by an appeal to an infallible rule, expressible in a few words, whose simple application can decide all cases, including whether drugs should be freely available to the entire adult population. Philosophical fundamentalism is not preferable to the religious variety; and because the desiderata of human life are many, and often in conflict with one another, mere philosophical inconsistency in policy—such as permitting the consumption of alcohol while outlawing cocaine—is not a sufficient argument against that policy. We all value freedom, and we all value order; sometimes we sacrifice freedom for order, and sometimes order for freedom. But once a prohibition has been removed, it is hard to restore, even when the newfound freedom proves to have been ill-conceived and socially disastrous.

Even Mill came to see the limitations of his own principle as a guide for policy and to deny that all pleasures were of equal significance for human existence. It was better, he said, to be Socrates discontented than a fool satisfied. Mill acknowledged that some goals were intrinsically worthier of pursuit than others.

This being the case, not all freedoms are equal, and neither are all limitations of freedom: some are serious and some trivial. The freedom we cherish—or should cherish—is not merely that of satisfying our appetites, whatever they happen to be. We are not Dickensian Harold Skimpoles, exclaiming in protest that "Even the butterflies are free!" We are not children who chafe at restrictions *because* they are restrictions. And we even recognize the apparent paradox that some limitations to our freedoms have the consequence of making us freer overall. The freest man is not the one who slavishly follows his appetites and desires throughout his life—as all too many of my patients have discovered to their cost.

We are prepared to accept limitations to our freedoms for many reasons, not just that of public order. Take an extreme hypothetical case: public exhibitions of necrophilia are quite rightly not permitted, though on Mill's principle they should be. A corpse has no interests and cannot be harmed, because it is no longer a person; and no member of the public is harmed if he has agreed to attend such an exhibition.

Our resolve to prohibit such exhibitions would not be altered if we discovered that millions of people wished to attend them or even if we discovered that millions already were attending them illicitly. Our objection is not based upon pragmatic considerations or upon a head count: it is based upon the wrongness of the would-be exhibitions themselves. The fact that the prohibition represents a genuine restriction of our freedom is of no account.

It might be argued that the freedom to choose among a variety of intoxicating substances is a much more important freedom and that millions of people have derived innocent fun from taking stimulants and narcotics. But the consumption of drugs has the effect of reducing men's freedom by circumscribing the range of their interests. It impairs their ability to pursue more important human aims, such as raising a family and fulfilling civic obligations. Very often it impairs their ability to pursue gainful employment and promotes parasitism. Moreover, far from being expanders of consciousness, most drugs severely limit it. One of the most striking characteristics of drug-takers is their intense and tedious self-absorption; and their journeys into inner space are generally forays into inner vacuums. Drug-taking is a lazy man's way of pursuing happiness and wisdom, and the shortcut turns out to be the deadest of dead ends. We lose remarkably little by not being permitted to take drugs.

The idea that freedom is merely the ability to act upon one's whims is surely very thin and hardly begins to capture the complexities of human existence; a man whose appetite is his law strikes us not as liberated but enslaved. And when such a narrowly conceived freedom is made the touchstone of public policy, a dissolution of society is bound to follow. No culture that makes publicly sanctioned self-indulgence its highest good can long survive: a radical egotism is bound to ensue, in which any limitations upon personal behavior are experienced as infringements of basic rights. Distinctions between the important and the trivial, between the freedom to criticize received ideas and the freedom to take LSD, are precisely the standards that keep societies from barbarism.

So the legalization of drugs cannot be supported by philosophical principle. But if the pragmatic argument in favor of legalization were strong enough, it might overwhelm other objections. It is upon this argument that proponents of legalization rest the larger part of their case.

The argument is that the overwhelming majority of the harm done to society by the consumption of currently illicit drugs is caused not by their pharmacological properties but by their prohibition and the resultant criminal activity that prohibition always calls into being. Simple reflection tells us that a supply invariably grows up to meet a demand; and when the demand is widespread, suppression is useless. Indeed, it is harmful, since—by raising the price of the commodity in question—it raises the profits of middlemen, which gives them an even more powerful incentive to stimulate demand further. The vast profits to be made from cocaine and heroin—which, were it not for their illegality, would be cheap and easily affordable even by the poorest in affluent societies—exert a deeply corrupting effect on producers, distributors, consumers, and law enforcers alike. Besides, it is well known that illegality in itself has attractions for youth already inclined to disaffection. Even many of the harmful physical effects of illicit drugs stem from their illegal status: for example, fluctuations in the purity of heroin bought on the street are responsible for many of the deaths by overdose. If the sale and consumption of such drugs were legalized, consumers would know how much they were taking and thus avoid overdoses.

Moreover, since society already permits the use of some mind-altering substances known to be both addictive and harmful, such as alcohol and nicotine, in prohibiting others it appears hypocritical, arbitrary, and dictatorial. Its hypocrisy, as well as its patent failure to enforce its prohibitions successfully, leads inevitably to a decline in respect for the law as a whole. Thus things fall apart, and the center cannot hold.

It stands to reason, therefore, that all these problems would be resolved at a stroke if everyone were permitted to smoke, swallow, or inject anything he chose. The corruption of the police, the luring of children of eleven and twelve into illegal activities, the making of such vast sums of money by drug dealing that legitimate work seems pointless and silly by comparison, and the turf wars that make poor neighborhoods so exceedingly violent and dangerous, would all cease at once were drug taking to be decriminalized and the supply regulated in the same way as alcohol.

But a certain modesty in the face of an inherently unknowable future is surely advisable. That is why prudence is a political virtue: what stands to reason *should* happen does not necessarily happen in practice. As Goethe said, all theory (even of the monetarist or free-market variety) is grey, but green springs the golden tree of life. If drugs were legalized, I suspect that the golden tree of life might spring some unpleasant surprises.

It is of course true, but only trivially so, that the present illegality of drugs is the cause of the criminality surrounding their distribution. Likewise, it is the illegality of stealing cars that creates car thieves. In fact the ultimate cause of all criminality is law. As far as I am aware, no one has ever suggested that law should therefore be abandoned. Moreover, the impossibility of winning the "war" against theft, burglary, robbery, and fraud has never been used as an argument that these categories of crime should be abandoned. And so long as the demand for material goods outstrips supply, people will be tempted to commit criminal acts against the owners of property. This is not an argument, in my view, against private property or in favor of the common ownership of all goods. It does suggest, however, that we shall need a police force for a long time to come.

In any case, there are reasons to doubt whether the crime rate would fall quite as dramatically as advocates of legalization have suggested. Amsterdam, where access to drugs is relatively unproblematic, is among the most violent and squalid cities in Europe. The idea behind crime—of getting rich, or at least richer, quickly and without much effort—is unlikely to disappear once drugs are freely available to all who want them. And it may be that officially sanctioned anti-social behavior—the official lifting of taboos— breeds yet more anti-social behavior, as the "broken windows" theory would suggest.

Having met large numbers of drug dealers in prison, I doubt that they would return to respectable life if the principal article of their commerce were to be legalized. Far from evincing a desire to be reincorporated into the world of regular work, they express a deep contempt for it and regard those who accept the bargain of a fair day's work for a fair day's pay as cowards and fools. A life of crime has its attractions for many who would otherwise lead a mundane existence. So long as there is the possibility of a lucrative racket or illegal traffic, such people will find it and extend its scope. Therefore, since even legalizers would hesitate to allow children to take drugs, decriminalization might easily result in dealers turning their attentions to younger and younger children, who—in the permissive atmosphere that even now prevails—have already been inducted into the drug subculture in alarmingly high numbers.

Those who do not deal in drugs but commit crimes to fund their consumption of them are, of course, more numerous than large-scale dealers. And it is true that once opiate addicts, for example, enter a treatment program, which often includes maintenance doses of methadone, the rate at which they commit crimes falls markedly. The drug clinic in my hospital claims an 80 percent reduction in criminal convictions among heroin addicts once they have been stabilized on methadone.

This is impressive, but it is not certain that the results should be generalized. First, the patients are self-selected: they have some motivation to change, otherwise they would not have attended the clinic in the first place. Only a minority of addicts attend, and therefore it is not safe to conclude that, if other addicts were to receive methadone, their criminal activity would similarly diminish.

Second, a decline in convictions is not necessarily the same as a decline in criminal acts. If methadone stabilizes an addict's life, he may become a more efficient, harder-to-catch criminal. Moreover, when the police in our city do catch an addict, they are less likely to prosecute him if he can prove that he is undergoing anything remotely resembling psychiatric treatment. They return him directly to his doctor. Having once had a psychiatric consultation is an all-purpose alibi for a robber or a burglar; the police, who do not want to fill in the forty-plus forms it now takes to charge anyone with anything in England, consider a single contact with a psychiatrist sufficient to deprive anyone of legal responsibility for crime forever.

Third, the rate of criminal activity among those drug addicts who receive methadone from the clinic, though reduced, remains very high. The deputy director of the clinic estimates that the number of criminal acts committed by his average patient (as judged by self-report) was 250 per year before entering treatment and 50 afterward. It may well be that the real difference is considerably less than this, because the patients have an incentive to exaggerate it to secure the continuation of their methadone. But clearly, opiate addicts who receive their drugs legally and free of charge continue to commit large numbers of crimes. In my clinics in prison, I see numerous prisoners who were on methadone when they committed the crime for which they are incarcerated.

Why do addicts given their drug free of charge continue to commit crimes? Some addicts, of course, continue to take drugs other than those prescribed and have to fund their consumption of them. So long as any restriction whatever regulates the consumption of drugs, many addicts will seek them illicitly, regardless of what they receive legally. In addition, the drugs themselves exert a long-term effect on a person's ability to earn a living and severely limit rather than expand his horizons and mental repertoire. They sap the will or the ability of an addict to make long-term plans. While drugs are the focus of an addict's life, they are not all he needs to live, and many addicts thus continue to procure the rest of what they need by criminal means.

For the proposed legalization of drugs to have its much-vaunted beneficial effect on the rate of criminality, such drugs would have to be both cheap and readily available. The legalizers assume that there is a natural limit to the demand for these drugs, and that if their consumption were legalized, the demand would not increase substantially. Those psychologically unstable persons currently taking drugs would continue to do so, with the necessity to commit crimes removed, while psychologically stabler people (such as you and I and our children) would not be enticed to take drugs by their new legal status and cheapness. But price and availability, I need hardly say, exert a profound effect on consumption: the cheaper alcohol becomes, for example, the more of it is consumed, at least within quite wide limits.

I have personal experience of this effect. I once worked as a doctor on a British government aid project to Africa. We were building a road through remote African bush. The contract stipulated that the construction company could import, free of all taxes, alcoholic drinks from the United Kingdom. These drinks the company then sold to its British workers at cost, in the local currency at the official exchange rate, which was approximately one-sixth the black-market rate. A liter bottle of gin thus cost less than a dollar and could be sold on the open market for almost ten dollars. So it was theoretically possible to remain dead drunk for several years for an initial outlay of less than a dollar.

Of course, the necessity to go to work somewhat limited the workers' consumption of alcohol. Nevertheless, drunkenness among them far outstripped anything I have ever seen, before or since. I discovered that, when alcohol is effectively free of charge, a fifth of British construction workers will regularly go to bed so drunk that they are incontinent both of urine and feces. I remember one man who very rarely got as far as his bed at night: he fell asleep in the lavatory, where he was usually found the next morning. Half the men shook in the mornings and resorted to the hair of the dog to steady their hands before they drove their bulldozers and other heavy machines (which they frequently wrecked, at enormous expense to the British taxpayer); hangovers were universal. The men were either drunk or hung over for months on end.

Sure, construction workers are notoriously liable to drink heavily, but in these circumstances even formerly moderate drinkers turned alcoholic and eventually suffered from delirium tremens. The heavy drinking occurred not because of the isolation of the African bush: not only did the company provide sports facilities for its workers, but there were many other ways to occupy oneself there. Other groups of workers in the bush whom I visited, who did not have the same rights of importation of alcoholic drink but had to purchase it at normal prices, were not nearly as drunk. And when the company asked its workers what it could do to improve their conditions, they unanimously asked for a further reduction in the price of alcohol, because they could think of nothing else to ask for.

The conclusion was inescapable: that a susceptible population had responded to the low price of alcohol, and the lack of other effective restraints upon its consumption, by drinking destructively large quantities of it. The health of many men suffered as a consequence, as did their capacity for work; and they gained a well-deserved local reputation for reprehensible, violent, antisocial behavior.

It is therefore perfectly possible that the demand for drugs, including opiates, would rise dramatically were their price to fall and their availability to increase. And if it is true that the consumption of these drugs in itself predisposes to criminal behavior (as data from our clinic suggest), it is also possible that the effect on the rate of criminality of this rise in consumption would swamp the decrease that resulted from decriminalization. We would have just as much crime in aggregate as before, but many more addicts.

The intermediate position on drug legalization, such as that espoused by Ethan Nadelmann, director of the Lindesmith Center, a drug policy research institute sponsored by financier George Soros, is emphatically not the answer to drug-related crime. This view holds that it should be easy for addicts to receive opiate drugs from doctors, either free or at cost, and that they should receive them in municipal injecting rooms, such as now exist in Zurich. But just look at Liverpool, where 2,000 people of a population of 600,000 receive official prescriptions for methadone: this once proud and prosperous city is still the world capital of drug-motivated burglary, according to the police and independent researchers.

Of course, many addicts in Liverpool are not yet on methadone, because the clinics are insufficient in number to deal with the demand. If the city expended more money on clinics, perhaps the number of addicts in treatment could be increased five- or tenfold. But would that solve the problem of burglary in Liverpool? No, because the profits to be made from selling illicit opiates would still be large: dealers would therefore make efforts to expand into parts of the population hitherto relatively untouched, in order to protect their profits. The new addicts would still burgle to feed their habits. Yet more clinics dispensing yet more methadone would then be needed. In fact Britain, which has had a relatively liberal approach to the prescribing of opiate drugs to addicts since 1928 (I myself have prescribed heroin to addicts), has seen an explosive increase in addiction to opiates and all the evils associated with it since the 1960s, despite that liberal policy. A few hundred have become more than a hundred thousand.

At the heart of Nadelmann's position, then, is an evasion. The legal and liberal provision of drugs for people who are already addicted to them will not reduce the economic benefits to dealers of pushing these drugs, at least until the entire susceptible population is addicted and in a treatment program. So long as there are addicts who have to resort to the black market for their drugs, there will be drug-associated crime. Nadelmann assumes that the number of potential addicts wouldn't soar under considerably more liberal drug laws. I can't muster such Panglossian optimism.

The problem of reducing the amount of crime committed by individual addicts is emphatically not the same as the problem of reducing the amount of crime committed by addicts as a whole. I can illustrate what I mean by an analogy: it is often claimed that prison does not work because many prisoners are recidivists who, by definition, failed to be deterred from further wrongdoing by their last prison sentence. But does any sensible person believe that the abolition of prisons in their entirety would not reduce the numbers of the law-abiding? The murder rate in New York and the rate of drunken driving in Britain have not been reduced by a sudden upsurge in the love of humanity, but by the effective threat of punishment. An institution such as prison can work for society even if it does not work for an individual.

The situation could be very much worse than I have suggested hitherto, however, if we legalized the consumption of drugs other than opiates. So far I have considered only opiates, which exert a generally tranquilizing effect. If opiate addicts commit crimes even when they receive their drugs free of charge, it is because they are unable to meet their other needs any other way; but there are, unfortunately, drugs whose consumption directly leads to violence because of their psychopharmacological properties and not merely because of the criminality associated with their distribution. Stimulant drugs such as crack cocaine provoke paranoia, increase aggression, and promote violence. Much of this violence takes place in the home, as the relatives of crack-takers will testify. It is something I know from personal acquaintance by working in the emergency room and in the wards of our hospital. Only someone who has not been assaulted by drug-takers rendered psychotic by their drug could view with equanimity the prospect of the further spread of the abuse of stimulants.

And no one should underestimate the possibility that the use of stimulant drugs could spread very much wider, and become far more general, than it is now, if restraints on their use were relaxed. The importation of the mildly stimulant khat is legal in Britain, and a large proportion of the community of Somali refugees there devotes its entire life to chewing the leaves that contain the stimulant, miring these refugees in far worse poverty than they would otherwise experience. The reason that the khat habit has not spread to the rest of the population is that it takes an entire day's chewing of disgustingly bitter leaves to gain the comparatively mild pharmacological effect. The point is, however, that once the use of a stimulant becomes culturally acceptable and normal, it can easily become so general as to exert devastating social effects. And the kinds of stimulants on offer in Western cities—cocaine, crack, amphetamines—are vastly more attractive than khat.

In claiming that prohibition, not the drugs themselves, is the problem, Nadelmann and many others—even policemen—have said that "the war on drugs is lost." But to demand a yes or no answer to the question "Is the war against drugs being won?" is like demanding a yes or no answer to the question "Have you stopped beating your wife yet?" Never can an unimaginative and fundamentally stupid metaphor have exerted a more baleful effect upon proper thought.

Let us ask whether medicine is winning the war against death. The answer is obviously no, it isn't winning: the one fundamental rule of human existence remains, unfortunately, one man one death. And this is despite the fact that 14 percent of the gross domestic product of the United States (to say nothing of the efforts of other countries) goes into the fight against death. Was ever a war more expensively lost? Let us then abolish medical schools, hospitals, and departments of public health. If every man has to die, it doesn't matter very much when he does so.

If the war against drugs is lost, then so are the wars against theft, speeding, incest, fraud, rape, murder, arson, and illegal parking. Few, if any, such wars are winnable. So let us all do anything we choose.

Even the legalizers' argument that permitting the purchase and use of drugs as freely as Milton Friedman suggests will necessarily result in less governmental and other official interference in our lives doesn't stand up. To the contrary, if the use of narcotics and stimulants were to become virtually universal, as is by no means impossible, the number of situations in which compulsory checks upon people would have to be carried out, for reasons of public safety, would increase enormously. Pharmacies, banks, schools, hospitals—indeed, all organizations dealing with the public—might feel obliged to check regularly and randomly on the drug consumption of their employees. The general use of such drugs would increase the *locus standi* of innumerable agencies, public and private, to interfere in our lives; and freedom from interference, far from having increased, would have drastically shrunk.

The present situation is bad, undoubtedly; but few are the situations so bad that they cannot be made worse by a wrong policy decision.

The extreme intellectual elegance of the proposal to legalize the distribution and consumption of drugs, touted as the solution to so many problems at once (AIDS, crime, overcrowding in the prisons, and even the attractiveness of drugs to foolish young people) should give rise to skepticism. Social problems are not usually like that. Analogies with the Prohibition era, often drawn by those who would legalize drugs, are false and inexact: it is one thing to attempt to ban a substance that has been in customary use for centuries by at least nine-tenths of the adult population, and quite another to retain a ban on substances that are still not in customary use, in an attempt to ensure that they never do become customary. Surely we have already slid down enough slippery slopes in the last thirty years without looking for more such slopes to slide down.

1997

All Sex, All the Time

◈ IF THERE IS one thing of which modern man is utterly convinced, it is that he has reached a state of sexual enlightenment.
Gone forever are the days of unhealthy concealment, of absurd
Victorian taboos that led to the application of cruel and cumber-
some devices to children to prevent masturbation, to prudish cir-
cumlocutions about sexual matters, to the covering of piano legs
to preserve the purity of the thoughts of men in the drawing room.
We are at ease with our sexuality, and the poet Philip Larkin's famous ironic lines

> *Sexual intercourse began*
> *In nineteen sixty-three . . .*

express for us an important truth: that for the first time in history
we can now enjoy sexual relations without any of the unnecessary
social and psychological accretions of the past that so complicated
and diminished life. No more guilt, shame, jealousy, anxiety, frus-
tration, hypocrisy, and confusion. "Free at last, free at last, thank
God Almighty, I'm free at last!"

Yet, enlightened as we believe ourselves to be, a golden age of
contentment has not dawned—very far from it. Relations between
the sexes are as fraught as ever they were. The sexual revolution
has not yielded peace of mind but confusion, contradiction, and
conflict. There is certainty about nothing except the rightness, inevitability, and irrevocability of the path we have gone down.

A hundred yards from where I write this, twelve-year-old prostitutes often stand under streetlamps on the corner at night, wait-

ing for customers. The chief of the local police has said that he will not remove them because he considers that they are sufficiently victimized already, and he is not prepared to victimize them further (his job, apparently, being to empathize rather than to enforce the law). The local health authorities send a van round several times at night to distribute condoms to the girls, the main official concern being to ensure that the sex in which the girls take part is safe, from the bacteriological and virological point of view. It is the authorities' proud boast that 100 percent of local prostitutes now routinely use condoms, at a cost to the city's taxpayers of $135,000 a year, soon to be increased by the employment of a further outreach worker, whose main qualification, according to the recent job advertisement in the local press, will be "an ability to work non-judgmentally"—that is, to have no moral qualms about aiding and abetting child prostitution. Meanwhile, local residents (such as my neighbors, a banker, a lawyer, an antiquarian bookseller, and two university professors) who object to the presence of discarded condoms in their gardens and in the street outside their homes have been offered a special instrument with which to pick them up, in lieu of any attempt to prevent them from arriving there in the first place. And at the same time, the overwhelming majority of the work done by the social workers of the city concerns the sexual abuse of children, principally by stepfathers and mothers' boyfriends who move in after biological fathers move out.

Evidence of sexual chaos is everywhere. Not a day passes without several of my patients providing ample testimony of it. For example, yesterday I saw a woman who had tried to kill herself after her daughter, nearly sixteen years old, moved out of her home with her eight-month-old child to live with her new twenty-two-year-old boyfriend. It goes without saying that this boyfriend was not the father of her baby but a man she had met recently in a nightclub. The father of the baby was "off the scene," as the end of a liaison is invariably described: fathers round here having their exits and their entrances, their exits usually following their entrances with indecent haste.

The mother was fourteen when the father, age twenty-one, made his entrance. On discovering that she was pregnant, he did what many young men do nowadays in such a situation: he beat her up. This not only relieves the feelings but occasionally produces a miscarriage. In this case, however, it failed to do so; instead the father was caught *in flagrante delicto* (that is to say, while beating her) by my patient, who promptly attacked him, managing to injure him so severely that he had to go to the hospital. While there, he and she did a little informal plea-bargaining: she would not inform on him for having had sex with an underage girl if he did not press charges against her for having assaulted him.

My patient subsequently spent what little money she had upon her grandchild's clothes, stroller, crib, bedding, and so on, even going $1,500 into debt to fund its comfort. Then her daughter decided to move out, and my patient was mortified.

Mortified, that is, by the absence of her grandchild, for whom she thought she had sacrificed so much. This was the first objection she had made in the whole affair. She had not considered the sexual conduct of her daughter, or that of either of the two men, to be in any way reprehensible. If the father of her grandchild had not turned violent, it would never have crossed her mind that he had done anything wrong in having sex with her daughter; and indeed, having done nothing to discourage the liaison, she in effect encouraged him. And her daughter had behaved only as she would have expected any girl of her age to behave.

It might be argued, of course, that such obviously wrongful behavior has occurred always: for when it comes to sexual misdemeanor there is nothing new under the sun, and history shows plentiful examples of almost any perversion or dishonorable conduct. But this is the first time in history there has been mass denial that sexual relations are a proper subject of moral reflection or need to be governed by moral restrictions. The result of this denial, not surprisingly, has been soaring divorce rates and mass illegitimacy, among other phenomena. The sexual revolution has been above all a change in moral sensibility, in the direction of a thorough coarsening of feeling, thought, and behavior.

Watching a British comedy from the mid-1950s recently, I grasped the speed and completeness of that change. In the film was a scene in which the outraged working-class father of a pregnant teenage daughter demanded that the middle-class boy who had made love to her must now marry her. The present-day audience giggled helplessly at this absurdly old-fashioned demand, which only forty-five years previously would still have seemed perfectly normal, indeed unarguable. Such naiveté is not for us in our superior, enlightened state, however, and we prove our sophistication by finding it ridiculous.

But who, one might ask, had the deeper and subtler moral understanding of human relations: the audience of the mid-1950s or that of today? To the 1950s audience it would have been unnecessary to point out that, once a child had been conceived, the father owed a duty not only to the child but to the mother; that his own wishes in the matter were not paramount, let alone all-important, and that he was not simply an individual but a member of a society whose expectations he had to meet if he were to retain its respect; and that a sense of moral obligation toward a woman was not inimical to a satisfying relationship with her but a precondition of it. To the present-day audience, by contrast, the only considerations in such a situation would be the individual inclinations of the parties involved, floating free of all moral or social constraints. In the modern view, unbridled personal freedom is the only good to be pursued; any obstacle to it is a problem to be overcome.

And yet at the same time—in the same audience—there are many young people yearning for precisely the certainties they feel obliged to mock: young women who hope to find a man who will woo her, love her, respect her, stand by her, and be a father to her children, while there are many men with the reciprocal wish. How many times have I heard from my patients of their aching desire to settle down and live in a normal family, and yet who have no idea whatever how to achieve this goal that was once within the reach of almost everyone!

Our newspapers confirm daily the breakdown of the last vestiges of the traditional mores governing sexual relations. Last weekend, for instance, the British papers reported the third baby born to a homosexual couple by surrogate motherhood, and a liberal paper reported (with implicit approval and admiration, of course) a growing trend among women to make themselves pregnant by artificial insemination, like cattle. Of course, human sexual activity has never been very closely confined to procreation, even before the advent of birth control; but surely this is the first time that procreation has been dissociated from human sexual activity.

Thanks to the sexual revolution, current confusions are manifold. In a society that forms sexual liaisons with scarcely a thought, a passing suggestive remark can result in a lawsuit; the use of explicit sexual language is *de rigueur* in literary circles, but medical journals fear to print the word "prostitute" and use the delicate euphemism "sex worker" instead; commentators use the word "transgressive," especially in connection with sex, as a term of automatic approbation when describing works of art, while such sex offenders as reach prison have to be protected from the murderous assaults of their fellow prisoners; anxiety about the sexual abuse of children subsists with an utter indifference to the age of consent; compulsory sex education and free contraception have proved not incompatible with the termination of a third of all pregnancies in Britain and with unprecedented numbers of teenage pregnancies; the effective elimination of the legal distinction between marriage and cohabitation is contemporary with the demand that homosexual couples be permitted to marry and enjoy the traditional legal rights of marriage; and while it has become ever more difficult for married but childless parents to adopt, homosexual couples now have the right to do so. The right of lesbians to artificially aided conception by the sperm of homosexual men has likewise been conceded on the principle of nondiscrimination, and sixty-year-old women naturally enough claim the same rights to in vitro fertilization. Sexual liberty has led to an increase, not to a diminution, in violence between the sexes, both by men and by women: for people rarely grant the object of their affection the freedom they claim and practice for themselves, with a consequent rise in mistrust and jealousy—one of the great, age-old provokers of violence, as *Othello* attests. Our era admires sexual athleticism but condemns predatory conduct. Boundaries between the sexes have melted away, as men become women by surgical means, and women men, while demands for tolerance and understanding grow ever more shrill and imperious. The only permissible judgment in polite society is that no judgment is permissible.

A century-long reaction against Victorian prudery, repression, and hypocrisy, led by intellectuals who mistook their personal problems for those of society as a whole, has created this confusion. It is as though these intellectuals were constantly on the run from their stern, unbending, and joyless forefathers—and as if they took as an unfailing guide to wise conduct either the opposite of what their forefathers said and did, or what would have caused them most offense, had they been able even to conceive of the possibility of such conduct.

Revolutions are seldom the spontaneous mass upheaval of the downtrodden, provoked beyond endurance by their miserable condition, and the sexual revolution was certainly no exception in this respect. The revolution had its intellectual progenitors, as shallow, personally twisted, and dishonest a parade of people as one could ever wish to encounter. They were all utopians, lacking understanding of the realities of human nature; they all thought that sexual relations could be brought to the pitch of perfection either by divesting them of moral significance altogether or by reversing the moral judgment that traditionally attached to them; all believed that human unhappiness was solely the product of laws, customs, and taboos. They were not the kind of people to take seriously Edmund Burke's lapidary warning that "it is ordained in the eternal constitution of things that men of intemperate minds cannot be free": on the contrary, just as appetites often grow with the feeding, so the demands of the revolutionaries escalated whenever the last demand was met. When the expected happiness failed to emerge, the analysis of the problem and the proposed solution were always the same: more license, less self-control. By 1994, John Money, perhaps the most influential academic sexologist of the last third of the twentieth century, was still able to write in all seriousness that we live in an anti-sexual and taboo-ridden society. Get rid of the remaining taboos, he implied, and human unhappiness will take care of itself.

Not that there are many taboos left to destroy. In my hospital, for example, adolescent and young adult visitors to their hospitalized boyfriends or girlfriends not infrequently climb into bed and indulge in sexual foreplay with them, in full view of the staff and of old people occupying the beds opposite. This gross disinhibition would once have been taken as a sign of madness but is now accepted as perfectly normal: indeed, objection to such behavior would now appear objectionable and ridiculous. No one seems to have noticed, however, that a loss of a sense of shame means a loss of privacy; a loss of privacy means a loss of intimacy; and a loss of intimacy means a loss of depth. There is, in fact, no better way to produce shallow and superficial people than to let them live their lives entirely in the open, without concealment of anything.

There is virtually no aspect of modern society's disastrous sexual predicament that does not find its apologist and perhaps its "onlie" begetter in the work of the sexual revolutionaries fifty or a hundred years earlier. It is impossible to overlook the connection between what they said should happen and what has actually happened. Ideas have their consequences, if only many years later.

Take the question of adolescent sexuality. It has long been an orthodoxy among the right-thinking that it is perfectly natural and therefore to be welcomed. Any attempt to promote self-control would be killjoy and would drive such sexuality underground once again, resulting in a renewal of furtiveness and yet more teenage pregnancy. That is why British doctors must now connive at illegal sexual acts by distributing contraceptives to underage children without informing their parents.

The patron saint of these ideas is Margaret Mead. In 1928, when she was 27, she published her *Coming of Age in Samoa*, which made her famous for the rest of her life. When she died 50 years later, her book was still selling 100,000 copies a year. Few university students during that half-century did not read it or at least know its message.

Mead was a pupil of the anthropologist Franz Boas, an extreme cultural determinist who wanted to prove that the angst of adolescence was, like most important human realities, the product of culture, not of biology, as was then generally believed. If a society could be found somewhere in the world in which adolescents felt no angst, QED: hormones were not the cause. Mead, intellectually infatuated with Boas and dependent upon him for her academic advancement, was preordained to find in Samoa what he wanted her to find.

And find it she did—or thought she did. Here was a South Sea paradise in which adolescents spent the years between puberty and marriage in uninhibited sexual activity, as much as possible with as many as possible. There was no jealousy, no rivalry, no anxiety, no guilt, just fun—and, *mirabile dictu*, no unwanted pregnancy, a somewhat surprising fact that did not arrest Mead's attention then or at any time later. So Mead added a value judgment to Boas's proposition: here was a culture that dealt with sex better than we, as the absence of Samoan adolescent unhappiness proved.

Of course her depiction of Samoa was in error: she was taken in by her ironical informants. Sexual morality in Samoa was puritanical rather than liberal, and owed much to the efforts of the London Missionary Society, no advocate of free love during adolescence or at any other time.

But few people are averse to the message that one can indulge appetites freely without bad consequences to oneself or others, and so Mead's book passed as authoritative. And if youthful sexual libertinism was possible in Samoa with only beneficial social and psychological effects, why not in Sheffield and Schenectady? Even had her depiction of Samoa, *per impossibile*, been accurate, no one paused to wonder whether Samoa was a plausible model for Europe or America or whether the mere existence of a sexual custom—the celibacy of religious communities down the ages, say—should warrant its universal adoption.

So generations of educated people accepted Mead's ideas about adolescent sexuality as substantially correct and reasonable. They took the Samoan way of ordering these matters as natural, enjoyable, healthy, and psychologically beneficial. No doubt Mead's ideas were somewhat distorted as they filtered down into the class of people who had not read her (or any other) book: but it does not altogether surprise me now to meet people who started living in sexual union with a boyfriend or girlfriend from the age of eleven or twelve, under the complaisant eyes of their parents. Only someone completely lacking in knowledge of the human heart—someone, in fact, a little like Margaret Mead—would have failed to predict the consequences: gross precocity followed by permanent adolescence and a premature world-weariness.

For example, an intelligent young woman patient of twenty came to me last week complaining of the dreariness of life. She had given up on education at the age of thirteen to pursue sexual encounters full-time, as it were, but the initial excitement had worn off, leaving only greyness and a vague self-disgust behind. At the time of her induction into the sexual life, of course, she had been led to believe that it was the key to happiness and fulfillment, that nothing else counted: but as with all monochromatic descriptions of the ends of life, this had proved bitterly disappointing.

And, of course, once boundaries, such as the age of consent, that are to some extent arbitrary but nonetheless socially necessary are breached, they tend to erode entirely. Thus children inhabit a highly sexualized world earlier and earlier, and social pressure upon them to exhibit sexualized behavior starts earlier and earlier. A schoolteacher friend recently told me how she had comforted a seven-year-old who was in tears because a girl in his class had insulted him, calling him a virgin. She asked whether he knew what the word meant.

"No," replied the little boy. "But I know it's something horrible."

The sexual revolutionaries' ideas about the relations between men and women—entailing ever greater sexual liberty, ever less mastery of the appetite—were so absurd and utopian that it is hard to understand how anyone could have taken them seriously. But mere absurdity has never prevented the triumph of bad ideas, if they accord with easily aroused fantasies of an existence freed of human limitations.

One of the earliest of the sexual revolutionaries, the English doctor and litterateur Havelock Ellis, had strong opinions about marriage and relations between the sexes in general. For many years this supremely strange and repulsive, though learned, man— who looked like a tripartite cross between Tolstoy, Rasputin, and Bernard Shaw; who was one of the many semi-pagan ideological nudists that England produced at the end of the nineteenth century; and who never achieved full sexual arousal until his second wife urinated on him in his late middle age—won respect on both sides of the Atlantic as a sexual sage. His works enjoyed immense prestige and wide circulation during the first third of the twentieth century. He attached supreme, almost mystical, importance to the sexual act (perhaps not surprisingly, given his great difficulties with it); his conception of ideal relations between men and women was completely untouched by any awareness of human reality and was at the same time implicitly sordid. Many venerated his views and made them the basis of an entire philosophy of life, as did D. H. Lawrence, another English sexual pagan.

Ellis believed in a complete fusion of two souls that, in the course of the sexual act, would achieve union with the creator of the universe (whom, being a modern pagan, he refrained from calling God). But for this mystical fusion to take place, the relations between men and women first had to be freed of all the dross of petty considerations, such as law, custom, and what was then considered morality. "Our thoughts of duty and goodness and chastity are the things that need to be altered and put aside; these are the barriers to true goodness," Ellis wrote. "I foresee the positive denial of *all* positive morals, the removal of *all* restrictions. I feel I do not know what license, as we should term it, may not belong to the perfect state of Man." Once freed from all restraint—social, moral, legal, and political—man would regain his natural beauty and generosity of character. He would become again the noble sexual savage. It never occurred to Ellis and his ilk that he might become instead the prototypical caveman of the cartoonists, dragging off his mate of the moment by the hair.

Ellis was not alone in this adolescent utopian dream of unlimited sex without tears as the key to both human happiness and goodness. Another English doctor who achieved world fame as a sexologist more than half a century later, Alex Comfort, whose sex manuals sold by the tens of millions, was of much the same opinion. Although he apparently had great difficulty in explaining the facts of life to his own son, he advised all fifteen-year-old boys—again, with the notable exception of his own son—to take condoms with them to parties, and he explained to adolescents in his manual *The Facts of Love* that pornography was "a long word for any kind of book or movie about sex which someone wants to prohibit." An anarchist and pacifist who saw all institutions merely as emanations of power, which he believed to be the supreme enemy of human happiness, he had opposed armed resistance to Nazism during World War II. In *Barbarism and Sexual Freedom* (which two phenomena he regarded as diametrically opposed) he wrote: "Normality of the biological kind . . . excludes religious coercion, economic pressure and social custom. Institutions based upon the State and other such bodies, civil or religious, have no place in biological sexuality." In other words, sex should float free from all considerations except the sexual attraction of the moment.

What is left but personal whim in the determination of sexual conduct? It is precisely the envelopment of sex (and all other natural functions) with an aura of deeper meaning that makes man human and distinguishes him from the rest of animate nature. To remove that meaning, to reduce sex to biology, as all the sexual revolutionaries did in practice, is to return man to a level of primitive behavior of which we have no record in human history. All animals have sex, but only man makes love. When sex is deprived of the meaning with which only the social conventions, religious taboos, and personal restraints so despised by sexual revolutionaries such as Ellis and Comfort can infuse it, all that is left is the ceaseless—and ultimately boring and meaningless—search for the transcendent orgasm. Having been issued the false prospectus of happiness through unlimited sex, modern man concludes, when he is not happy with his life, that his sex has not been unlimited enough. If welfare does not eliminate squalor, we need more welfare; if sex does not bring happiness, we need more sex.

It is a matter of curiosity that such puerile drivel could ever have been mistaken for serious thought; but the fact is that Ellis's and Comfort's view of the proper basis for the relationship between men and women is now the commonly accepted, even orthodox, one. Explaining their decision to part from the mother or father of their children, my patients routinely tell me that they do not experience with her or him the bliss they clearly expected to experience, and that their union had no cosmic significance *à la*

Ellis. The possibility that their union might serve other, slightly more mundane and other-regarding purposes has never occurred to them. That depth of feeling is at least as important as intensity (and in the long run, more important) is a thought completely alien to them. With no social pressure to keep them together, with religious beliefs utterly absent from their lives, and with the state through its laws and welfare provisions positively encouraging the fragmentation of the family, relationships become kaleidoscopic in their changeability but oddly uniform in their denouement.

I have seen Comfort's utopia, and it does not work.

One has only to compare the writings of the sexual revolutionaries with a single sonnet by Shakespeare (to take only one of literature's myriad subtle reflections on love) to see what a terrible retrocession in understanding and refinement those writings represent:

> *When my love swears that she is made of truth*
> *I do believe her though I know she lies,*
> *That she might think me some untutored youth*
> *Unlearned in the world's false subtleties. . . .*
> *O, love's best habit is in seeming trust,*
> *And age in love loves not to have years told.*
> *Therefore I lie with her, and she with me,*
> *And in our faults by lies we flattered be.*

The subtlety of this understanding of the human heart, to say nothing of the beauty with which it is expressed, has never been excelled. Everything is there: the human need for deep companionship throughout life, the inevitability of compromise if such companionship is to last, and the acceptance of the inherent limitations of existence that is essential to happiness. Shakespeare's view answers the needs of man as a physical, social, and spiritual being—and no one with the slightest acquaintance with his work could accuse him of being anti-sexual.

Another rhetorical technique the sexual revolutionaries favor (apart from the appeal to a fantasy of limitless eroticism) has been to try to dissolve sexual boundaries. They preached that all sexual behavior is, by nature, a continuum. And they thought that if they could show that sex had no natural boundaries, all legal prohibition or social restraint of it would at once be seen as arbitrary and artificial and therefore morally untenable: for only differences in nature could be legitimately recognized by legal and social taboos.

The arch-proponent of this viewpoint was Alfred Kinsey, author of the famous reports, a man who spent the first half of his professional life studying and classifying gall wasps and the second half studying and classifying orgasms: though in the event, he was to find the taxonomy of gall wasps far more complex than that of orgasms, since he came to the conclusion that all orgasms were created equal and endowed by their creator with certain inalienable rights, etc.

Kinsey's program had two pillars, designed to free people of the sexual restraint that he considered the cause of all their miseries. The first was to establish by means of extensive survey that the sexual behavior of Americans was very different from what it was supposed to have been according to traditional morality. Without doubt he skewed his survey to ensure this intensely desired result. He had a personal ax to grind, of course: he was himself a man of perverted sexual appetite, though like most sexual revolutionaries he was a very late developer. He pierced his own foreskin and put metal wires up his urethra, and his filming of two thousand men masturbating to ejaculation (ostensibly to discover how far they could project their semen) must rank as one of history's most prodigious feats of voyeurism.

Having established to his own very great satisfaction that 37 percent of American males had had a homosexual experience leading to orgasm, having expended three times as much space in his report on homosexuality as on heterosexuality, and having intimated that all forms of sexuality lie on a spectrum rather than existing as separate, discrete activities, Kinsey then established the second pillar of his sexual philosophy: what might be termed the Forty Million Frenchmen Can't Be Wrong argument. Our sexual morality, he said, must be based not upon a striving toward goodness, toward an ideal, but upon what actually happens here and now. Otherwise we are merely chasing chimeras. The fact that such a morality extends the scope of what actually happens by providing an instant justification for whatever anybody does whenever he does it appears not to have struck Kinsey; but if it had, it wouldn't have worried him.

Applied in the sphere of financial honesty, Kinsey's argument would have been seen as preposterous at once. A survey of the kind he conducted into financial probity would surely have revealed that there is hardly a person in the world who has never in his life been dishonest—who has never taken so much as a paper clip or overestimated expenses on a tax return. No sensible person would conclude from this that the striving for honesty is a sham, that it is pointless to have any laws regarding financial conduct, that it is perfectly all right for shopkeepers to shortchange their customers and for their customers to steal from them. And yet this is precisely what the sexual revolutionaries, Kinsey foremost among them, have argued in the realm of sex.

The work of dissolving the boundaries continues, never satisfied that it has gone quite far enough—as if to accept one limitation or taboo would be to admit the legitimacy of all. I recently read in a criminological journal that the only conclusive argument against bestiality with chickens was that the chickens were non-consenting to the liaison, and that therefore their (human? avian?) rights were infringed. And while Kinsey wanted to make all sexual activity equal, psychologist and sex therapist John Money went even further, insisting upon the almost infinite plasticity of what he termed "gender identity." He wrote that: "Beyond the four basic reproductive functions [impregnation, menstruation, gestation, and lactation], nothing—nothing—of the differences between the sexes is immutably ordained along sex lines. . . . As long as the four basic reproductive functions are allowed for, . . . no particular gender stereotype is unalterable. A society has almost unlimited choice of role design or redesign." Thus there is no normal and no abnormal either: whatever we choose is good, or at least not bad.

Money became, needless to say, a hero of radical feminists who wished to claim that female "sex roles" had been imposed upon them arbitrarily by society. A self-proclaimed "missionary of sex," who advocated all sex, all the time, he left to each individual the free choice of creating his sexual identity. No perversion was alien to him, pedophilia included, which only those in a state of "moralistic ignorance," he asserted, would condemn. Money became the multi-culturalist of sex: with polymorphous perversity replacing cultural diversity as a good in itself.

Money was not only a theoretician but a practitioner, head of the Johns Hopkins Gender Identity Clinic. It was his belief in the unlimited malleability of human sexuality that led him, in his most famous case, to advise the parents of a baby whose penis was nearly cut off during a botched circumcision that he should henceforth be brought up as a girl. After all, what was a girl but a boy in skirts? And what was a boy but a girl given toy guns to play with? The requisite operations once performed on the unfortunate child, to complete what the botched circumcision had nearly accomplished, all would be well.

The boy brought up as a girl continued to show the boylike qualities familiar to any mother. He or she fought like a trooper, was more interested in cars and trains than in dolls, was adventurous and boisterous, and, given a jump rope as a gift, used it only to tie up his or her twin brother. As he or she grew older, he or she expressed no sexual interest whatever in boys. Professor Money continued to describe the case as an unqualified success, and for a long time the scientific and journalistic worlds were fooled. Yes, it was possible to turn little boys into little girls by fiat. No, sexual identity was not fixed by biology but was socially constructed, a product of convention and custom. Money's view was accepted uncritically as true and therefore it became orthodox (I remember being taught it as a medical student).

When at age fourteen the subject of Money's experiment was told of what had happened to him or her in early life, he or she immediately determined to revert to masculinity, for he or she, depressed and maladjusted all through childhood, had known all along in inchoate fashion that something was wrong: and, with yet more reconstructive surgery, he made a sound readjustment to masculinity and is now happily married to a woman. This was a part of the story that Money never told, for it contradicted the philosophy to which he had devoted his entire life's work. It suggested that we cannot construct a sexual utopia of the kind that he, a once-repressed farm boy from New Zealand, had dreamed about.

Such theories could only license and encourage ever more bizarre conduct and appetites, of course. And the escalation of appetite that Jeffrey Dahmer experienced, eventually finding sexual release only in congress with the intestines of his increasing numbers of murdered victims, can occur on a mass scale also, as witness a recent film, funded by the Canadian Arts Council, "normalizing" necrophilia.

And so now, when I meet lesbian patients who have used a syringe full of a male friend's semen to impregnate themselves, they challenge me to dare to pass judgment on them. For who am I to judge what is natural or unnatural, normal or abnormal, good or bad? Transsexuals, in my experience, exude a triumphalist moral superiority, conscious of having forced the world to accept what it previously deemed unacceptable. Perhaps, if they haven't read John Money, they have read the eerily similar opinion of Havelock Ellis, that sexual perversions (which he called "erotic symbolisms") are what most distinguish man from the animals, and are his supreme achievement: "[O]f all the manifestations of sexual psychology, . . . they are the most specifically human. More than any others they involve the potently plastic force of the imagination. They bring us the individual man, not only apart from his fellows, but in opposition, himself creating his own paradise." They constitute the supreme triumph of idealism.

Here is the gnostic reversal of good and evil in the realm of sex, the technique that Sartre and Mailer employed in the realm of criminality, transforming Jean Genet and Jack Abbott into existential heroes. Of course it is true that human sexuality is different from that of the beasts, but surely not because men can desire intercourse with chickens while chickens cannot reciprocate. We must go to literature, not to sexologists, if we want to understand the difference.

It isn't necessary, of course, for people to read the original sources of ideas for those ideas to become part of their mental furniture. But the ideas and sensibilities of the sexual revolutionaries have now so thoroughly permeated our society that we are scarcely aware any longer of the extent to which they have done so. The Dionysian has definitively triumphed over the Apollonian. No grace, no reticence, no measure, no dignity, no secrecy, no depth, no limitation of desire is accepted. Happiness and the good life are conceived as prolonged sensual ecstasy and nothing more. When, in my work in an English slum, I observe what the sexual revolution has wrought, I think of the words commemorating the architect Sir Christopher Wren in the floor of St. Paul's Cathedral: *si monumentum requiris, circumspice.*

2000

Who Killed Childhood?

◈ THERE IS nothing so absurd, wrote Macaulay in the middle of the nineteenth century, as the spectacle of the British public in one of its periodic fits of morality; but now the spectacle is sinister as well as absurd. To make up for its lack of a moral compass, the British public is prey to sudden gusts of kitschy sentimentality followed by vehement outrage, encouraged by the cheap and cynical sensationalism of its press. Spasms of self-righteousness are its substitute for the moral life.

On no subject is the British public more fickle and more prone to attacks of intense but shallow emotion than childhood. Not long ago, for example, a pediatrician's house in South Wales was attacked by a mob unable to distinguish a pediatrician from a pedophile. The attackers, of course, came from precisely the social milieu in which every kind of child abuse and neglect flourishes, in which the age of consent has been de facto abolished, and in which adults are afraid of their own offspring once they reach the age of violence. The upbringing of children in much of Britain is a witches' brew of sentimentality, brutality, and neglect, in which overindulgence in the latest fashions, toys, or clothes and a television in the bedroom are regarded as the highest—indeed only— manifestations of tender concern for a child's welfare.

There is no more powerful stimulus to emotional dishonesty than a guilty conscience, which perhaps explains why for a few days—but a few days only—the country was transfixed by the joint trial of Ian Huntley and Maxine Carr. Huntley was accused of the abduction and murder of two ten-year-old girls, Holly Wells and Jessica Chapman, in the hitherto tranquil, or at least unnoticed, town of Soham in Cambridgeshire. Carr stood trial for perverting the course of justice by giving Huntley a false alibi.

It was the second time that the case had caught the nation's attention, to the exclusion of almost everything else. The first time was when the two little girls, who were best friends, went missing, on the evening of August 4, 2002. They slipped out of Holly's house, probably to buy candy, at about 5 P.M., and never returned. The two-week search for them, which finally uncovered their bodies in a ditch near the Lakenheath Air Force Base, was the largest manhunt in British history. The press extensively reported every false lead; people who hardly believed in God lit candles in churches around the country and prayed for the girls in public. Because the two were wearing T-shirts in the Manchester United colors when they disappeared, a huge banner, asking for information about their whereabouts, was unfurled in the Budapest stadium where Manchester United was playing in the European Cup. The *Daily Express*, a newspaper owned by Richard Desmond (who first made his fortune in pornography with titles such as *Horny Housewives* and *Asian Babes*), offered a reward of $1.8 million for information about the whereabouts of the two girls. This offer soon led to the arrival of thousands of sightseers in Soham, hoping to turn up the bodies in the fields surrounding the town and claim their reward. The police were inundated with thousands of calls of the flying-saucer-sighting variety.

Television stations aired an appeal to the abductor by David Beckham, the blond soccer superstar (the girls were wearing soccer shirts emblazoned with his number when they disappeared). Among the people of Soham who made tearful appeals on television to the abductor to return the children to their homes was the man who killed them, Ian Huntley. He emerged as an activist in the search, helping to arrange the police press conferences in Soham and even consoling the father of one of the girls. The window of his house displayed a banner asking the abductor for the safe return of the girls.

Huntley, the caretaker of the school they attended, was discovered almost at once to be the last man undoubtedly to see them alive, but his girlfriend, Maxine Carr, misled the police by claiming to have been with him for the whole evening on which they disappeared. But after ten days it emerged not only that there was material evidence to connect Huntley with the disappearance, but also that Carr had lied to the police. That day she had gone to Grimsby, her hometown, to visit her mother. The police took Huntley and Carr into custody; the bodies were discovered soon afterward.

Such was the scale of the publicity and ersatz emotion generated by the murder of the girls that British soccer crowds, notorious throughout the world for their propensity to drunken vulgarity and primitive violence, observed a minute's silence before the following weekend's games. Ten thousand bouquets, liberally admixed with teddy bears and poetic effusions, were laid around Soham Church, often by people who had come hundreds of miles: it was Princess Diana all over again. Before long, a nursery offered a new pink rose named after the Soham tragedy (at an introductory price of only thirty-six dollars).

The case revealed the moral swamp that is contemporary Britain. Embarrassingly for the police, two of the investigating officers were themselves arrested soon after the discovery of the bodies for having child pornography downloaded onto their laptop computers. The press treated Huntley and Carr as if their guilt were already established beyond reasonable doubt—as if no presumption of innocence were necessary in their case—so much so that the trial judge had to consider whether they could receive a fair trial at all. And true to the principles of mob rule, whenever the accused appeared in court at preliminary hearings, a crowd of several hundred gathered outside the courtrooms, screaming, shouting, hurling eggs, and demanding the reinstitution of the death penalty. They would have torn the accused limb from limb had they been allowed to do so.

Oddly enough, many mothers saw fit to bring their young children into this melee. The children were clearly terrified, and many burst into tears, but the vengefully self-righteous crowd did not see its conduct as a form of mass child abuse. On the contrary, the mothers said they had come to demand the protection of children from perverts and monsters.

In one of the more minor scandals of the case, a photographer from the *News of the World*, a sensationalist Sunday newspaper, got himself hired as a guard in the high-security prison where Huntley was awaiting trial and succeeded in taking forbidden photographs of the most hated man in Britain. In his job application, the photographer had given a nonexistent company as a character reference and used a false personal address. Moreover, those who hired him had failed to notice that his passport stated that he was a journalist.

The trial took place fifteen months after the murder. It dominated the press and the airwaves for the six weeks it lasted. Huntley's defense was that he found the girls outside his house; Holly Wells was having a nosebleed. He took the girls indoors, to his bathroom, where he had run a bath for himself. Sitting on the edge of the bath while holding a tissue to her nose, Holly slipped into the water and drowned. Jessica Chapman screamed, and to quiet her Huntley put his hand over her mouth. The next thing he knew, she had slipped to the ground, dead.

Maxine Carr, his girlfriend, who had been away in Grimsby, said that she misled the police because she believed Huntley to be innocent, and because he had told her that he had once been accused of rape. He said that he could not face false accusations again. Blinded by love—or possibly in mortal fear of him were he acquitted—she said she had been with him at the time the girls disappeared. Despite the fact that she had not participated in the actual killings, she was quickly branded a second Myra Hindley, the notorious Moors murderess, who with her associate Ian Brady had kidnapped, tortured, killed, and buried at least five children on the Lancashire Moors in the early 1960s, and who, until her death in prison last year, had remained a symbol of absolute evil.

The jury took a surprising length of time to come to its verdict. Doubtless it had trouble deciding whether Maxine Carr knew of Huntley's guilt when she lied to the police. If she did, she was guilty of a more serious offense than if she didn't. In the end, the jury opted for the less grave offense. But it found Huntley guilty of the two murders, and the judge duly sentenced him to two life terms.

It goes without saying that his crimes were appalling—but it did not go without saying. On the contrary, one commentator in the *Daily Mirror*, a Labour-supporting tabloid, wrote what was virtually an incitement to murder. "Hanging is too good for him," he wrote, as if to recall the infamous anonymous pamphlet of 1701, "Hanging Not Punishment Enough." "He knows what prison dishes out to those who abuse and kill children. Hopefully now that justice has been done, he will receive it."

He appeared, in other words, to be appealing to prisoners to kill, rape, or maim Huntley, apparently unaware that the great majority of prisoners in Britain have themselves fathered and then abandoned their own children, leaving them to a social environment in which neglect is the best they can hope for, and abuse is what they most likely will receive. Perhaps it is not entirely a co-incidence that the *Daily Mirror* has a large circulation in that market niche.

After the trial ended, much came out in the press about Huntley's past. He was, it appeared, a sexual offender who had never actually been convicted of anything, but who had been once charged with rape and had come to the notice of his local police on several occasions. He and his girlfriend had moved to Soham for a new start in life; and when he applied for the job of school caretaker there, a police check, now mandatory for all would-be school employees, failed to reveal any of the suspicions raised about him in the past. The public seamlessly transferred its fury, at least if the press was to be believed, from the man himself to the police, for having failed to prevent the monster from having been hired. Hysterical fears of Ian Huntleys lurking everywhere raged: surveys demonstrated that a majority of parents feared more than ever for the safety of their children, and a tenth of adults even said that the Soham murders would discourage them from ever having children.

The stories told about Huntley to the papers hardly reflected well on British parents or British society. One girl, Laura, revealed how Huntley, then aged eighteen, had sex with her when she was twelve, more or less by force. Her mother, when she discovered what had happened, did not call the police.

Another girl, Janine, related how she had moved in with Huntley when she was fifteen. Where, one might ask (but no one in the British press did ask), were the parents when this happened? The relationship did not last, however: "He was cheating on me with a lot of other girls as well, including some of my friends at school," Janine reported. She left him just after her sixteenth birthday.

Karen told a touching story. When he was eighteen and she was sixteen, she "fell for him," but he was so rough with her when they had sex that "it put me off doing it again." Nevertheless she continued to see him until he became too jealous and possessive. "Those gorgeous eyes that girls always spotted could be evil as well as charming," she recalled. Unfortunately, though, she met him again in a pub five years later, by which time she was engaged to be married. "Now he was a man. We were laughing and getting drunk. He was charming me again, and I fell for it again." The happy couple went back to his home. "He locked the bedroom door. Then his mood changed. He overpowered me, got on top of me, and forced me to have intercourse."

You might have thought that by then she had had enough of Mr. Huntley: but no. Their relationship continued, though not for long. "It only lasted a short time before his then current girlfriend threw stones at the window." Karen added, "I couldn't tell anyone [about him] because I was engaged."

Louise, when aged eleven, met Huntley at a fun fair and was flattered to be attractive to a man of twenty-two. He took her home and had sex with her. He persisted in his sexual activities with her until she threatened to scream. But Louise continued to see Huntley until "the relationship petered out as he chased other girls." He was then living in the kind of town where everyone knows everyone else.

Huntley threw Alison down the stairs when she was sixteen and had told Huntley that she was pregnant by him. They had already been living together for several months (that is to say, before the legal age of consent), and he had already beaten her unconscious with a pool cue. So far as anyone knows, Alison's parents had done nothing to intervene in the relationship, nor did they exercise any kind of control over her.

Chantel was fifteen when she met Huntley (then twenty-one) and moved in with him. Her parents actually helped her to set up a home with him, thus being willing and knowing accessories to what the law says is a sexual crime. Her father, a plumber, said, "We did everything we could to help them set up home together. . . . He even worked with me for a while."

Huntley then imprisoned and starved Chantel, locking her in their dingy bedsit for two weeks. In the end, she collapsed from weakness, exhaustion, and dehydration, and went to a hospital. Her father continues the story: "I was so livid when I found out, but I did not want to get into any trouble with the police by dealing with Huntley myself." What did he do, then? "We just had him run out of town. He was told he had better move out in no uncertain terms." It takes no great effort of imagination to know what those terms would have been. Actually, the father did not want to go to the police because he had acted as his daughter's pander: for, unlike Huntley, he could not plausibly have claimed not to know his own daughter's age.

Yet another woman had a child by Huntley. She was fifteen when she and Huntley moved into a bedsit together, "despite protests from her parents, who were alarmed at their daughter having underage sex with a man six years older than she," according to the story she related to the *Daily Mirror*. They did not go to the police, however, and the couple soon moved in with Huntley's mother, who was apparently perfectly prepared for her son to live with a fifteen-year-old girl. (After the trial she called for the death penalty for her son.) The girl's parents were not quite as powerless as the story suggests, however, because once Huntley had been accused of rape, they banned him from seeing the child he had had with their daughter.

The police tried to investigate another case of a girl who had sex with Huntley before the age of consent, but neither she nor her mother would cooperate with them.

Huntley was once married. His wife knew that he had been violent to other women but married him nonetheless. Within a short time he had performed a termination of pregnancy on her by the method usually employed by men like him: he kicked her repeatedly in the stomach.

She left him soon after, going to live with his father. There she realized that "she had strong feelings for his brother"—whom she subsequently married.

The one charge of rape lodged against Huntley had to be dropped for lack of evidence. The complainant alleged that he had raped her while she was on her way home from a nightclub. But she had been videotaped dancing with him earlier that evening in the nightclub, an episode that she was too drunk to remember. The police decided, not without reason, that a witness who could not remember important periods of the material time because she was too drunk to do so would not cut a very convincing figure in the witness box, especially in a case in which it was her word against that of the accused.

All his victims describe Huntley as a jealous, possessive, controlling kind of man, who wanted to be the sole focus of a girl's attention, no matter how flagrantly unfaithful he was to her. This, certainly, was one of the reasons commentators offered as to why Maxine Carr should have been prepared to lie on his behalf: in effect, they theorized, she had ceased to be an autonomous, thinking being and had merely carried out his will. Her mother, on the other hand, suggested another reason: that she was so deeply and madly in love with him that she wanted to protect him at all costs.

On the evening when Huntley was murdering the two girls, however, Carr went out to a nightclub in Grimsby where, after a few drinks, she attempted to have sex with a seventeen-year-old boy and a twenty-two-year-old man, baring her breasts to them both. She had gone to the club in the company of her mother, who saw everything. Nevertheless her mother did not see anything in her daughter's conduct to make her revise her view that the love of her life was a hundred miles away, in Soham. The headline of the article in the *Times* about Maxine Carr on the day following her and Huntley's conviction was: A QUIET HOMELOVING GIRL WITH THE FATAL KNACK OF FALLING FOR THE WRONG MEN.

After the trial was over, press commentary concentrated exclusively on the failure of the Grimsby police to inform the Cambridgeshire police of Huntley's proclivities. It is true that they failed, with lamentable inefficiency, to carry out their statutory tht:

duties. But the press devoted not a single word to the social meaning of Huntley's encounters with underage girls, to the existence of so many complaisant and complicit parents, or to the sluttish public drunkenness among young women that is to be seen in the center of all British cities and towns and that makes so many allegations of rape impossible to investigate. (The police often ask my opinion in such cases, the latest one being a young mother of three, who, entrusting her children by different men to a babysitter, went out for the night, got so drunk that she could not remember how she arrived in a strange man's bedroom, and then, on waking, cried rape.) There was no commentary, either, on the reasons why so many young British males are jealous, possessive, and controlling in the fashion of Ian Huntley, or why, with the exception of the murders themselves, his behavior was not so very much out of the ordinary. In a democratic age, only the behavior of the authorities is subject to public criticism; that of the people themselves, never. This is a modern version of Rousseau's doctrine: if it weren't for the authorities, the people would be good.

As for the national outpouring of ersatz grief, reminiscent of the scenes that followed the death of Princess Diana, it surely spoke not of feeling but of an egotistical inability to feel, compensated for by outward show. The British seem not only to have forgotten but would no longer even be able to understand the words of their national poet:

> Nor are those empty-hearted whose low sound
> Reverbs no hollowness.

Insofar as there were people—other than the girl's relatives and friends, of course—who truly mourned, it was not only for the death of the children but for the death of childhood.

2004

A Horror Story

IN THE psychotherapeutic worldview to which all good liberals subscribe, there is no evil, only victimhood. The robber and the robbed, the murderer and the murdered, are alike the victims of circumstance, united by the events that overtook them. Future generations (I hope) will find it curious how, in the century of Stalin and Hitler, we have been so eager to deny man's capacity for evil. Every now and again, however, a case arises that stirs a faint memory of this capacity—forgotten soon afterward.

The case of Frederick and Rosemary West is an example of this phenomenon. It began with public levity, passed through a brief stage of appalled disgust, and is now principally a commercial opportunity for publishers and tour operators. But rightly considered it reminds us of what men are capable, once all restraints are removed; and because the Wests' crimes were so much worse than can be explained by their personal circumstances, the case reminds us also of what should be obvious, but alas is not, that no conceivable perfection of society will ever render redundant all external restraints upon human conduct.

As soon as the police had dug up the first human remains in the backyard of Number 25, Cromwell Street, Gloucester, in February 1994, bookmakers all over the country started to take bets on how many bodies would eventually be found there. There is nothing that lifts English national morale as effectively as a really gruesome murder, and murders do not come any more gruesome than those that took place on Cromwell Street.

In the end, nine sets of human remains were uncovered at that address, including those of the daughter of the proud houseowners, Mr. Frederick and Mrs. Rosemary West (born in 1943 and 1953, respectively). The remains of their stepdaughter were found at their previous address, Number 25, Midland Road, Gloucester, while those of Mr. West's first wife, Rena, and those of one of his mistresses—pregnant at the time of her demise—were discovered in two fields near Mr. West's birthplace, the picturesquely named village of Much Marcle. As Agatha Christie once so perceptively remarked, there is a deal of wickedness in an English village.

Before he hanged himself on New Year's Day 1994, in Winson Green Prison, Birmingham, Mr. West confessed to a confidante—who has since been offered more than $150,000 to relay the confidences, as yet unpublished, to a newspaper—that he had killed at least twenty others. It is difficult, however, to place much credence in his confession, for Fred was never very good at figures and, according to members of his family, could never remember exactly how many children he had, or their names. I have heard a rumor that the true number of his victims was nearer to sixty than twenty. Admittedly, the bearer of the rumor was a man with reason to be nervous: he was a doctor whose office extension had recently been completed by Fred, a small-time builder. Fred had obligingly offered to prepare the foundations for the extension while the doctor was away on vacation: a thoughtfulness that, in retrospect, may have been motivated by more than a mere desire to spare the doctor the noise that construction inevitably entails.

Another acquaintance of mine turned down Fred's offer to build him a conservatory: the builder's manner put him off. Indeed, there was something distinctly odd about the murderer's appearance: he looked like an intermediate stage in the transformation of man into werewolf. Extremely hirsute, he was short and had a limp from an early motorbike accident; he had the traditional bad teeth of the English working class, but his eyes glittered brightly, and there is no doubt that, despite his poor education, bucolic accent, and limited vocabulary, he was able to exert a hypnotic charm over susceptible and inexperienced young women.

Rosemary's appearance was rather more ordinary. She put on weight early and looked matronly before her time. There was nothing in her face or bearing that suggested a voracious sexual appetite or uncontrolled sadism. While she was in prison awaiting trial, she looked every bit the fond grandmother who knitted socks for her grandchildren.

It is unlikely we shall ever know for certain how many lives Fred and Rose cut short: an entire county would have to be dug up, and since the relatively limited excavations so far undertaken by the police, comprising two hundred square yards at most, have already cost $2.25 million, a really thorough investigation would bankrupt the nation. Whatever the true number of victims, the Gloucester of the Wests is now as firmly etched onto the national consciousness as the Whitechapel of Jack the Ripper. Rose's trial monopolized the attention of the public as O. J. Simpson's trial had done in America, though only through the medium of the press: cameras (quite rightly) not being allowed in British courtrooms, to preserve whatever little remains of the majesty of the law.

Gloucester is a small cathedral city of about 100,000, where the city council has conclusively demonstrated that with the right combination of 1960s urban planning and an undiscriminating welfare policy, the degraded inner-city conditions of much larger conurbations may be successfully reproduced in small country towns. The ancient but decayed medieval city center has been re-placed almost in its entirety by concrete buildings that would have gladdened the hearts of another famous couple, the Ceauşes-cus. As for Cromwell Street itself, once decent and even elegant nineteenth-century housing has degenerated into near slum, where a shifting population of drifters rent dismal rooms by the week, and everything looks uncared for: the paint peels off the woodwork, the stucco crumbles, and litter—the packaging of junk food—flutters in the breeze. On the end wall of another ter-race of houses nearby, a muralist has depicted the glorious march of the British masses from unemployment during the depression to single parenthood in the nineties, headed by a Rastafarian with dreadlocks who holds aloft a banner saying "Give Us a Future": by which is meant, according to the smaller banners held aloft behind him by the single mothers, more generous welfare payments. Next door to the Wests' house is a mean little Seventh-Day Adventist church, whose noticeboard offers passersby "peace and sanity in a mad, mad world."

Number 25, Cromwell Street, does hold out promise of urban renewal, however. Some have suggested that it be turned into a memorial for the Wests' victims. Others, more commercial-minded, have suggested that it be made into a waxwork museum, which would undoubtedly transform it into one of the principal tourist attractions of these islands, stimulating the economy of Gloucester as a whole. Some idea of Cromwell Street's touristic potential can be gauged from the fact that, even two years after the first uncovering of the bodies there, a steady and never-ending stream of the curious passes the house: this despite the windows' having been filled in by cinder block and the doors securely fastened against entry, so that there is nothing whatever to see. Local storekeepers are now so accustomed to the prurience of strangers that they direct them to Cromwell Street even before they have opened their mouths to ask the way.

The revelations during the recent trial of Mrs. West (she was found guilty on three counts of murder on November 21, and on a further seven the following day) were deemed so deeply shocking that even the British gutter press, no enemy to sensation or salaciousness, unanimously declined to print the grimmer details. The jurors were offered psychotherapy after the trial, and some of them may have accepted; the crime reporters present rejected a similar offer with contumely. This solicitousness on the part of the authorities for the emotional welfare of witnesses to the trial was in marked contrast to their previous indifference to the evidence that the Wests were murdering their way through a multitude, almost—but not quite—unmolested for a quarter of a century.

The Wests committed their murders both for practical reasons and for sexual gratification. At first, Fred killed alone. The dismembered body of his pregnant mistress, who was last seen alive in July 1967 (when Fred was twenty-four), was discovered buried in a field in June 1994. As far as is known, she was the first person he had killed—apart from a three-year-old child whom he had accidentally run over in a van and crushed to death in Glasgow. He killed his mistress because his first wife, a prostitute and petty criminal from Glasgow, with whom he lived only intermittently, was becoming jealous. He then killed, dismembered, and buried his first wife in 1970. By this time, he was living with Rosemary, who was fifteen when they had first met at a bus stop. Her parents had been so alarmed by her liaison with a man ten years older than she (though her father had himself sexually abused her) that they delivered her up to the care of the local social services department, which, however, permitted her to continue to see Fred. Aged sixteen, she gave birth to their daughter, Heather, whom they were jointly to murder sixteen years later.

In 1971, Rosemary West killed Charmaine, the eight-year-old daughter of Fred's first wife by an Indian bus driver in Glasgow, who lived with the Wests when she was not in the care of the local social services. Fred was then serving a prison sentence for minor property offenses. "Darling, about Char," Rosemary wrote to him in prison. "I think she likes to be handled rough. But darling, why do I have to be the one to do it. I would keep her for her own sake, if it wasn't for the rest of the children." The rest of the children, at that stage, were Fred's own daughter by his first wife (Charmaine's mother) and the Wests' first child.

When Charmaine no longer appeared at her school, the teachers and her friends (one of whom had witnessed Mrs. West beating her severely with a wooden spoon while her wrists were tied behind her back with a leather belt) were told that she had been taken away by her real mother—who by then had been decomposing for two years in a field. No further efforts to trace Charmaine were ever made: a child had simply vanished without a trace.

Fred and Rose were married in 1972, Fred describing himself in the marriage register as a bachelor. Soon thereafter they first sexually assaulted Charmaine's half-sister, Anna Marie, then eight years old, Fred's daughter by his first wife. They took her down into the cellar, her hands already tied and her mouth gagged; Mrs. West sat on her face while Fred raped her. They told her that she should be grateful to have such caring parents and that it had all been for her own good. They kept her out of school for a few days and told her that if she informed anyone of what had happened, she would receive a severe beating. Thereafter she was repeatedly and regularly strapped to a metal frame, erected in the cellar by Fred, so that his wife could indulge in lesbian sexual acts with her. At school, Anna Marie would often refuse to participate in sports, lest the injuries inflicted by her parents on her be revealed; but no one realized that anything was wrong or thought to intervene.

It was in late 1972 that Fred and Rose first abducted a young woman from the streets. The presence of a woman in the cruising car reassured their victims that nothing was amiss with the offered ride. Their first such victim was sexually assaulted in the car by Rose, then punched unconscious by Fred, then tied up in masking tape, then dragged into the cellar of Number 25, Cromwell Street, then further assaulted by Rose, then raped by Fred (while Rose was upstairs making a cup of tea for them all, a peculiarly English touch to the story), and finally released on condition—to which she assented—that she return in the near future for more. Instead she went to the police.

The police convinced her that it would be better to charge the Wests with indecent assault rather than with kidnap and rape: that way the Wests would plead guilty, and she would not have to make a traumatic appearance in court. In the event, the Wests were fined seventy-five dollars each, a leniency of sentencing that even the most ardent of liberals would, I trust, find unfortunate in the light of subsequent events.

It was after their lucky escape that the Wests got down to some serious killing, deciding that if their sexual playmates were going to go to the police, it would be better to dispose of them altogether. They abducted a number of single girls—six at the very least—whom they sexually tortured, binding them up with masking tape (and, in one case, inserting plastic tubes into her nostrils so that she could continue to breathe—a technique they learned, most probably, from a pornographic magazine later found in their possession), finally killing, dismembering, and burying them in the cellar that was later used as their children's bedroom.

These were by no means the Wests' only activities. They took in lodgers, to many of whom Mrs. West, with her husband's active encouragement, made love, and some of whom heard the nocturnal screams of the tortured downstairs; they refrained from intervening, however, because they accepted the Wests' explanation that the screams arose from their daughter's nightmares. Occasionally the police would raid Number 25 and would prosecute some of the lodgers for possession of small quantities of marijuana—an ironic attention to detail, under the circumstances.

The Wests also ran a brothel (patronized by the local police, according to rumor), in which Mrs. West was the sole prostitute. The Wests repeatedly placed advertisements in local magazines seeking W.E.—i.e., Well-Endowed—West Indian Males for Sex with Housewife. (Of Mrs. West's eventual eight children, only four were by Fred, and four by her clients, three of them being of mixed race.) Initially Mrs. West entertained men only for pleasure, both her own and her husband's; but with so many mouths to feed, she soon turned professional. Fred enjoyed watching and listening to his wife at work, and installed an intercom system so that he could hear her wherever he happened to be in the house. He also installed spy holes and videotaped his wife on many occasions, later showing the films to his children on one of the seven video machines in the house (all of them stolen, for Fred was a petty thief as well as a mass murderer, with eleven convictions for theft). He also offered tapes of women being tortured to the local video store, but the store owner declined the offer and went to the police instead, who, anxious in the then-new permissive moral climate to demonstrate that they were as broad-minded as anybody, did nothing.

This was far from the only missed clue that something strange was going on at Cromwell Street. The Wests' sadistic treatment of their children led to thirty-one visits to the emergency room of the local hospital, for conditions as disparate as peculiar puncture marks on the feet to female genital injuries allegedly caused by having to stop suddenly while riding a bicycle. One daughter, age fifteen, attended the hospital with an ectopic pregnancy (Fred was the father, of course), but although this meant that, legally speaking, a rape *must* have taken place, the age of consent being sixteen, no one thought to investigate further or even to ask the simple question as to who the father was: for to have done so would have been regarded as implicitly *judgmental.*

Rosemary was so angered by her son one day that she grabbed him round the throat and throttled him nearly to unconsciousness. There were bruises on his neck afterward—clearly finger marks— and the blood vessels had burst in the whites of his eyes; but when he was asked about these signs at school, he said that he came by them while playing in a tree with a rope around his neck, when he accidentally fell. This was regarded as a perfectly adequate and acceptable explanation. He regularly appeared in school covered in bruises.

The Wests switched from male to female lodgers. Mrs. West, being bisexual, found them as much fun to be with as men; and Mr. West (who, incidentally, had often boasted of his ability to perform abortions and may actually have performed a few) re- garded them as more reliable payers of rent than casually em- ployed males, especially if the girls were single, pregnant, and in receipt of welfare.

But most of the Wests' victims were picked up by the wayside. The majority of them—though not quite all—were rebellious and difficult teenagers from broken homes, who had either run away from home or had been in the care of the social services. One, however, was a university student of medieval English, the niece of the novelist Kingsley Amis, while another was the daughter of a well-to-do Swiss businessman, hitchhiking her way to Ireland. Ex- tensive searches by the police failed to find them: there was noth- ing to connect them to the Wests.

More typical were the cases of Lynda Gough and Juanita Mott. Lynda was a rebellious and headstrong girl from Gloucester who suddenly left home, leaving behind a note for her parents: "Please don't worry about me. I have got a flat and will come and see you sometime."

Three Saturdays later, having heard nothing from her daughter, Mrs. Gough managed to trace her via her friends to Cromwell Street. By then, Lynda had been tortured, raped, cut up, and buried. Rosemary West came to the front door wearing Lynda's slippers; moreover, Mrs. Gough recognized her daughter's clothes hanging on the washing line. Mrs. West told Mrs. Gough that her daughter had departed for the seaside resort of Weston-super-Mare, leaving her belongings behind. After a further lapse of time, Mrs. Gough and her husband searched Weston for Lynda but of course did not find her. They sought the help of several organizations, including the Salvation Army, but never reported her as missing to the police. Thereafter they made no further efforts to trace their daughter: perhaps they did not really care, or thought that their daughter, who had attended a school for the mentally backward, had the right and duty to make a life for herself at the age of nineteen (the age at which she disappeared), untrammeled by parental guidance.

Juanita Mott was the daughter of an American serviceman whose parents split up when she was very young. She left both school and home at age fifteen; three years later, having already lodged with the Wests earlier, she accepted a lift from them and was abducted by them, suspended from the beams in their cellar, and then murdered. She too was never reported as missing.

As the number of the West children grew, and as they matured, it became more difficult to conduct burials at home. The abuse of the older children, however, escalated, so that their son, then age thirteen, ran away from home and stayed for a while with friends. When he returned home he was beaten and told that he would soon be old enough to have intercourse with his mother (the normal thing for a boy, his father told him). Heather, the eldest daughter, then age sixteen, vehemently rejected the advances of her father and was told that this meant she was a lesbian. She was then tied up, raped, killed, and buried in the backyard rather than the cellar. The eldest son was asked to help with the digging, under the impression that it was for a fishpond. The Wests explained Heather's disappearance to the other children as her decision to work away at a holiday camp. She was the last person to be buried at 25 Cromwell Street, and her parents set up the family barbecue precisely over the site of her grave.

Five years later—and probably many murders later—the Wests were arrested for the rape of a fourteen-year-old girl. The court case collapsed because the girl ultimately refused to testify in public; but during the police investigation an immense quantity of pornographic material, including ninety-nine homemade videos, was found at Cromwell Street. The police destroyed the videos, apparently without ever having watched them; they may well have contained recordings of the murders.

The detective in charge of the investigation (who was later officially reprimanded when she tried to sell her story to a publisher for $1.5 million) had by now uncovered evidence of terrible abuse and wanted urgently to interview Heather. No one, however, knew her whereabouts, though one of the children had told a social worker that there was a family rumor that she was buried under the patio. The social worker did not think to inform the police; but in any case the detective was by now highly suspicious. She attempted to convince her superiors that there was a good case for searching—indeed, excavating—the West house, but they procrastinated for more than a year, worried about the expense of it. Meanwhile, Fred had gone from Gloucester Prison, where he had been held on a charge of rape, to a bail hostel in Birmingham (where, he later boasted, he had killed a woman), to complete freedom after acquittal in court. It was not very long, however, before the game was over, this time for good.

After their final arrest, on February 25, 1994, the Wests chose different paths. Fred confessed—though only gradually and teasingly, with many different versions, no doubt to taunt the police—while Rosemary maintained a posture of injured innocence. When she was asked by the police why, if she were innocent, she had not reported her daughter as missing, she replied, "So I have to snitch on my own daughter now, do I?"—thus revealing that, for her, to resort to the help of the police when a sixteen-year-old daughter was missing was a form of betrayal, rather than the natural response of a worried mother.

Both the Wests showed a sentimental streak, however, confirming Jung's aphorism that sentimentality is a superstructure covering brutality. Fred was writing his memoirs at the time he hanged himself, which he entitled "I Was Loved by an Angel"; and he gave his son advice in his letters from prison, letters that incidentally throw a lurid light upon the level of education in England: "Working all day and night like I did . . . you cud end up in hear, all ways no What going on in your home pliase son all Ways spend as much time With your Wife and children as you can and love your Wife and children, there the most valuable thing you will ever have in your life so look after it son." His suicide note included the following suggestion for the epitaph on his tombstone, as if his death had brought to an end a modern version of *Romeo and Juliet*:

In loving memory
FRED WEST   ROSE WEST
Rest in peace where no shadow falls
In perfect peace
he waits for Rose, his wife

Rose, on the other hand, turned to poetry. From prison she wrote to her daughter, whom she had repeatedly beaten, raped, and abused:

I love you like the birds and bee's
I love you like the flower's sweet,
I love you like the deep blue sea's,
And memories dear to keep.

It was as if the pair of them believed that the utterance of a cloying sentiment or two could establish the purity of their hearts, irrespective of their actions.

Of course, speculation began at once in all the British newspapers as to what social and psychological forces might have molded this extraordinarily depraved couple. For example, both of them came from large and poor families in which violence was commonplace. But none of their siblings approached Fred or Rose in their ferocity or cruelty, even if some of Rose's brothers were petty criminals. Fred was brought up in a rural cottage without electricity; at the age of nine he was required to slaughter animals. His brothers were raised in similar fashion, however, and they did not end up slaughtering humans. And if the so-called cycle of deprivation explained everything, or indeed anything, how are we to account for the strong moral sense their eldest and worst-abused children appear to have developed?

No doubt there have always been deeply perverted people, and it was a mischance that two of them such as the Wests should have found each other. But reflecting on their story, it is difficult not to conclude that their path was smoothed by the increasing uncertainty during the last three decades as to the line between acceptable and unacceptable conduct, or even whether such a line exists at all. Increasing sexual permissiveness was taken by the Wests, whose libidos were a great deal stronger than their powers of reason, to entail a complete absence of limits; they told those whom they raped that what they were doing was only "natural" and therefore unobjectionable. And they operated in an atmosphere in which, increasingly, self-discipline was not accepted as a necessary condition of freedom—in which everyone's merest whim was law. Moreover the majority of their victims were young people cast adrift without the guidance of adults, of whom they believed themselves to have no need, and of whom they were in any case highly intolerant.

The West case revealed how easily, in the anonymity of the modern urban environment, and in the midst of crowds, people may disappear; and how such disappearances are made all the easier by a collective refusal—in the name of individual liberty—of parents to take responsibility for their children, of neighbors to notice what is happening around them, of anyone to brave the mockery of libertines in the defense of some standard of decency. And the various public agencies—the police, the schools, the social services, the hospitals—proved no substitute for the personal concern that families were once supposed to have provided, but that, in a permissive climate in which tolerance all too often shades into indifference, many provide no longer. The failure of these agencies was not accidental, but inherent in their nature as bureaucracies: the state is not, and never will be, a substitute for an old-fashioned Mum and Dad.

I meet adolescents each day in my hospital whose conduct renders them vulnerable to any Wests who might present themselves. These adolescents think they are streetwise, but if so, they are streetwise, life foolish. Last week, for example, I spoke to the fourteen-year-old daughter of Indian parents, who had repeatedly run away from home because her parents insisted that she go out not more than one evening a week and return by ten at night.

"I want them to be like an English family," she said to me.

"And what is an English family like?" I asked.

"They look after you till you're sixteen," she replied. "Then you find a flat on your own."

I sincerely hope she never meets her West: for were she ever to do so, no one would come to her rescue. All that is necessary for evil to triumph, said Burke, is for good men to do nothing; and most good men nowadays can be relied upon to do precisely that. Where a reputation for intolerance is more feared than a reputation for vice itself, all manner of evil may be expected to flourish.

1996

The Man Who Predicted
the Race Riots

◈   NOT SINCE I lived and worked briefly in South Africa under
the apartheid regime have I seen a city as racially segregated as
Bradford in the north of England. In South Africa, of course, the
racial segregation was a matter of law: and the single road that
separated the African townships from the white residential and
business districts could be sealed off easily by an armored car or
two. Then, if the blacks rioted, they would (in the words of my
Afrikaner informant) "only foul their own nest."

It goes without saying that there is no law to separate the races
in Bradford. But stone walls do not a ghetto make: which is why it
is possible in one part of Bradford to conclude that it is a typical
northern British city, dominated almost completely by a white
working class, and in another (reached by driving along a single
major road that bisects the city) that it is an outpost of Islam,
whose people have changed their hemisphere of residence but not
their culture or way of life.

Once a thriving woolen-manufacturing town, Bradford
reached an acme of prosperity in the second half of the nineteenth
century, before its success evaporated, leaving behind a legacy of
municipal pride and magnificence, of splendid public buildings in
the Gothic and Renaissance-revival styles. (It was on the head of a
Bradford millionaire that Eliot sarcastically stuck a silk hat in
"The Waste Land.") Even many of the terraced working-class
homes are elegantly and expensively faced in stone, so that large

areas of the city resemble nothing so much as Bath with textile mills added.

One beautiful part of the city, Hanover Square, is a small masterpiece of Victorian town architecture: it was long the residence of Margaret McMillan, who some ninety years ago founded the British nursery-school movement and agitated for improvements in working-class education. Nowadays there is not a white face to be seen in the square, nor that of any woman. It is strictly men only on the street, dressed as for the Northwest frontier (apart, incongruously, from their sneakers); a group of them perpetually mills around outside the house that functions as a *madrassa*, or Muslim school. Horace's famous line of two millennia ago comes to mind: they change their skies, not their souls, who run across the sea.

The informal ghetto that separates the races almost as effectively as South Africa's formal ones nevertheless makes interracial rioting much easier. And in July last year, only a few weeks before September 11, serious riots (the worst in Britain for twenty years) did in fact break out in Bradford and other similar northern English cities, such as Blackburn and Oldham. White gangs clashed with Pakistani ones, indulging for several days in the pleasures of looting and arson, under the comforting illusion that they were fighting for a cause. The young whites believed themselves to have been dispossessed of something by the young Muslims, without the young Muslims believing they had inherited anything from the young whites. Both groups were united in—though not, of course, by—their resentment.

One man was not at all surprised at this outbreak of inchoate racial fury. He was Ray Honeyford, the headmaster of a middle school in an immigrant area of Bradford in the early 1980s. He knew that the official multi-culturalist educational policies that he was expected to implement would sooner or later lead to social disaster such as these riots: and when he repeatedly exposed the folly of these policies in print, the advocates of "diversity"—who maintain that all cultures are equal but that opinions other than their own are forbidden—mounted a vicious and vituperative campaign against him. For at least two years the Honeyford Affair, as it was known, was a national preoccupation, calling forth endless newspaper and broadcast commentary, the man himself often branded a near-murderous racist and ultimately drummed out of his job. Hell, it seems, hath no fury like a multi-culturalist contradicted.

Of course, the events of September 11 have concentrated at least some British minds a little harder on questions of cultural diversity and group loyalties. A disturbingly large number of British Muslims, from a variety of backgrounds, supported al-Qaeda. Three of the captives now held at Guantanamo were from Britain, all of them products of the kind of home that now exists in Bradford and elsewhere by the thousands. Two chemistry Ph.D.s of Bangladeshi origin are on trial in Birmingham, accused (not for the first time) of conspiracy to manufacture explosives for terrorist ends, and they are unlikely to have been acting merely as individuals. Several British Islamic charities were found to have been channeling money to terrorists. Richard Reid, who tried to blow up a transatlantic airliner with Semtex in his sneakers, had converted to Islam in a British jail. The newly alert intelligence service in the prison in which I work now believes that fully half the Muslim prisoners there sympathize with the World Trade Center attacks: and since Muslim prisoners are by far the fastest-growing group of prisoners in Britain, already far overrepresented in the prison population, this is enough to disturb even the most complacent. The British elites, it appears, would have done far better to have heeded rather than vilified Honeyford almost two decades ago.

Honeyford's fundamental ideas were as logical, sensible, and coherent as they were unfashionable. He argued that the 20 percent of Bradford's population who were Islamic immigrants were in Britain to stay, with no intention of returning home; and that both for their own sake and for Britain's, they needed to be integrated fully into British society. The children of immigrants needed to feel that they were truly British, if they were to participate fully in the nation's life; and they could acquire a British identity only if their education stressed the primacy of the English language, along with British culture, history, and traditions.

Honeyford did not believe that the cultural identity necessary to prevent the balkanization of our cities into warring ethnic and religious factions implied a deadening cultural or religious uniformity. On the contrary, he used the example of the Jews (who emigrated to Britain, including to Bradford and nearby Manchester, in substantial numbers at the end of the nineteenth century) as an example of what he meant. Within a generation of arrival, Jews succeeded, despite the initial prejudice against them, in making a hugely disproportionate contribution to the upper reaches of national life as academics, cabinet ministers, entrepreneurs, doctors and lawyers, writers and artists. The upkeep of their own traditions was entirely their own affair, and they relied not at all on official patronage or the doctrines of multi-culturalism. This was Honeyford's ideal, and he saw no reason why the formula should not work again, given a chance.

When the storm broke over his head in 1984, Honeyford had been headmaster of Drummond Middle School for four years. His school was another magnificent piece of high Victorian public architecture, grand without being overbearing, and conveying implicit aesthetic and moral lessons to its pupils, however humble the homes from which they came. The collapse of the cultural confidence that had produced such a school building was soon complete, however: after his departure as headmaster, Drummond Middle School quickly received a new Urdu name and then was burned down beyond repair by an arsonist, as also happened to a similar, neighboring school, now completely boarded up. All children in the area now go to school in the preternaturally hideous buildings of modern British architecture, whose combination of Le Corbusian functionalism, financial stringency, and bad taste are a complete visual education in brutality.

Honeyford brought his troubles down upon him when he published an article exposing the follies of multi-cultural education in the conservative *Salisbury Review*, after the worthy but dull *Times Educational Supplement*, for which he had previously written, turned it down. That the article appeared in the *Salisbury Review* gave almost as much offense as its content: for in the new, officially diverse Britain, the *Review*'s brand of cultural conservatism is beyond the pale. The *Review*'s name hardly ever appears without the qualification that it is rabidly right wing, thereby implying that no intellectual engagement with the ideas expressed in it is ever necessary—only the kind of opposition appropriate to dealing with brown- and blackshirts. All opinion is free, of course, but some opinions are freer than others.

In his article, Honeyford enumerated some of multi-culturalism's problems and contradictions. The debasement of language that multi-culturalist and anti-racist bureaucrats have brought about, he argued, has made it extremely difficult to talk honestly or clearly about racial and cultural matters. By lumping together all ethnic minorities as "black" in order to create a false dichotomy between white oppressors on the one hand and all minorities on the other, for example, these bureaucrats could obscure such complex and unpleasant realities as the continued hostility between Sikhs and Muslims, or the Muslim ill-treatment of women. Only by means of such deliberate blindness can the tenets of multi-culturalism, feminism, and universal human rights be reconciled. Honeyford quoted Orwell to the effect that politicized language "is designed to make lies sound truthful" and "to give an impression of solidity to pure wind."

He held up a very concrete example of how the multi-culturalist mind-set was damaging education. Immigrant parents, he observed, frequently sent their children back to Pakistan and Bangladesh for months or even years at a time, often precisely to keep them from acquiring any British cultural characteristics. Though this practice had obvious social and educational disadvantages for people destined to spend their adult lives in Britain—and though it was entirely illegal as well—the authorities turned a blind eye to it.

British law obliges a parent, once his child is registered at a school, to ensure that he attends regularly; any white parent who kept his child away for so long would undoubtedly be prosecuted and punished. In the case of the children of immigrants, however, school authorities never pressed charges but instead directed teachers to keep absentees' places open indefinitely and to regard their absence as a culturally, and therefore educationally, enriching experience. As Honeyford summed up: "I am left with the ethically indefensible task of complying with a school attendance policy which is determined not, as the law requires, on the basis of individual parental responsibility, but by the parent's country of origin—a blatant and officially sanctioned policy of racial discrimination." Seventeen years after he described the problem, it remains unsolved.

Honeyford's article also called into question the unwarranted but widespread assumption that differences in educational achievement between groups reflect unfair discrimination and nothing else. In the *Times Educational Supplement*, Honeyford had already mentioned the great and growing educational success of some subgroups of Indian immigrants, which he linked to their system of values—with the obvious corollary that the educational failure of other groups was not attributable to British racial prejudice. As a result, a black pressure group in London branded him a "blatant racist" and demanded his dismissal if he did not accept "massive in-service training courses to purge [him] of [his] racist ideology and outlook."

Finally, and even less forgivably, Honeyford made mention of the plight of another ethnic minority in his school: the white children, who, when the article appeared, made up a mere 5 percent of the pupils. Their education suffered in a school dominated by pupils from non-English-speaking homes, he said, and he suggested that officials disregarded their plight because their parents, ill-educated and inarticulate, had formed no pressure group, and no political capital could be made of them. (Once, in the 1960s, the city council had tried to disperse the children of non-English-speaking immigrants to schools throughout the city, precisely to prevent the development of ghetto schools such as Drummond, but race-relations experts and bureaucrats declared this practice to be discriminatory and therefore stopped it—to Honeyford's regret.)

No one would have noticed Honeyford's article—the *Salisbury Review*'s circulation being extremely small—had the local newspaper not drawn attention to it; but then an unremitting campaign against him gathered steam, under the leadership of local politicians and pressure groups, some of which sprang up expressly to get him fired. He received several death threats, which the police took seriously enough to connect his home by alarm directly to the local police station. (I repeat: he had proposed only that Muslim children should be fully integrated into British society—the very opposite of suggesting that they should be discriminated against or in any way maltreated.) For months he had to enter his own school under police protection from the small but militant group of pickets that formed outside and grew in size and volume whenever a television camera appeared. A few small children, too young to understand what was at issue, learned from their parents to chant "Ray-cist! Ray-cist!" at him and to hold up denunciatory placards, some with a skull and crossbones above his name. The Bradford Education Authority considered the possibility of a court order against the demonstrators, since children who continued to attend the school were likewise insulted as stooges and sellouts, but it decided that such an order would only inflame passions further. Thus political extremists learned a valuable lesson: intimidation pays.

No insult was deemed too scurrilous to hurl at Honeyford. A press release issued by an extremist group calling itself the Bradford Drummond Parents' Support Group is a case in point: "One wonders," it read, "whether Mr. Honeyford will be the next person to be advocating bird shots [sic] fired at the black children at the school." Several months into the affair, Honeyford's employer, the Bradford Education Authority, ordered him to attend a kind of public trial in a local college on the charge of disloyalty. Fortunately the eminent lawyer representing him argued so vigorously that those intending to convict him had to acquit him.

The affair took its toll on him: after all, he was not a career politician but merely a schoolmaster who had spoken out against what he thought was wrong. His health, and his wife's, began to suffer; and when his employer arranged to meet him secretly and offered him $30,000 in cash to agree to publish no further articles for three years, he was tempted to accept. His wife dissuaded him, however, telling him that he would never be able to live with himself if he concluded so sordid a deal.

Intimidation spread and became a tool against anyone who supported Honeyford. A Sikh shopkeeper told him that he supported his stand, to which Honeyford replied, "Why don't you say so to the television people?" The answer was that the man's business would be stoned or burned down if he were to do so. For very similar reasons, the majority of school headmasters in Bradford who agreed with Honeyford in private remained silent in public.

The campaign against Honeyford disregarded entirely the fact that no complaint had ever been received about his competence as a teacher, or the fact that there were always far more applications to his school (mainly by Muslim parents) than there were places. Several attempts by political zealots on the city council to have him dismissed failed for lack of legal cause. Eventually, however, he accepted early retirement: constant abuse, however unjustified, is wearing—and he wanted to spare his pupils, who, like him, had to enter the school through a daily gauntlet of forty vituperative pickets. Although teaching was his vocation, Honeyford never returned to it. Instead he wrote several books about race relations and education, and became a freelance journalist.

It is difficult, meeting him now, to believe that he was ever a natural controversialist. He lives in modest retirement. He is mild-mannered and unexcitable. He was once a naive believer in the freedom of expression and the virtues of plain speaking—formerly a tradition in the north of England. He thought that different opinions might be tolerated, not having grasped that the purpose of those who argue for cultural diversity is to impose ideological uniformity. In his naiveté, he also enunciated some painful truths that were tangential to his central argument: for example, that Pakistan (the country of origin of most of the immigrants in his area) had been unable throughout its history to develop either democratic institutions or a culture of tolerance. However accurate, such an inflammatory statement enabled his detractors to pretend that he was motivated by prejudice: a useful diversionary tactic from Honeyford's underlying argument, that the induction of immigrant children into British culture and traditions was necessary both for their own personal good and for the nation's future social harmony.

But it is impossible to meet Honeyford for long without realizing that he is a passionate believer in the redemptive power of education and in the duty of schools to give the children of immigrants the same educational opportunities as everyone else. His only regret about the affair was that it drastically shortened his teaching career. It is a tribute to the power of Orwellian language that a man who believes these things should successfully have been labeled a racist.

His own personal history would suggest some direct insight into the problems of the disadvantaged. His father was an unskilled laborer injured in the First World War and able to work only intermittently thereafter. His mother was the daughter of penniless Irish immigrants. His parents had eleven children, six of whom died in childhood. They lived in a small house in Manchester with no indoor lavatory (and not a single book). He was brought up in a place and in times when the next meal was not guaranteed to appear. Yet despite the poverty, theft was unheard of: everyone felt able to leave his front door unlocked.

Through nervousness rather than lack of ability, Honeyford failed the examination, given at the age of eleven, for entrance to the local selective, state-run grammar school, a guaranteed (and by far the easiest) route out of the slums. He recalls having been disappointed by his failure, but it was not the blow to his self-esteem that today's educationists claim that all such failure must be—so that the principal goal of education should be the preservation of the child's self-esteem from the slings and arrows of outrageous competition.

As was the British working-class custom of the time, he left school at the earliest opportunity to find work, an office job that bored him. Restless, he decided to go to night school to get a high school education, and he then gained acceptance for teacher training. After receiving his teaching diploma, he obtained a B.A. by correspondence course and finally a master's degree (in linguistics). Such a man is unlikely to wish to deny opportunity to others: and his experience led him to conclude that only educational traditionalism can offer the severely disadvantaged such opportunity.

Though he failed to gain admission to a selective grammar school himself, he bitterly regrets the passing of these quintessentially meritocratic institutions, which allowed so many poor but talented children a chance to join the mainstream and even to excel in Britain's open society. (This fact alone suggests his large-mindedness: how many people can resist erecting a general principle out of their personal disappointments?) Such schools, which ideologues condemned as elitist, might have helped prevent the strife that convulses Bradford today by creating a common culture and an interracial elite. They would have drawn (by and large, though not of course with 100 percent accuracy) the most intelligent children from diverse areas, allowing lasting friendships to form across the races among people likely to grow up to be the most prominent citizens of their respective groups.

Instead, today the schools draw children of every level of ability, but from a single geographical area only. If that area is white only, then the school will be white only; if Muslim, the school will be Muslim. Different ethnic and cultural groups—their differences preserved in educational aspic—live in geographical proximity but without any real contact. It does not require a Nostradamus to predict the consequences.

Of course the forces that deny a British education to the Muslims of Bradford have also denied it to the whites, who—on the grounds of the new need for a multi-culturalist outlook—receive schooling that leaves them virtually as ignorant of British history and traditions as their Muslim counterparts, without giving them any useful knowledge of any other history or traditions. They are thus left to float free in the sea of popular culture, without cultural or moral bearings and prey to the inchoate but deep resentments that this popular culture so successfully inculcates.

The children of Bradford's Muslim immigrants also bear the stamp of popular culture and the sense of loss and of entitlement denied that it fosters: indeed, this is the only aspect of the West with which, inescapably, they have any contact. In one Muslim community center that I visited in Bradford, the Muslim Youth League advertised a course of lectures: Islam for the 21st-Century Dude.

The scene is set for a battle of competing resentments. If we had only listened to Ray Honeyford, we should not have sown what we are now reaping and what we (and others) shall reap for many years to come.

2002

When Islam Breaks Down

◆ MY FIRST CONTACT with Islam was in Afghanistan. I had been through Iran overland to get there, but it was in the days of the shah's White Revolution, which had given rights to women and had secularized society (with the aid of a little detention without trial and torture). In my naive, historicist way, I assumed that secularization was an irreversible process, like the breaking of eggs: that once people had seen the glory of life without compulsory obeisance to the men of God, they would never turn back to them as the sole guides to their lives and politics.

Afghanistan was different, quite clearly a pre-modern society. The vast, barren landscapes in the crystalline air were impossibly romantic, and the people (that is to say the men, for women were not much in evidence) had a wild dignity and nobility. Their mien was aristocratic. Even their hospitality was fierce. They carried more weapons in daily life than the average British commando in wartime. You knew that they would defend you to the death, if necessary—or cut your throat like a chicken's, if necessary. Honor among them was all.

On the whole I was favorably impressed. I thought they were freer than we. I thought nothing of such matters as the clash of civilizations, and experienced no desire, and felt no duty, to redeem them from their way of life in the name of any of my own civilization's ideals. Impressed by the aesthetics of Afghanistan and unaware of any fundamental opposition or tension between the modern and the pre-modern, I saw no reason why the West and Afghanistan should not rub along pretty well together, each in its own little world, provided only that each respected the other.

I was with a group of students, and our appearance in the middle of a country then seldom visited was almost a national event. At any rate, we put on extracts of *Romeo and Juliet* in the desert, in which I had a small part, and the crown prince of Afghanistan (then still a kingdom) attended. He arrived in Afghanistan's one modern appurtenance: a silver convertible Mercedes sports car—I was much impressed by that. Little did I think then that lines from the play—those of Juliet's plea to her mother to abrogate an unwanted marriage to Paris, arranged and forced on her by her father, Capulet—would so uncannily capture the predicament of some of my Muslim patients in Britain more than a third of a century after my visit to Afghanistan, and four centuries after they were written:

> Is there no pity sitting in the clouds
> That sees into the bottom of my grief?
> O sweet my mother, cast me not away!
> Delay this marriage for a month, a week,
> Or if you do not, make the bridal bed
> In that dim monument where Tybalt lies.

How often have I been consulted by young Muslim women patients, driven to despair by enforced marriages to close relatives (usually first cousins) back "home" in India and Pakistan, who have made such an unavailing appeal to their mothers, followed by an attempt at suicide!

Capulet's attitude to his refractory daughter is precisely that of my Muslim patients' fathers:

> Look to't, think on't, I do not use to jest
> Thursday is near, lay hand on heart, advise:
> And you be mine, I'll give you to my friend;
> And you be not, hang, beg, starve, die in the streets,
> For by my soul, I'll ne'er acknowledge thee,
> Nor what is mine shall ever do thee good.

In fact the situation of Muslim girls in my city is even worse than Juliet's. Every Muslim girl in my city has heard of the killing of such as she back in Pakistan, on refusal to marry her first cousin, betrothed to her by her father, all unknown to her, in the earliest years of her childhood. The girl is killed because she has impugned family honor by breaking her father's word, and any halfhearted official inquiry into the death by the Pakistani authorities is easily and cheaply bought off. And even if she is not killed, she is expelled from the household—*O sweet my mother, cast me not away!*—and regarded by her "community" as virtually a prostitute, fair game for any man who wants her.

This pattern of betrothal causes suffering as intense as any I know of. It has terrible consequences. One father prevented his daughter, highly intelligent and ambitious to be a journalist, from attending school, precisely to ensure her lack of Westernization and economic independence. He then took her, aged sixteen, to Pakistan for the traditional forced marriage (silence, or a lack of open objection, amounts to consent in these circumstances, according to Islamic law) to a first cousin whom she disliked from the first and who forced his attentions on her. Granted a visa to come to Britain, as if the marriage were a bona fide one—the British authorities having turned a cowardly blind eye to the real nature of such marriages in order to avoid the charge of racial discrimination—he was violent toward her.

She had two children in quick succession, both of whom were so severely handicapped that they would be bedridden for the rest of their short lives and would require nursing twenty-four hours a day. (For fear of giving offense, the press almost never alludes to the extremely high rate of genetic illnesses among the offspring of consanguineous marriages.) Her husband, deciding that the blame for the illnesses was entirely hers, and not wishing to devote himself to looking after such useless creatures, left her, divorcing her after Islamic custom. Her family ostracized her, having concluded that a woman whose husband had left her must have been to blame and was the next thing to a whore. She threw herself off a cliff, but was saved by a ledge.

I've heard a hundred variations of her emblematic story. Here, for once, are instances of unadulterated female victimhood, yet the silence of the feminists is deafening. Where two pieties—feminism and multi-culturalism—come into conflict, the only way of preserving both is an indecent silence.

Certainly such experiences have moderated the historicism I took to Afghanistan—the naive belief that monotheistic religions have but a single, "natural" path of evolution, which they all eventually follow. By the time Christianity was Islam's present age, I might once have thought, it had still undergone no Reformation, the absence of which is sometimes offered as an explanation for Islam's intolerance and rigidity. Give it time, I would have said, and it will evolve, as Christianity has, to a private confession that acknowledges the legal supremacy of the secular state—at which point Islam will become one creed among many.

That Shakespeare's words express the despair that oppressed Muslim girls feel in a British city in the twenty-first century with much greater force, short of poisoning themselves, than that with which they can themselves express it, that Shakespeare evokes so vividly their fathers' sentiments as well (though condemning rather than endorsing them), suggests—does it not?—that such oppressive treatment of women is not historically unique to Islam, and that it is a stage that Muslims will leave behind. Islam will even outgrow its religious intolerance, as Christian Europe did so long ago, after centuries in which the Thirty Years' War, for example, resulted in the death of a third of Germany's population, or when Philip II of Spain averred, "I would rather sacrifice the lives of a hundred thousand people than cease my persecution of heretics."

My historicist optimism has waned. After all, I soon enough learned that the shah's revolution from above was reversible—at least in the short term, that is to say the term in which we all live, and certainly long enough to ruin the only lives that contemporary Iranians have. Moreover, even if there were no relevant differences between Christianity and Islam as doctrines and civilizations in their ability to accommodate modernity, a vital difference in the historical situations of the two religions also tempers my historicist optimism. Devout Muslims can see (as Luther, Calvin, and others could not) the long-term consequences of the Reformation and its consequent secularism: a marginalization of the Word of God, except as an increasingly distant cultural echo—as the "melancholy, long, withdrawing roar" of the once full "Sea of faith," in Matthew Arnold's precisely diagnostic words.

And there is enough truth in the devout Muslim's criticism of the less attractive aspects of Western secular culture to lend plausibility to his call for a return to purity as the answer to the Muslim world's woes. He sees in the West's freedom nothing but promiscuity and license, which is certainly there; but he does not see in freedom, especially freedom of inquiry, a spiritual virtue as well as an ultimate source of strength. This narrow, beleaguered consciousness no doubt accounts for the strand of reactionary revolt in contemporary Islam. The devout Muslim fears, and not without good reason, that to give an inch is sooner or later to concede the whole territory.

This fear must be all the more acute among the large and growing Muslim population in cities like mine. Except for a small, highly educated middle class, who live de facto as if Islam were a private religious confession like any other in the West, the Muslims congregate in neighborhoods that they have made their own, where the life of the Punjab continues amid the architecture of the Industrial Revolution. The halal butcher's corner shop rubs shoulders with the terra cotta municipal library, built by the Victorian city fathers to improve the cultural level of a largely vanished industrial working class.

The Muslim immigrants to these areas were not seeking a new way of life when they arrived; they expected to continue their old lives, but more prosperously. They neither anticipated, nor wanted, the inevitable cultural tensions of translocation, and they certainly never suspected that in the long run they could not maintain their culture and their religion intact. The older generation is only now realizing that even outward conformity to traditional codes of dress and behavior by the young is no longer a guarantee of inner acceptance (a perception that makes their vigilantism all the more pronounced and desperate). Recently I stood at the taxi stand outside my hospital, beside two young women in full black costume, with only a slit for the eyes. One said to the other, "Give us a light for a fag, love; I'm gasping." Release the social pressure on the girls, and they would abandon their costume in an instant.

Anyone who lives in a city like mine and interests himself in the fate of the world cannot help wondering whether, deeper than this immediate cultural desperation, there is anything intrinsic to Islam—beyond the devout Muslim's instinctive understanding that secularization, once it starts, is like an unstoppable chain reaction—that renders it unable to adapt itself comfortably to the modern world. Is there an essential element that condemns the Dar al-Islam to permanent backwardness with regard to the Dar al-Harb, a backwardness that is felt as a deep humiliation, and is exemplified, though not proved, by the fact that the whole of the Arab world, minus its oil, matters less to the rest of the world economically than the Nokia telephone company of Finland?

I think the answer is yes, and that the problem begins with Islam's failure to make a distinction between church and state. Unlike Christianity, which had to spend its first centuries developing institutions clandestinely and so from the outset clearly had to separate church from state, Islam was from its inception both church and state, one and indivisible, with no possible distinction between temporal and religious authority. Muhammad's power was seamlessly spiritual and secular (though the latter grew ultimately out of the former), and he bequeathed this model to his followers. Since he was, by Islamic definition, the last prophet of God upon earth, his was a political model whose perfection could not be challenged or questioned without the total abandonment of the pretensions of the entire religion.

But his model left Islam with two intractable problems. One was political. Muhammad unfortunately bequeathed no institutional arrangements by which his successors in the role of omnicompetent ruler could be chosen (and, of course, a schism occurred immediately after the Prophet's death, with some—today's Sunnites—following his father-in-law, and some—today's Shi'ites—his son-in-law). Compounding this difficulty, the legitimacy of temporal power could always be challenged by those who, citing Muhammad's spiritual role, claimed greater religious purity or authority; the fanatic in Islam is always at a moral advantage vis-à-vis the moderate. Moreover Islam—in which the mosque is a meetinghouse, not an institutional church—has no established, anointed ecclesiastical hierarchy to decide such claims authoritatively. With political power constantly liable to challenge from the pious, or the allegedly pious, tyranny becomes the only guarantor of stability, and assassination the only means of reform. Hence the Saudi time bomb: sooner or later, religious revolt will depose a dynasty founded upon its supposed piety but long since corrupted by the ways of the world.

The second problem is intellectual. In the West the Renaissance, the Reformation, and the Enlightenment, acting upon the space that had always existed, at least potentially, in Christianity between church and state, liberated individual men to think for themselves, and thus set in motion an unprecedented and still unstoppable material advancement. Islam, with no separate, secular sphere where inquiry could flourish free from the claims of religion, if only for technical purposes, was hopelessly left behind: as, several centuries later, it still is.

The indivisibility of any aspect of life from any other in Islam is a source of strength, but also of fragility and weakness, for individuals as well as for polities. Where all conduct, all custom, has a religious sanction and justification, any change is a threat to the whole system of belief. Certainty that their way of life is the right one thus coexists with fear that the whole edifice—intellectual and political—will come tumbling down if it is tampered with in any way. Intransigence is a defense against doubt and makes living on terms of true equality with others who do not share the creed impossible.

Not coincidentally, the punishment for apostasy in Islam is death: apostates are regarded as far worse than infidels, and punished far more rigorously. In every Islamic society, and indeed among Britain's Muslim immigrants, there are people who take this idea quite literally, as their rage against Salman Rushdie testified.

The Islamic doctrine of apostasy is hardly favorable to free inquiry or frank discussion, to say the least, and surely it explains why no Muslim, or former Muslim, in an Islamic society would dare to suggest that the Qu'ran was not divinely dictated through the mouth of the Prophet but rather was a compilation of a charismatic man's words made many years after his death, and incorporating, with no very great originality, Judaic, Christian, and Zoroastrian elements. In my experience, devout Muslims expect and demand a freedom to criticize, often with perspicacity, the doctrines and customs of others, while demanding an exaggerated degree of respect and freedom from criticism for their own doctrines and customs. I recall, for example, staying with a Pakistani Muslim in East Africa, a very decent and devout man, who nevertheless spent several evenings with me deriding the absurdities of Christianity: the paradoxes of the Trinity, the impossibility of Resurrection, and so forth. Though no Christian myself, had I replied in kind, alluding to the pagan absurdities of the pilgrimage to Mecca, or to the gross, ignorant, and primitive superstitions of the Prophet with regard to jinn, I doubt that our friendship would have lasted long.

The unassailable status of the Qu'ran in Islamic education, thought, and society is ultimately Islam's greatest disadvantage in the modern world. Such unassailability does not debar a society from great artistic achievement or charms of its own: great and marvelous civilizations have flourished without the slightest intellectual freedom. I myself prefer a souk to a supermarket any day, as a more human, if less economically efficient, institution. But until Muslims (or former Muslims, as they would then be) are free in their own countries to denounce the Qu'ran as an inferior hodgepodge of contradictory injunctions, without intellectual unity (whether it is so or not)—until they are free to say with Carlyle that the Qu'ran is "a wearisome confused jumble" with "endless iterations, longwindedness, entanglement"—until they are free to remake and modernize the Qu'ran by creative interpretation, they will have to reconcile themselves to being, if not helots, at least in the rearguard of humanity, as far as power and technical advance are concerned.

A piece of pulp fiction by Sir Arthur Conan Doyle, first published in 1898, when followers of the charismatic fundamentalist leader Muhammad al-Mahdi tried to establish a theocracy in Sudan by revolting against Anglo-Egyptian control, makes precisely this point and captures the contradiction at the heart of contemporary Islam. Called *The Tragedy of the Korosko*, the book is the story of a small tourist party to Upper Egypt who are kidnapped and held to ransom by some Mahdists, and then rescued by the Egyptian Camel Corps. (I hesitate, as a Francophile, to point out to American readers that there is a French character in the book, who, until he is himself captured by the Mahdists, believes that they are but a figment of the British imagination, to give perfidious Albion a pretext to interfere in Sudanese affairs.) A mullah among the Mahdists who capture the tourists attempts to convert the Europeans and Americans to Islam, deriding as unimportant and insignificant their technically superior civilization: "'As to the [scientific] learning of which you speak . . .' said the Moolah . . . 'I have myself studied at the University of Al Azhar at Cairo, and I know that to which you allude. But the learning of the faithful is not as the learning of the unbeliever, and it is not fitting that we pry too deeply into the ways of Allah. Some stars have tails . . . and some have not; but what does it profit us to know which are which? For God made them all, and they are very safe in His hands. Therefore . . . be not puffed up by the foolish learning of the West, and understand that there is only one wisdom, which consists in following the will of Allah as His chosen prophet has laid it down for us in this book.'"

This is by no means a despicable argument. One of the reasons we can appreciate the art and literature of the past, and sometimes of the very distant past, is that the fundamental conditions of human existence remain the same, however much we advance in the technical sense: I have myself argued that human self-understanding, except in purely technical matters, reached its apogee with Shakespeare. In a sense, the mullah is right.

But if we made a fetish of Shakespeare (much richer and more profound than the Qu'ran, in my view), if we made him the sole object of our study and the sole guide of our lives, we would soon enough fall into backwardness and stagnation. And the problem is that so many Muslims want both stagnation and power: they want a return to the perfection of the seventh century and to dominate the twenty-first, as they believe is the birthright of their doctrine, the last testament of God to man. If they were content to exist in a seventh-century backwater, secure in a quietist philosophy, there would be no problem for them or us; their problem, and ours, is that they want the power that free inquiry confers, without either the free inquiry or the philosophy and institutions that guarantee that free inquiry. They are faced with a dilemma: either they abandon their cherished religion or they remain forever in the rear of human technical advance. Neither alternative is very appealing; and the tension between their desire for power and success in the modern world on the one hand, and their desire not to abandon their religion on the other, is resolvable for some only by exploding themselves as bombs.

People grow angry when faced with an intractable dilemma; they lash out. Whenever I have described in print the cruelties my young Muslim patients endure, I receive angry replies: I am either denounced outright as a liar, or the writer acknowledges that such cruelties take place but are attributable to a local culture, in this case Punjabi, not to Islam, and that I am ignorant not to know it.

But Punjabi Sikhs also arrange marriages: they do not, however, force consanguineous marriages of the kind that take place from Madras to Morocco. Moreover—and not, I believe, coincidentally—Sikh immigrants from the Punjab, of no higher original social status than their Muslim confrères from the same provinces, integrate far better into the local society once they have immigrated. Precisely because their religion is a more modest one, with fewer universalist pretensions, they find the duality of their new identity more easily navigable. On the fiftieth anniversary of Queen Elizabeth's reign, for example, the Sikh temples were festooned with perfectly genuine protestations of congratulations and loyalty. No such protestations on the part of Muslims would be thinkable.

But the anger of Muslims, their demand that their sensibilities should be accorded a more than normal respect, is a sign not of the strength but of the weakness—or rather, the brittleness—of Islam in the modern world, the desperation its adherents feel that it could so easily fall to pieces. The control that Islam has over its populations in an era of globalization reminds me of the hold that the Ceaușescus appeared to have over the Romanians: an absolute hold, until Ceaușescu appeared one day on the balcony and was jeered by the crowd that had lost its fear. The game was over, as far as Ceaușescu was concerned, even if there had been no pre-existing conspiracy to oust him.

One sign of the increasing weakness of Islam's hold over its nominal adherents in Britain—of which militancy is itself but another sign—is the throng of young Muslim men in prison. They will soon overtake the young men of Jamaican origin in their numbers and in the extent of their criminality. By contrast, young Sikhs and Hindus are almost completely absent from prison, so racism is not the explanation for such Muslim overrepresentation.

Confounding expectations, these prisoners display no interest in Islam whatsoever; they are entirely secularized. True, they still adhere to Muslim marriage customs, but only for the obvious personal advantage of having a domestic slave at home. Many of them also dot the city with their concubines—sluttish white working-class girls or exploitable young Muslims who have fled forced marriages and do not know that their young men are married. This is not religion, but having one's cake and eating it.

The young Muslim men in prison do not pray; they do not demand halal meat. They do not read the Qu'ran. They do not ask to see the visiting imam. They wear no visible signs of piety: their main badge of allegiance is a gold front tooth, which proclaims them members of the city's criminal subculture—a badge (of honor, they think) that they share with young Jamaicans, though their relations with the Jamaicans are otherwise fraught with hostility. The young Muslim men want wives at home to cook and clean for them, concubines elsewhere, and drugs and rock 'n' roll. As for Muslim proselytism in the prison—and Muslim literature has been insinuated into nooks and crannies there far more thoroughly than any Christian literature—it is directed mainly at the

Jamaican prisoners. It answers their need for an excuse to go straight while not at the same time surrendering to the morality of a society they believe has wronged them deeply. Indeed, conversion to Islam is their revenge upon that society, for they sense that their newfound religion is fundamentally opposed to it. By conversion, therefore, they kill two birds with one stone.

But Islam has no improving or inhibiting effect upon the behavior of my city's young Muslim men, who, in astonishing numbers, have taken to heroin, a habit almost unknown among their Sikh and Hindu contemporaries. The young Muslims not only take heroin but deal in it, and have adopted all the criminality attendant on the trade.

What I think these young Muslim prisoners demonstrate is that the rigidity of the traditional code by which their parents live, with its universalist pretensions and emphasis on outward conformity to them, is all or nothing; when it dissolves, it dissolves completely and leaves nothing in its place. The young Muslims then have little defense against the egotistical licentiousness they see about them and that they all too understandably take to be the *summum bonum* of Western life.

Observing this, of course, there are among Muslim youth a tiny minority who reject this absorption into the white lumpenproletariat and turn militant or fundamentalist. It is their perhaps natural, or at least understandable, reaction to the failure of our society, kowtowing to absurd and dishonest multi-culturalist pieties, to induct them into the best of Western culture: into that spirit of free inquiry and personal freedom that has so transformed the life chances of every person in the world, whether he knows it or not.

Islam in the modern world is weak and brittle, not strong: that accounts for its so frequent shrillness. The shah will, sooner or later, triumph over the ayatollah in Iran, because human nature decrees it, though meanwhile millions of lives will have been ruined and impoverished. The Iranian refugees who have flooded into the West are fleeing Islam, not seeking to extend its dominion, as I know from speaking to many in my city. To be sure, fundamentalist Islam will be very dangerous for some time to come, and all of us, after all, live only in the short term; but ultimately the fate of the Church of England awaits it. Its melancholy, withdrawing roar may well (unlike that of the Church of England) be not just long but bloody, but withdraw it will. The fanatics and the bombers do not represent a resurgence of unreformed, fundamentalist Islam, but its death rattle.

2004

The Barbarians at the
Gates of Paris

◈ EVERYONE KNOWS *la douce France*: the France of wonderful food and wine, beautiful landscapes, splendid *châteaux* and
cathedrals. More tourists (sixty million a year) visit France than
any country in the world by far. Indeed, the Germans have a saying, not altogether reassuring for the French: "to live as God in
France." Half a million Britons have bought second homes there;
many of them bore their friends back home with how they order
these things better in France.

But there is another growing, and much less reassuring, side
to France. I go to Paris about four times a year and thus have a
sense of the evolving preoccupations of the French middle
classes. A few years ago it was schools: the much vaunted French
educational system was falling apart; illiteracy was rising; children were leaving school as ignorant as they entered and much
worse-behaved. For the last couple of years, though, it has been
crime: *l'insécurité, les violences urbaines, les incivilités*. Everyone
has a tale to tell, and no dinner party is complete without a hor-
rifying story. Every crime, one senses, means a vote for Le Pen or
whoever replaces him.

I first saw *l'insécurité* for myself about eight months ago. It
was just off the Boulevard Saint-Germain, in a neighborhood
where a tolerably spacious apartment would cost $1 million.
Three youths—Romanians—were attempting quite openly to
break into a parking meter with large screwdrivers to steal the

coins. It was four o'clock in the afternoon; the sidewalks were crowded, and the nearby cafés were full. The youths behaved as if they were simply pursuing a normal and legitimate activity, with nothing to fear.

Eventually two women in their sixties told them to stop. The youths, laughing until then, turned murderously angry, insulted the women, and brandished their screwdrivers. The women retreated, and the youths resumed their "work."

A man of about seventy then told them to stop. They berated him still more threateningly, one of them holding a screwdriver as if to stab him in the stomach. I moved forward to help the man, but the youths, still shouting abuse and genuinely outraged at being interrupted in the pursuit of their livelihood, decided to run off. But it all could have ended very differently.

Several things struck me about the incident: the youths' sense of invulnerability in broad daylight; the indifference to their behavior of large numbers of people who would never dream of behaving in the same way; that only the elderly tried to do anything about the situation, though physically least suited to do so. Could it be that only they had a view of right and wrong clear enough to wish to intervene? That everyone younger than they thought something like: "Refugees . . . hard life . . . very poor . . . too young to know right from wrong and anyway never taught . . . no choice for them . . . punishment cruel and useless"? The real criminals, indeed, were the drivers whose coins filled the parking meters: were they not polluting the world with their cars?

Another motive for inaction was that, had the youths been arrested, nothing would have happened to them. They would have been back on the streets within the hour. Who would risk a screwdriver in the liver to safeguard the parking meters of Paris for an hour?

The *laxisme* of the French criminal justice system is now notorious. Judges often make remarks indicating their sympathy for the criminals they are trying (based upon the usual generalizations about how society, not the criminal, is to blame); and the day before I witnessed the scene on the Boulevard Saint-Germain, eight thousand police had marched to protest the release from prison on bail of an infamous career armed robber and suspected murderer before his trial for yet another armed robbery, in the course of which he shot someone in the head. Out on bail before this trial, he then burgled a house. Surprised by the police, he and his accomplices shot two of them dead and seriously wounded a third. He was also under strong suspicion of having committed a quadruple murder a few days previously, in which a couple who owned a restaurant, and two of their employees, were shot dead in front of the owners' nine-year-old daughter.

The left-leaning *Libération*, one of the two daily newspapers the French intelligentsia reads, dismissed the marchers, referring with disdainful sarcasm to *la fièvre flicardiaire*—cop fever. The paper would no doubt have regarded the murder of a single journalist— that is to say, of a *full* human being—differently, let alone the murder of two journalists or six; and of course no one in the newspaper acknowledged that an effective police force is as vital a guarantee of personal freedom as a free press, and that the thin blue line that separates man from brutality is exactly that: thin. This is not a decent thing for an intellectual to say, however true it might be.

It is the private complaint of everyone, however, that the police have become impotent to suppress and detect crime. Horror stories abound. A Parisian acquaintance told me how one recent evening he had seen two criminals attack a car in which a woman was waiting for her husband. They smashed her side window and tried to grab her purse, but she resisted. My acquaintance went to her aid and managed to pin down one of the assailants, the other running off. Fortunately some police passed by, but to my acquaintance's dismay they let the assailant go, giving him only a warning.

My acquaintance said to the police that he would make a complaint. The senior among them advised him against wasting his time. At that time of night there would be no one to complain to in the local commissariat. He would have to go the following day and would have to wait on line for three hours. He would have to return several times, with a long wait each time. And in the end, nothing would be done.

As for the police, he added, they did not want to make an arrest in a case like this. There would be too much paperwork. And even if the case came to court, the judge would give no proper punishment. Moreover, such an arrest would retard their careers. The local police chiefs were paid by results—by the crime rates in their areas of jurisdiction. The last thing they wanted was for policemen to go around finding and recording crime.

Not long afterward I heard of another case in which the police simply refused to record the *occurrence* of a burglary, much less try to catch the culprits.

Now crime and general disorder are making inroads into places where, not long ago, they were unheard of. At a peaceful and prosperous village near Fontainebleau that I visited—the home of retired high officials and of a former cabinet minister—criminality had made its first appearance only two weeks before. There had been a burglary and a "rodeo"—an impromptu race of youths in stolen cars around the village green, whose fence the car thieves had knocked over to gain access.

A villager called the police, who said they could not come at the moment but who politely called back half an hour later to find out how things were going. Two hours later still, they finally appeared, but the rodeo had moved on, leaving behind only the remains of a burned-out car. The blackened patch on the road was still visible when I visited.

The official figures for this upsurge, doctored as they no doubt are, are sufficiently alarming. Reported crime in France has risen from 600,000 annually in 1959 to 4 million today, while the population has grown by less than 20 percent (and many think today's crime number is an underestimate by at least a half). In 2000 one crime was reported for every sixth inhabitant of Paris, and the rate has increased by at least 10 percent a year for the last five years. Reported cases of arson in France have increased 2,500 percent in seven years, from 1,168 in 1993 to 29,192 in 2000; robbery with violence rose by 15.8 percent between 1999 and 2000, and 44.5 percent since 1996 (itself no golden age).

Where does the increase in crime come from? The geographical answer: from the public housing projects that encircle and increasingly besiege every French city or town of any size, Paris especially. In these housing projects lives an immigrant population numbering several million, from North and West Africa mostly, along with their French-born descendants and a smattering of the least successful members of the French working class. From these projects, the excellence of the French public transport system ensures that the most fashionable *arrondissements* are within easy reach of the most inveterate thief and vandal.

Architecturally, the housing projects sprang from the ideas of Le Corbusier, the Swiss totalitarian architect—and still the untouchable hero of architectural education in France—who believed that a house was a machine for living in, that areas of cities should be entirely separated from one another by their function, and that the straight line and the right angle held the key to wisdom, virtue, beauty, and efficiency. The mulish opposition that met his scheme to pull down the whole of the center of Paris and rebuild it according to his "rational" and "advanced" ideas baffled and frustrated him.

The inhuman, unadorned, hard-edged geometry of these vast housing projects in their unearthly plazas brings to mind Le Corbusier's chilling and tyrannical words: "The despot is not a man. It is the . . . *correct, realistic, exact plan* . . . that will provide your solution once the problem has been posed clearly. . . . *This plan has been drawn up well away from . . . the cries of the electorate or the laments of society's victims.* It has been drawn up by serene and lucid minds."

But what is the problem to which these housing projects, known as *cités*, are the solution, conceived by serene and lucid minds like Le Corbusier's? It is the problem of providing an *Habitation de Loyer Modéré*—a House at Moderate Rent, shortened to HLM—for the workers, largely immigrant, whom the factories needed during France's great industrial expansion from the 1950s to the 1970s, when the unemployment rate was 2 percent and cheap labor was much in demand. By the late eighties, however, the demand had evaporated, but the people whose labor had satisfied it had not; and together with their descendants and a constant influx of new hopefuls, they made the provision of cheap housing more necessary than ever.

An apartment in this publicly owned housing is also known as a *logement*, a lodging, which aptly conveys the social status and degree of political influence of those expected to rent them. The *cités* are thus social marginalization made concrete: bureaucratically planned from their windows to their roofs, with no history of their own or organic connection to anything that previously existed on their sites, they convey the impression that, in the event of serious trouble, they could be cut off from the rest of the world by switching off the trains and by blockading with a tank or two the highways that pass through them (usually with a concrete wall on either side), from the rest of France to the better parts of Paris.

The average visitor gives not a moment's thought to these *Cités* of Darkness as he speeds from the airport to the City of Light. But they are huge and important—and what the visitor would find there, if he bothered to go, would terrify him.

A kind of anti-society has grown up in them—a population that derives the meaning of its life from the hatred it bears for the other, "official," society in France. This alienation, this gulf of mistrust—greater than any I have encountered anywhere else in the world, including in the black townships of South Africa during the apartheid years—is written on the faces of the young men, most of them permanently unemployed, who hang out in the pocked and potholed open spaces between their *logements*. When you approach to speak to them, their immobile faces betray not a flicker of recognition of your shared humanity; they make no gesture to smooth social intercourse. If you are not one of them, you are against them.

Their hatred of official France manifests itself in many ways that scar everything around them. Young men risk life and limb to adorn the most inaccessible surfaces of concrete with graffiti— BAISE LA POLICE, fuck the police, being the favorite theme. The iconography of the *cités* is that of uncompromising hatred and aggression: a burned-out and destroyed community-meeting place in the Les Tarterets project, for example, has a picture of a science-fiction humanoid, his fist clenched as if to spring at the person who looks at him, while to his right is an admiring portrait of a huge slavering pit bull, a dog by temperament and training capable of tearing out a man's throat—the only breed of dog I saw in the *cités*, paraded with menacing swagger by their owners.

There are burned-out and eviscerated carcasses of cars everywhere. Fire is now fashionable in the *cités*: in Les Tarterets, residents had torched and looted every store—with the exceptions of one government-subsidized supermarket and a pharmacy. The underground parking lot, charred and blackened by smoke like a vault in an urban hell, is permanently closed.

When agents of official France come to the *cités*, the residents attack them. The police are hated: one young Malian, who comfortingly believed that he was unemployable in France because of the color of his skin, described how the police invariably arrived like a raiding party, with batons swinging—ready to beat whoever came within reach, irrespective of who he was or of his innocence of any crime, before retreating to safety to their commissariat. The conduct of the police, he said, explained why residents threw Molotov cocktails at them from their windows. Who could tolerate such treatment at the hands of *une police fasciste*?

Molotov cocktails also greeted the president of the republic, Jacques Chirac, and his interior minister when they recently campaigned at two *cités*, Les Tarterets and Les Musiciens. The two dignitaries had to beat a swift and ignominious retreat, like foreign overlords visiting a barely held and hostile suzerainty: they came, they saw, they scuttled off.

Antagonism toward the police might appear understandable, but the conduct of the young inhabitants of the *cités* toward the firemen who come to rescue them from the fires that they have themselves started gives a dismaying glimpse into the depth of their hatred for mainstream society. They greet the admirable firemen (whose motto is *Sauver ou périr*, save or perish) with Molotov cocktails and hails of stones when they arrive on their mission of mercy, so that armored vehicles frequently have to protect the fire engines.

Benevolence inflames the anger of the young men of the *cités* as much as repression, because their rage is inseparable from their being. Ambulance men who take away a young man injured in an incident routinely find themselves surrounded by the man's "friends," and jostled, jeered at, and threatened: behavior that, according to one doctor I met, continues right into the hospital, even as the friends demand that their associate should be treated at once, before others.

Of course they also expect him to be treated as well as anyone else, and in this expectation they reveal the bad faith, or at least ambivalence, of their stance toward the society around them. They are certainly not poor, at least by the standards of all previously existing societies: they are not hungry; they have cell phones, cars, and many other appurtenances of modernity; they are dressed fashionably—according to their own fashion—with a uniform disdain of bourgeois propriety and with gold chains round their necks. They believe they have rights, and they know they will receive medical treatment, however they behave. They enjoy a far higher standard of living (or consumption) than they would in the countries of their parents' or grandparents' origin, even if they labored there fourteen hours a day to the maximum of their capacity.

But this is not a cause for gratitude—on the contrary: they feel it as an insult or a wound, even as they take it for granted as their due. But like all human beings, they want the respect and approval of others, even—or rather especially—of the people who carelessly toss them the crumbs of Western prosperity. Emasculating dependence is never a happy state, and no dependence is more absolute, more total, than that of most of the inhabitants of the *cités*. They therefore come to believe in the malevolence of those who maintain them in their limbo: and they want to keep alive the belief in this perfect malevolence, for it gives meaning—the only possible meaning—to their stunted lives. It is better to be opposed by an enemy than to be adrift in meaninglessness, for the simulacrum of an enemy lends purpose to actions whose nihilism would otherwise be self-evident.

That is one of the reasons that, when I approached groups of young men in Les Musiciens, many of them were not just suspicious (though it was soon clear to them that I was no member of the enemy) but hostile. When a young man of African origin agreed to speak to me, his fellows kept interrupting menacingly.

"Don't talk to him," they commanded, and they told me, with fear in their eyes, to go away. The young man was nervous too: he said he was afraid of being punished as a traitor. His associates feared that "normal" contact with a person who was clearly not of the enemy, and yet not one of them either, would contaminate their minds and eventually break down the them-and-us worldview that stood between them and complete mental chaos. They needed to see themselves as warriors in a civil war, not mere ne'er-do-wells and criminals.

The ambivalence of the *cité* dwellers matches "official" France's attitude toward them: overcontrol and interference, alternating with utter abandonment. Bureaucrats have planned every item in the physical environment, for example, and no matter how many times the inhabitants foul the nest (to use the Afrikaner's expression), the state pays for renovation, hoping thereby to demonstrate its compassion and concern. To assure the immigrants that they and their offspring are potentially or already truly French, the streets are named for French cultural heroes: for painters in Les Tarterets (rue Gustave Courbet, for example) and for composers in Les Musiciens (rue Gabriel Fauré). Indeed, the only time I smiled in one of the *cités* was when I walked past two concrete bunkers with metal windows, the école maternelle Charles Baudelaire and the école maternelle Arthur Rimbaud. Fine as these two poets are, theirs are not names one would associate with kindergartens, let alone with concrete bunkers.

But the heroic French names point to a deeper official ambivalence. The French state is torn between two approaches: Courbet, Fauré, *nos ancêtres, les gaullois,* on the one hand, and the shibboleths of multi-culturalism on the other. By compulsion of the Ministry of Education, the historiography that the schools purvey is that of the triumph of the unifying, rational, and benevolent French state through the ages, from Colbert onward, and Muslim girls are not allowed to wear headscarves in schools. After graduation, people who dress in "ethnic" fashion will not find jobs with major employers. But at the same time, official France also pays a cowering lip service to multi-culturalism—for example, to the "culture" of the *cités.* Thus French rap music is the subject of admiring articles in *Libération* and *Le Monde* as well as of pusil-lanimous expressions of approval from the last two ministers of culture.

One rap group, the *Ministère amer* (Bitter Ministry), won special official praise. Its best-known lyric: "Another woman takes her beating. / This time she's called Brigitte. / She's the wife of a cop. / The novices of vice piss on the police. / It's not just a firework, scratch the clitoris. / Brigitte the cop's wife likes nig-gers. / She's hot, hot in her pants." This vile rubbish receives ac-colades for its supposed authenticity: for in the multi-culturalist's mental world, in which the savages are forever noble, there is no criterion by which to distinguish high art from low trash. And if intellectuals, highly trained in the Western tradition, are prepared to praise such degraded and brutal pornography, it is hardly sur-prising that those who are not so trained come to the conclusion that there cannot be anything of value in that tradition. Cow-ardly multi-culturalism thus makes itself the handmaiden of anti-Western extremism.

Whether or not rap lyrics are the authentic voice of the *cités*, they are certainly its authentic ear: you can observe many young men in the *cités* sitting around in their cars aimlessly, listening to it for hours on end, so loud that the pavement vibrates to it a hun-dred yards away. The imprimatur of the intellectuals and of the French cultural bureaucracy no doubt encourages them to believe that they are doing something worthwhile. But when life begins to imitate art, and terrible gang rapes occur with increasing fre-quency, the same official France becomes puzzled and alarmed. What should it make of the eighteen young men and two young women currently being tried in Pontoise for allegedly abducting a girl of fifteen and for four months raping her repeatedly in base-ments, stairwells, and squats? Many of the group seem not merely unrepentant or unashamed but proud.

Though most people in France have never visited a *cité*, they dimly know that long-term unemployment among the young is so rife there that it is the normal state of being. Indeed, French youth unemployment is among the highest in Europe—and higher the further you descend the social scale, largely because high minimum wages, payroll taxes, and labor protection laws make employers loath to hire those whom they cannot easily fire, and whom they must pay beyond what their skills are worth.

Everyone acknowledges that unemployment, particularly of the permanent kind, is deeply destructive, and that the devil really does find work for idle hands; but the higher up the social scale you ascend, the more firmly fixed is the idea that the labor-market rigidities that encourage unemployment are essential both to distinguish France from the supposed savagery of the Anglo-Saxon neo-liberal model (one soon learns from reading the French newspapers what *anglo-saxon* connotes in this context) and to protect the downtrodden from exploitation. But the labor-market rigidities protect those who least need protection while condemning the most vulnerable to utter hopelessness: and if sexual hypocrisy is the vice of the Anglo-Saxons, economic hypocrisy is the vice of the French.

It requires little imagination to see how, in the circumstances, the burden of unemployment should fall disproportionately on immigrants and their children: and why, already culturally distinct from the bulk of the population, they should feel themselves vilely discriminated against. Having been enclosed in a physical ghetto, they respond by building a cultural and psychological ghetto for themselves. They are of France, but not French.

The state, while concerning itself with the details of their housing, their education, their medical care, and the payment of subsidies for them to do nothing, abrogates its responsibility completely in the one area in which the state's responsibility is absolutely inalienable: law and order. In order to placate, or at least not to inflame, disaffected youth, the Ministry of the Interior has instructed the police to tread softly (that is to say, virtually not at all, except by occasional raiding parties when inaction is impossible) in the more than eight hundred *zones sensibles*— sensitive areas—that surround French cities and that are known collectively as *la Zone*.

But human society, like nature, abhors a vacuum, and so authority of a kind, with its own set of values, occupies the space where law and order should be—the authority and brutal values of psychopathic criminals and drug dealers. The absence of a real economy and of law means, in practice, an economy and an informal legal system based on theft and drug-trafficking. In Les Tarterets, for example, I observed two dealers openly distributing drugs and collecting money while driving around in their highly conspicuous BMW convertible, clearly the monarchs of all they surveyed. Both of northwest African descent, one wore a scarlet baseball cap backward while the other had dyed blond hair, contrasting dramatically with his complexion. Their faces were as immobile as those of potentates receiving tribute from conquered tribes. They drove everywhere at maximum speed in low gear and high noise: they could hardly have drawn more attention to themselves if they tried. They didn't fear the law: rather, the law feared them.

I watched their proceedings in the company of old immigrants from Algeria and Morocco, who had come to France in the early 1960s. They too lived in Les Tarterets and had witnessed its descent into a state of low-level insurgency. They were so horrified by daily life that they were trying to leave, to escape their own children and grandchildren: but once having fallen into the clutches of the system of public housing, they were trapped. They wanted to transfer to a *cité*, if such existed, where the new generation did not rule: but they were without leverage—or *piston*—in the giant system of patronage that is the French state. And so they had to stay put, puzzled, alarmed, incredulous, and bitter at what their own offspring had become, so very different from what they had hoped and expected. They were better Frenchmen than either their children or grandchildren: they would never have whistled and booed at the *Marseillaise*, as their descendants did before the soccer match between France and Algeria in 2001, alerting the rest of France to the terrible canker in its midst.

Whether France was wise to have permitted the mass immigration of people culturally very different from its own population to solve a temporary labor shortage and to assuage its own abstract liberal conscience is disputable: there are now an estimated 8 or 9 million people of North and West African origin in France, twice the number in 1975—and at least 5 million of them are Muslims. Demographic projections (though projections are not predictions) suggest that their descendants will number 35 million before this century is out, more than a third of the likely total population of France.

Indisputably, however, France has handled the resultant situation in the worst possible way. Unless it assimilates these millions successfully, its future will be grim. But it has separated and isolated immigrants and their descendants geographically into dehumanizing ghettos; it has pursued economic policies to promote unemployment and create dependence among them, with all the inevitable psychological consequences; it has flattered the repellent and worthless culture they have developed; and it has withdrawn the protection of the law from them, allowing them to create their own lawless order.

No one should underestimate the danger that this failure poses, not only for France but also for the world. The inhabitants of the *cités* are exceptionally well armed. When the professional robbers among them raid a bank or an armored car delivering cash, they do so with bazookas and rocket launchers, and dress in paramilitary uniforms. From time to time the police discover whole arsenals of Kalashnikovs in the *cités*. There is a vigorous informal trade between France and post-Communist Eastern Europe: workshops in underground garages in the *cités* change the serial numbers of stolen luxury cars before export to the East, in exchange for sophisticated weaponry.

A profoundly alienated population is thus armed with serious firepower; and in conditions of violent social upheaval, such as France is in the habit of experiencing every few decades, it could prove difficult to control. The French state is caught in a dilemma between honoring its commitments to the more privileged section of the population, many of whom earn their livelihoods from administering the *dirigiste* economy, and freeing the labor market sufficiently to give the hope of a normal life to the inhabitants of the *cités*. Most likely the state will solve the dilemma by attempts to buy off the disaffected with more benefits and rights, at the cost of higher taxes that will further stifle the job creation that would most help the *cité* dwellers. If that fails, as in the long run it will, harsh repression will follow.

But among the third of the population of the *cités* that is of North African Muslim descent, there is an option that the French, and not only the French, fear. For imagine yourself a youth in Les Tarterets or Les Musiciens, intellectually alert but not well educated, believing yourself to be despised because of your origins by the larger society that you were born into, permanently condemned to unemployment by the system that contemptuously feeds and clothes you, and surrounded by a contemptible nihilistic culture of despair, violence, and crime. Is it not possible that you would seek a doctrine that would simultaneously explain your predicament, justify your wrath, point the way toward your revenge, and guarantee your salvation, especially if you were imprisoned? Would you not seek a "worthwhile" direction for the energy, hatred, and violence seething within you, a direction that would enable you to do evil in the name of ultimate good? It would require only a relatively few of like mind to cause havoc. Islamist proselytism flourishes in the prisons of France (where 60 percent of the inmates are of immigrant origin), as it does in British prisons; and it takes only a handful of Zacarias Moussaouis to start a conflagration.

The French knew of this possibility well before September 11: in 1994 their special forces boarded a hijacked aircraft that landed in Marseilles and killed the hijackers—an unusual step for the French, who have traditionally preferred to negotiate with, or give in to, terrorists. But they had intelligence suggesting that, after refueling, the hijackers planned to fly the plane into the Eiffel Tower. In this case, no negotiation was possible.

A terrible chasm has opened up in French society, dramatically exemplified by a story that an acquaintance told me. He was driving along a six-lane highway with housing projects on both sides when a man tried to dash across the road. My acquaintance hit him at high speed and killed him instantly.

According to French law, the participants in a fatal accident must stay as near as possible to the scene until officials have elucidated all the circumstances. The police therefore took my informant to a kind of hotel nearby, where there was no staff and the door could be opened only by inserting a credit card into an automatic billing terminal. Reaching his room, he discovered that all the furniture was of concrete, including the bed and washbasin, and attached either to the floor or walls.

The following morning the police came to collect him, and he asked them what kind of place this was. Why was everything made of concrete?

"But don't you know where you are, *monsieur*?" they asked. "*C'est la Zone, c'est la Zone.*"

La Zone is a foreign country: they do things differently there.

2002

After Empire

⬧ AS SOON AS I qualified as a doctor, I went to Rhodesia, which was to transform itself into Zimbabwe five years or so later. In the next decade I worked and traveled a great deal in Africa and couldn't help but reflect upon such matters as the clash of cultures, the legacy of colonialism, and the practical effects of good intentions unadulterated by any grasp of reality. I gradually came to the conclusion that the rich and powerful can indeed have an effect upon the poor and powerless—perhaps can even remake them—but not necessarily (in fact, necessarily not) in the way they wanted or anticipated. The law of unintended consequences is stronger than the most absolute power.

I went to Rhodesia because I wanted to see the last true outpost of colonialism in Africa, the final gasp of the British Empire that had done so much to shape the modern world. True, it had now rebelled against the mother country and was a pariah state: but it was still recognizably British in all but name. As Sir Roy Welensky, the prime minister of the short-lived and ill-fated Federation of Rhodesia and Nyasaland, once described himself, he was "half-Polish, half-Jewish, one hundred percent British."

Until my arrival at Bulawayo Airport, the British Empire had been for me principally a philatelic phenomenon. When I was young, Britain's still-astonishing assortment of far-flung territories—from British Honduras and British Guiana to British North Borneo, Basutoland, Bechuanaland, and Swaziland—each issued beautiful engraved stamps, with the queen's profile in the right upper corner, looking serenely down upon exotic creatures such as orangutans or frigate birds, or upon natives (as we still called and thought of them) going about their natively tasks, tapping rubber or climbing coconut palms. To my childish mind, any political entity that issued such desirable stamps must have been a power for good. And my father—a Communist by conviction—also encouraged me to read the works of G. A. Henty, late-nineteenth-century adventure stories extolling the exploits of empire builders, who by bravery, sterling character, superior intelligence, and *force majeure* overcame the resistance of such spirited but doomed peoples as the Zulu and the Fuzzy-Wuzzies. Henty might seem an odd choice for a Communist to give his son, but Marx himself was an imperialist of a kind, believing that European colonialism was an instrument of progress toward History's happy denouement; only at a later stage, after it had performed its progressive work, was empire to be condemned.

And condemned Rhodesia most certainly was, loudly and insistently, as if it were the greatest threat to world peace and the security of the planet. By the time I arrived, it had no friends, only enemies. Even South Africa, the regional colossus with which Rhodesia shared a long border and which might have been expected to be sympathetic, was highly ambivalent toward it: for South Africa sought to ingratiate itself with other nations by being less than wholehearted in its economic cooperation with the government of Ian Smith.

I expected to find on my arrival, therefore, a country in crisis and decay. Instead I found a country that was, to all appearances, thriving: its roads were well maintained, its transport system functioning, its towns and cities clean and manifesting a municipal pride long gone from England. There were no electricity cuts or shortages of basic food commodities. The large hospital in which I was to work, while stark and somewhat lacking in comforts, was extremely clean and ran with exemplary efficiency. The staff, mostly black except for its most senior members, had a vibrant *esprit de corps*, and the hospital, as I discovered, had a reputation for miles around for the best of medical care. The rural poor would make immense and touching efforts to reach it: they arrived covered in the dust of their long journeys. The African nationalist leader and foe of the government, Joshua Nkomo, was a patient there and trusted the care implicitly, for medical ethics transcended all political antagonisms.

The surgeon for whom I worked, who came from England, was the best I have ever known and a man of exemplary character. Devoting his enormous technical accomplishment to the humblest of patients, he seemed not only capable of every surgical procedure, but he was a brilliant diagnostician, his clinical intuition honed by a relative lack of high-tech aids: so much so that others in the hospital regarded him as the final court of appeal. I never knew him to be mistaken, though like every other doctor he must have made errors in his time. He saved the lives of hundreds every year and inspired the most absolute trust and confidence in his patients. He never panicked, even in the direst emergency; and he knew what to do when a man had been half eaten by a crocodile or mauled by a leopard, when a child had been bitten in the leg by a puff adder, or when a man appeared with a spear driven through his skull. When called in the early hours of the morning, as he frequently was, he was as even-tempered as if attending a social event. Greater love hath no man. . . .

He was not a missionary, however; he was infused by nothing resembling a religious spirit, only by a profound medical ethic and an enthusiasm for his art and science. He wanted a varied and interesting surgical practice, and he wanted to save human life; and the Rhodesia of the time offered him ideal conditions for using his skills to maximum benefit (even the best of surgeons relies on a well-organized hospital to achieve results). Within a short time of the political handover in 1980, however, he returned to England—not because of any racial feeling or political antagonism but simply because the swift degeneration of standards in the hospital made the high-level practice of surgery impossible. The institution that had seemed to me on my arrival to be so solid and well founded fell apart in the historical twinkling of an eye.

In leaving Zimbabwe and returning to England, he accepted a much reduced standard of living, whatever the nominal value of his income. Talleyrand said that he who had not experienced the *ancien régime* (as an aristocrat, of course) knew nothing of the sweetness of life. The same might be said of him who had not ex-perienced life as a colonial in Africa. I, whose salary was by other standards small, lived at a level that I have scarcely equaled since. It is true that Rhodesia lacked many consumer goods at that time, due to the economic sanctions imposed upon it: but what I learned from this lack is how little consumer goods add to the quality of life, at least in an equable climate such as Rhodesia's. Life was no poorer for being lived without them.

The real luxuries were space and beauty—and the time to en-joy them. With three other junior doctors, I rented a large and ele-gant colonial house, old by the standards of a country settled by whites only eighty years previously, set in beautiful grounds tended by a garden "boy" called Moses (the "boy" in garden boy or houseboy implied no youth: once, in East Africa, I was served by a houseboy who was ninety-four, who had lived in the same family for seventy years, and who would have seen the suggestion of retirement as insulting). Surrounding the house was a red flag-stone veranda where breakfast was served on linen in the cool of the morning, the soft light of the sunrise spreading through the fo-liage of the flame and jacaranda trees; even the harsh cry of the go-away bird seemed grateful on the ear. It was the only time in my life when I have arisen from bed without a tinge of regret.

We worked hard: I have never worked harder, and I can still conjure up the heavy feeling in my head, as if it were full of lead shot and could snap off my neck under its own weight, brought about by weekends on duty, when from Friday morning to Mon-day evening I would get not more than three hours' sleep. The lux-ury of our life was this: that, our work once done, we never had to perform a single chore for ourselves. The rest of our time, in our most beautiful surroundings, was given over to friendship, sport, study, hunting—whatever we wished.

Of course our leisure rested upon a pyramid of startling in-equality and social difference. The staff who freed us of life's little inconveniences lived an existence that was opaque to us, though they had quarters only a few yards from where we lived. Their hopes, wishes, fears, and aspirations were not ours; their beliefs, tastes, and customs were alien to us.

Our very distance, socially and psychologically, made our relations with them unproblematical and easy. We studiously avoided that tone of spoiled and bored querulousness for which colonials were infamous. We never resorted to that supposed staple of colonial conversation, the servant problem, but were properly grateful. Like most of the people I met in Rhodesia, we tried to treat our staff well, providing extra help for them for the frequent emergencies of African life—for example illness among relatives. In return they treated us with genuine solicitude. We assuaged our conscience by telling ourselves—what was no doubt true—that they would be worse off without our employ, but we couldn't help feeling uneasy about the vast gulf between us and our fellow human beings.

By contrast, our relations with our African medical colleagues were harder-edged, because the social, intellectual, and cultural distance between us was far reduced. Rhodesia was still a white-dominated society, but for reasons of practical necessity, and in a vain attempt to convince the world that it was not as monstrous as made out, it had produced a growing cadre of educated Africans, doctors prominent among them. Unsurprisingly, they were not content to remain subalterns under the permanent tutelage of whites, so that our relations with them were superficially polite and collegial, but human warmth was difficult or impossible. Many belonged secretly to the African nationalist movement that was soon to take power; and two were to serve (if that is the word to describe their depredations) as ministers of health.

Unlike in South Africa, where salaries were paid according to a racial hierarchy (whites first, Indians and colored second, Africans last), salaries in Rhodesia were equal for blacks and whites doing the same job, so that a black junior doctor received the same salary as mine. But there remained a vast gulf in our standards of living, the significance of which at first escaped me; but it was crucial in explaining the disasters that befell the newly independent countries that enjoyed what Byron called, and eagerly anticipated as, the first dance of freedom.

The young black doctors who earned the same salary as we whites could not achieve the same standard of living for a very simple reason: they had an immense number of social obligations to fulfill. They were expected to provide for an ever-expanding circle of family members (some of whom may have invested in their education) and people from their village, tribe, and province. An income that allowed a white to live like a lord because of a lack of such obligations scarcely raised a black above the level of his family. Mere equality of salary, therefore, was quite insufficient to procure for them the standard of living that they saw the whites had and that it was only human nature for them to desire—and believe themselves entitled to, on account of the superior talent that had allowed them to raise themselves above their fellows. In fact a salary a thousand times as great would hardly have been sufficient to procure it: for their social obligations increased *pari passu* with their incomes.

These obligations also explain the fact, often disdainfully remarked upon by former colonials, that when Africans moved into the beautiful and well-appointed villas of their former colonial masters, the houses swiftly degenerated into a species of superior, more spacious slum. Just as African doctors were perfectly equal to their medical tasks, technically speaking, so the degeneration of colonial villas had nothing to do with the intellectual inability of Africans to maintain them. Rather, the fortunate inheritor of such a villa was soon overwhelmed by relatives and others who had a social claim upon him. They brought even their goats with them; and one goat can undo in an afternoon what it has taken decades to establish.

It is easy to see why a civil service, controlled and manned in its upper reaches by whites, could remain efficient and uncorrupt but could not long do so when manned by Africans who were supposed to follow the same rules and procedures. The same is true, of course, for every other administrative activity, public or private. The thick network of social obligations explains why, while it would have been out of the question to bribe most Rhodesian bureaucrats, yet in only a few years it would have been out of the question not to try to bribe most Zimbabwean ones, whose relatives would have condemned them for failing to obtain on their behalf all the advantages their official opportunities might provide. Thus do the very same tasks in the very same offices carried out by people of different cultural and social backgrounds result in very different outcomes.

Viewed in this light, African nationalism was a struggle as much for power and privilege as it was for freedom, though it co-opted the language of freedom for obvious political advantage. In the matter of freedom, even Rhodesia—certainly no haven of free speech—was superior to its successor state, Zimbabwe. I still have in my library the oppositionist pamphlets and Marxist analyses of the vexed land question in Rhodesia that I bought there when Ian Smith was premier. Such thoroughgoing criticism of the rule of Mr. Mugabe would be inconceivable—or else fraught with much greater dangers than opposition authors experienced under Ian Smith. And indeed, in all but one or two African states, the accession to independence brought no advance in intellectual freedom but rather, in many cases, a tyranny incomparably worse than the preceding colonial regimes.

Of course, the solidarity and inescapable social obligations that corrupted public and private administration in Africa also gave a unique charm and humanity to life there and served to protect people from the worst consequences of the misfortunes that buffeted them. There were always relatives whose unquestioned duty it was to help and protect them if they could, so that no one had to face the world entirely alone. Africans tend to find our lack of such obligations puzzling and unfeeling—and they are not entirely wrong.

These considerations help explain the paradox that strikes so many visitors to Africa: the evident decency, kindness, and dignity of the ordinary people, and the fathomless iniquity, dishonesty, and ruthlessness of the politicians and administrators. This contrast recently struck me anew when a lawyer asked me to prepare a report on a Zimbabwean woman who had stayed illegally in England.

She was in her forties and clearly in a disturbed state of mind. Mostly she looked down at the floor, avoiding all eye contact. When she looked up, her eyes seemed focused on infinity, or at least upon another world. She spoke hardly a word: her story was told me by her niece, a nurse who had come (or fled) to England some years before, and with whom she now stayed.

During the war of "liberation," her brother had enlisted in the Rhodesian army. One day the nationalist guerrillas came to her village and commanded her parents to tell them where he was, that they might kill him as a traitor to the African cause. But not knowing his whereabouts, her parents could not answer: and so, in front of her eyes, and making her watch (she was seventeen years old at the time), they tied her parents to trees, doused them in gasoline, and burned them to death. (At this point in the story, I could not help but recall the argument, common among radicals at the time, that those African countries that liberated themselves by force of arms faced a better, brighter future than those that had been handed independence on a plate, because the war of liberation would forge genuine leadership and national unity. Algeria? Mozambique? Angola?)

Whether or not it was witnessing this terrible scene that turned her mind, she was never able thereafter to lead a normal life. She did not marry, a social catastrophe for a woman in Zimbabwe. She was taken in and looked after by a cousin who worked for a white farmer, and she spent her life staring into space. Then the "war veterans" arrived, those who had allegedly fought for Zimbabwe's freedom—in reality, groups of party thugs intent upon dispossessing white farmers of their land in fulfillment of Mr. Mugabe's demagogic and economically disastrous instructions. The white farmer and his black manager were killed and all the workers whom the farm had supported driven off the land. Hearing of her aunt's plight, her niece in England sent her a ticket.

This story illustrates both the ruthless appetite for power and control unleashed in Africa by the colonial experience—an appetite made all the nastier by some of the technological appurtenances of the colonialists' civilization—and the generosity of the great majority of Africans. The niece would look after her aunt uncomplainingly for the rest of her life, demanding nothing in return and regarding it as her plain duty to do so, also asking nothing from the British state. Her kindness toward her aunt, who could contribute nothing, was moving to behold.

My Zimbabwean experiences sensitized me to the chaos I later witnessed throughout Africa. The contrast between kindness on the one hand and rapacity on the other was everywhere evident: and I learned that there is no more heartless saying than that the people get the government they deserve. Who, en masse, could deserve an Idi Amin or a Julius Nyerere? Certainly not the African peasants I encountered. The fact that such monsters could quite explicably emerge from the people by no means meant that the people deserved them.

The explanations usually given for Africa's post-colonial travails seemed to me facile. It was often said, for example, that African states were artificial, created by a stroke of a European's pen that took no notice of social realities; that boundaries were either drawn with a ruler in straight lines or at a natural feature such as a river, despite the fact that people of the same ethnic group lived on both sides.

This notion overlooks two salient facts: that the countries in Africa that do actually correspond to social, historical, and ethnic realities—for example Burundi, Rwanda, and Somalia—have not fared noticeably better than those that do not. Moreover in Africa, social realities are so complex that no system of boundaries could correspond to them. For example, there are said to be up to three hundred ethnic groups in Nigeria alone, often deeply intermixed geographically: only extreme balkanization followed by profound ethnic cleansing could have resulted in the kind of boundaries that would have avoided this particular criticism of the European mapmakers. On the other hand, pan-Africanism was not feasible: for the kind of integration that could not be achieved on a small national scale could hardly be achieved on a vastly bigger international one.

In fact it was the imposition of the European model of the nation-state upon Africa, for which it was peculiarly unsuited, that caused so many disasters. With no loyalty to the nation but only to the tribe or family, those who control the state can see it only as an object and instrument of exploitation. Gaining political power is the only way ambitious people see to achieving the immeasurably higher standard of living that the colonialists dangled in front of their faces for so long. Given the natural wickedness of human beings, the lengths to which they are prepared to go to achieve power—along with their followers, who expect to share in the spoils—are limitless. The winner-take-all aspect of Africa's political life is what makes it more than usually vicious.

But it is important to understand why another explanation commonly touted for Africa's post-colonial turmoil is mistaken— the view that the dearth of trained people in Africa at the time of independence is to blame. No history of the modern Congo catastrophe is complete without reference to the paucity of college graduates at the time of the Belgian withdrawal, as if things would have been better had there been more of them. And therefore the solution was obvious: train more people. Education in Africa became a secular shibboleth that it was impious to question.

The expansion of education in Tanzania, where I lived for three years, was indeed impressive. The literacy rate had improved dramatically, so that it was better than that of the former colonizing power, and it was inspiring to see the sacrifices villagers were willing to make to enable at least one of their children to continue his schooling. School fees took precedence over every other expenditure. If anyone doubted the capacity of the poor to make investments in their own future, the conduct of the Tanzanians should have been sufficient to persuade him otherwise. (I used to lend money to villagers to pay the fees, and—poor as they were—they never failed to repay me.)

Unfortunately there was a less laudable, indeed positively harmful, side to this effort. The aim of education was, in almost every case, that at least one family member should escape what Marx contemptuously called the idiocy of rural life and get into government service, from which he would be in a position to extort from the only productive people in the country—namely, the peasants from whom he had sprung. The son in government service was social security, old-age pension, and secure income rolled into one. Farming, the country's indispensable economic base, was viewed as the occupation of dullards and failures, and so it was hardly surprising that the education of an ever-larger number of government servants went hand in hand with an ever-contracting economy. It also explains why there is no correlation between a country's number of college graduates at independence and its subsequent economic success.

The naive supposition on which the argument for education rests is that training counteracts and overpowers a cultural worldview. A trained man is but a clone of his trainer, on this theory, sharing his every attitude and worldview. But in fact what results is a curious hybrid, whose fundamental beliefs may be impervious to the education he has received.

I had a striking example of this phenomenon recently, when I had a Congolese patient who had taken refuge in this country from the terrible war in Central Africa that has so far claimed up to three million lives. He was an intelligent man and had that easy charm that I remember well from the days when I traversed—not without difficulty or discomfort—the Zaire of Marshal Mobutu Sese Seko. He had two degrees in agronomy and had trained in Toulouse in the interpretation of satellite pictures for agronomic purposes. He recognized the power of modern science, therefore, and had worked for the UN Food and Agricultural Organization, and was used to dealing with Western aid donors and investors as well as academics.

The examination over, we chatted about the Congo: he was delighted to meet someone who knew his country, by no means easily found in England. I asked him about Mobutu, whom he had known personally.

"He was very powerful," he said. "He collected the best witch doctors from every part of Zaire. Of course, he could make himself invisible; that was how he knew everything about us. And he could turn himself into a leopard when he wanted."

This was said with perfect seriousness. For him the magical powers of Mobutu were more impressive and important than the photographic power of satellites. Magic trumped science. In this he was not at all abnormal, it being as difficult or impossible for a sub-Saharan African to deny the power of magic as for an inhabitant of the Arabian peninsula to deny the power of Allah. My Congolese patient was perfectly relaxed: usually Africans feel constrained to disguise from Europeans their most visceral beliefs, for which they know the Europeans usually feel contempt, as primitive and superstitious. And so, in dealing with outsiders, Africans feel obliged to play an elaborate charade, denying their deepest beliefs in an attempt to obtain the outsider's minimal respect. In deceiving others about their innermost beliefs, often very easily, and in keeping their inner selves hidden from them, they are equalizing the disparity of power. The weak are not powerless: they have the power, for instance, to gull the outsider.

Perhaps the most baleful legacy of British and other colonials in Africa was the idea of the philosopher-king, to whose role colonial officials aspired, and which they often actually played, bequeathing it to their African successors. Many colonial officials made great sacrifices for the sake of their territories, to whose welfare they were devoted, and they attempted to govern them wisely, dispensing justice evenhandedly. But they left for the nationalists the instruments needed to erect the tyrannies and kleptocracies that marked post-independence Africa. They bequeathed a legacy of treating ordinary uneducated Africans as children, incapable of making decisions for themselves. No attitude is more grateful to the aspiring despot.

Take one example: the marketing boards of West Africa. Throughout West Africa, millions of African peasants under British rule set up small plantations for crops such as palm oil and cocoa. (Since cocoa trees mature only after five years, this is another instance of the African peasant's ability both to think ahead and delay gratification by investment, despite great poverty.) Then the British colonial governments had the idea, benignly intended, of protecting the peasant growers from the fluctuations of the marketplace. They set up a stabilization fund, under the direction of a marketing board. In good years the marketing board would withhold from the peasants some of the money their crops produced; in bad years it would use the money earned in the good years to increase their incomes. With stable incomes, they could plan ahead.

Of course, for the system to work, the marketing boards would have to have monopoly purchasing powers. And it takes little imagination to see how such marketing boards would tempt an aspiring despot, such as Dr. Nkrumah, with grandiose ideas: he could use them in effect to tax Ghana's producers in order to fund his insane projects and to subsidize the urban population that was the source of his power, as well as to amass a personal fortune. A continent away, in Tanzania, Nyerere used precisely the same means to expropriate the peasant coffee growers, in the end causing them to pull up their coffee bushes and plant a little corn instead, which at least they could eat, to the great and further impoverishment of the country.

The idea behind the marketing boards was a paternalist colonial one: that peasant farmers were too simple to cope with fluctuating prices and that the colonial philosopher-kings had therefore to protect them from such fluctuations—this despite the fact that it was the simple peasants who grew the commodities in the first place.

After several years in Africa I concluded that the colonial enterprise had been fundamentally wrong and mistaken, even when, as was often the case in its final stages, it was benevolently intended. The good it did was ephemeral; the harm, lasting. The powerful can change the powerless, it is true; but not in any way they choose. The unpredictability of humans is the revenge of the powerless. What emerges politically from the colonial enterprise is often something worse, or at least more vicious because better equipped, than what existed before. Good intentions are certainly no guarantee of good results.

2003

Index

Index

Portrait of a Young Girl (Miró), 120
Portugal, 178
Poverty, ix, 13; and crime, 162, 212; and entitlement, 178; virtue of, 65
Price, Richard, 138
Prisoners, 5; anti-social behavior, reduction in, 211; as malnourished, 212; vitamin and mineral supplements, effect of on, 211
Prisons: Jamaicans in, 293, 294; Muslims in, 275, 293, 294, 309; overcrowding of, 233
Progress, ix
Prohibition, 233
Proletarian, 87; and *Communist Manifesto* (Marx and Engels), 85
Prostitution, 234, 235
Prussia, 131
Public housing, 14; in France, 299, 301, 304, 305, 307; in Great Britain, 195; in Paris, 299, 300, 301. *See also Cités.*
Punjabi Sikhs, 292
Punk, 149, 150
Puritans, 44
Pyongyang (North Korea), 114, 115, 166, 174

Quinn, Mary, 150

Raeburn, Henry, 140
Reason: vs. passion, 90, 91
Rebelde (newspaper), 182
Reformation, 289

Reid, Richard, 275
Renaissance, 289
La Repubblica (newspaper), 190
Responsibility: shift of, 178–179; and West case, 271
Reynolds, Joshua, 143, 147, 152
Rhodesia, 25, 311, 312, 313; African nationalist movement in, 315, 317; salaries in, 315; social inequality in, 314, 315, 316, 317; social obligations in, 316. *See also* Zimbabwe.
Richard II, 23
Richard III, 33
Right to Heresy: Castellio Against Calvin, The (Zweig), 101
Romania, 111, 191, 293
Rome Olympics, 190
Romeo and Juliet (Shakespeare), 284
Rosenthal, Norman, 144, 145, 146, 147, 150
Rousseau, Jean-Jacques, 259
Rover, 192
Rowlandson, Thomas, 149, 150
Royal Academy of Art (London), 144, 147, 152; "Sensation" exhibit at, 140, 141
Royal College of Physicians, 150
Royal Opera House (London): as elitist, accusations of, 150
Rushdie, Salman, 289
Ruskin, John, 88
Russell, Bertrand, 218
Russia, 89; behavior in, 168, 169, 176; character of, 175; communism, legacy of in, 175; despotism in, 169, 170,

Tragedy of the Korosko, The
(Doyle), 291
Transgressive act: admiration of,
40, 127
Transsexuals, 249
Travel, 159
Treatise of Heretics (Castellio),
101
Turgenev, Ivan, 77, 87;
downtrodden, sympathy
toward, 88; in exile, 78;
funeral of, 89; house arrest of,
78, 79; literary influences of,
78; Karl Marx, compared
with, 84; and "Mumu," 78,
79, 80, 81, 82, 83, 89
Turgeneva, Varvara Petrovna,
81
Turner, Joseph, 71
Twentieth century, 31; barbarism
of, 103; disasters of, x;
dystopias in, 103, 104, 113;
horrors of, 122; moral
relativism of, 179; optimism
during, ix; pessimism of,
106–107; prosperity of, 179;
and social engineering, 103
*Twenty-four Hours in the Life of
a Woman* (Zweig), 97, 98, 99,
100
Tyranny, 31, 74

Unamuno, Miguel de, 125
Unemployed: personal relations,
as diversion, 23
UNESCO, 184
Unhappiness, 15, 239; and
depression, 9

United Nations Food and
Agricultural Organization, 321
United States: Cuba, relationship
with, 187; social breakdown
in, 183; and Tocqueville, 175
Utamaro, Kitagawa, 119
Utopia, 103

Van Dong, Pham, 18, 19
Verhaeren, Emile, 95
Vermeer, 118, 119, 122
Viardot, Pauline, 78
Vienna, 95, 96, 97, 123; as
civilized, 91; political
decadence of, 92; social
conventions of, 93
Vietnam War, 17, 18, 19, 21, 24;
photographers, death of in, 20
Virtue, 51, 127; as
proportionate, 49
Von Westphalen, Jenny, 86

Wales: crime, increase in, 9. *See
also* Great Britain.
Wallace Collection (London),
119
Welfare state, 8, 13, 177; in
Britain, 11; evil, spread of, 14
Wellensky, Roy, 311
Wells, H. G., 104, 105
Wells, Holly, 251–252, 254
West Africa: marketing boards
of, 322
West, Frederick, 260, 261, 262,
263, 264, 265, 266, 271;
acquittal of, 269; arrest of,
268, 269; suicide of, 269,
270; victims of, 267

A NOTE ON THE AUTHOR

Theodore Dalrymple is a British doctor and writer, born in 1949, who has worked on four continents and now works in a British inner-city hospital and a prison. He has written a column for the London *Spectator* for fourteen years and is a contributing editor of *City Journal* in the United States. His writings have appeared in the *Wall Street Journal*, the *Daily Telegraph*, the *Guardian*, the *Daily Mail*, the *National Post* (Canada), *New Statesman*, *National Review*, and many other publications. He lives in Birmingham, England.